Zhong Yuan Qigong

The Third Stage of Ascent:
Pause, The Way to Wisdom

Mingtang Xu
Tamara Martynova

Zhong Yuan Qigong

The Third Stage of Ascent:
Pause, The Way to Wisdom

A Book for Reading and Practice

Zhong Yuan Qigong. Third Stage of Ascent: Pause; the Way to Wisdom.—
A Book for Reading and Practice.
Translated from the second Russian edition supplemented and revised.
K.: JV "Da-Yu"; "Sophia," 2008.—296 p. Illustrated/Series "Enter your inner world"

Translator: Benjamin J. Salzano, bsalzano@hotmail.com
Co-editor: Ksenya Medvedev, lamargarita@gmail.com

Enter your inner world

Truth

Wisdom

Pause

Quietness

Relaxation

This book is a logical extension of the first two volumes on Stages I and II of Zhong Yuan Qigong (ZYQ). It's based on material from Stage III seminars involving lectures and practice, as well as training workshops, including those in Shaolin (China), that have been conducted by Qigong Master Professor Xu Mingtang in various countries.

The book presents some aspects of the ancient views on the structure and evolution of the Universe[1] and way of the development of humans. Described here is the philosophical concept of the model of creation, with its different levels of worlds and the possible forms of life and development currents contained therein.

The reader will find exercises pertaining to the activating of energy in the upper Dan Tian for the opening of the Third Eye, methods of breathing and energy nourishment through the navel, and the practice of rejuvenation. Detailed descriptions are offered of the state of Pause and the guided journey of the soul. The book explains the stages of development of the Third Eye, as well as the technology of diagnosing with the Third Eye and distance treatment.

As with the previous volumes in this series, the book is intended for both the general reader and Qigong practitioners.

---

1 The capitalization of the word "Universe" refers to material (or substantial), energetic, and informational (or spiritual) aspects of the universe together with all possible forms of life, visible and invisible.

TABLE OF CONTENTS

WARNINGS AND DISCLAIMERS

This book is intended for general readers as an introduction to the system and for people who are graduates of the Zhong Yuan Qigong seminars and workshops and practice the system.

Although extremely unlikely, the exercises described in this book may cause excessive stress in some individuals.

Please consult your doctor and stay under his or her supervision, especially if you suffer from mental or cardiovascular diseases.

Neither the authors nor the publishers are responsible for any health problems that could occur as the result of incorrect practice, such as overextending the duration of the exercises, improperly selecting certain exercises, and misinterpreting the instructions.

IF

R. Kipling

If you can keep your head when all about you
Are losing theirs and blaming it on you,
If you can trust yourself when all men doubt you,
But make allowance for their doubting, too;
If you can wait and not be tired by waiting,
Or being lied about, don't deal in lies,
Or being hated, don't give way to hating,
And yet don't look too good, nor talk too wise:

If you can dream—and not make dreams your master;
If you can think—and not make thoughts your aim;
If you can meet with Triumph and Disaster
And treat those two impostors just the same;
If you can bear to hear the truth you've spoken
Twisted by knaves to make a trap for fools,
Or watch the things you gave your life to, broken,
And stoop and build 'em up with worn-out tools:

If you can make one heap of all your winnings
And risk it on one turn of pitch-and-toss,
And lose, and start again at your beginnings
And never breathe a word about your loss;
If you can force your heart and nerve and sinew
To serve your turn long after they are gone,
And so hold on when there is nothing in you
Except the Will which says to them: "Hold on!"

If you can talk with crowds and keep your virtue,
Or walk with Kings—nor lose the common touch,
If neither foes nor loving friends can hurt you,
If all men count with you, but none too much;
If you can fill the unforgiving minute
With sixty seconds' worth of distance run,
Yours is the Earth and everything that's in it,
And—which is more—you'll be a Man, my son!

FOREWORD

We all experience over our lifetime a variety of problems, some of which poison our lives. For example, nobody goes through life without ever having experienced illness.

Our world is structured this way, and so are we. Right now someone, somewhere, is in the midst of an argument...or feeling offended. And somewhere a war is breaking out. All of this is an integral part of our lives. Qigong practice can help soften the blows of fate. It can eliminate many internal causes of your problems and reduce the external.

Life, we know, is movement, and its quality often depends on the scope of our motions. And since Qigong involves both movements of the physical body and Qi energy internally, it's viewed as a health-maintenance system, science, and sport. Health, however, is also balance. To the extent that Qigong balances energy with your emotional state without ignoring regulation of your physical health, it can be seen as a useful sport that is accessible to all ages and has no side effects.

For life to become more interesting, for us to understand and do more, we must understand ourselves. This requires investigating ourselves. After all, many mysterious things and questions that remain unanswered are connected with us. For example, what is the energy that we employ to help ourselves and others? What are our dreams, and why in many situations are they things that inform us about the future? Why do some people suddenly recall a previous life of theirs and begin speaking a different language? Why are we able to dream about our deceased relatives and interact with them? Why...? Why...? Why...?

If you think about the world in which we live, different landscapes and cityscapes come to mind: fields, forests, seas—places you've been to or seen in movies—with the sky above it all. The variety on Earth is staggering: vast oceans, scorched desert, impenetrable woods, endless steppes, the icy silence of polar snow. Earth contains highly diverse scenery and many different cities and countries. However, at the very same time we know very well that Earth isn't really such a big planet, that when measured against the cosmos, it's only a tiny speck of dust.

The Moon is the celestial body closest to our Earth. We've learned a great deal about it in recent decades. The sun gives us life, but about *it* we know far less. At night we look at the sky, with its sprinkling of myriad stars. They attract and lure, leaving no one unaffected, be it lovers, poets, scientists… From time immemorial, humans have asked themselves the question "What is out there?" With advances in technology has come a deeper and deeper penetration on the part of humankind into the mysteries of the macro- and micro-world. In our existence on Earth, humankind has advanced many hypotheses, assumptions, fantasies, scientific paradigms. But do we really know a lot? How far advanced are our ideas today from those of the Ancients'?

Of course, the assertion that Earth is flat and held up by three elephants standing on a giant turtle or that it floats on whales prompts nothing more than a condescending smile today. We think of ourselves as having made major advances. We now know about everything there is to know concerning the structure of matter; we can investigate its molecular and atomic level. We created the notion of quarks and labeled as "black holes" sections in the cosmos we aren't able to penetrate with the help of modern science. But is this a lot? Do we understand *what Life[1] is, what being alive is?* Do we know *where the boundary line of Life passes* and *whether there is*, in general, *such a line*? And *what niche in this Life is allotted to humans?* Furthermore *what*, generally speaking, *are the levels of Life?*

Of course, in light of contemporary scientific notions, we can assume that there's some form of life on other planets. Further, we know that space isn't uniform and far from empty. Studying the universe with the help of modern technical means, we can fix and record various types of radiation. But the majority of scientists still don't suspect the existence of principally other kind of information that neither instruments nor our brain knows how to perceive.

In ancient times there were no microscopes and telescopes, radio and television, earth satellites and bathyscaphes, electricity and nuclear

---

1   The capitalization of the word "Life" refers to all possible living forms in the universe, including animals, plants, crystals, bacteria, souls, etc.

technology—everything that humankind is accustomed to utilizing today. But there are drawings and descriptions of other celestial bodies, and we have maps of the continents, evidence of the transformation of matter, and more. From where and by what means is this information received? We get it from ourselves. Humans represent a reliable, multifunctional research laboratory with truly unlimited possibilities. All that's required is the knowledge necessary to utilize this laboratory.

Here's an instructive Chinese tale: In a well there lived a frog. It was known for saying, "I know how vast the sky is, and I know how much water there is." One day the frog climbed out of the well and headed toward the sea. But it lost its mind because it saw how huge the sky was and how much water there was.

Therefore humankind can take one of two routes: (1) never go anywhere, never familiarize yourself with anything new, and remain where you are, or (2) step by step, get to know this big world.

Zhong Yuan Qigong (ZYQ) is the key than can open the doors to your own laboratory and in it switch on all necessary analyzers. At the very same time, ZYQ is a simple science of life, although Life itself is far from simple.

Zhong Yuan Qigong practice not only contributes to improving our health, and it not only expands our knowledge about the world. It also allows us to reach a qualitatively different level of Life, one independent of the physical body and the conditions of our place of habitation.

Mingtang Xu

The miraculous disappears as soon as it's investigated.

Voltaire

*It's futile to expect great additions to learning when we insert
and implant what is new in the old. If we wish to avoid going eternally
in circles with the most insignificant movement forward,
there must be nothing less than an earthshaking, total renewal.*

F. Bacon

Envisaging limits to scientific knowledge and prophecy is not possible.

D. Mendeleev

*He alone enriches humankind who helps it to know itself,
who deepens its creative Self-awareness.*

Stefan Zweig

*A fairy tale may be lies, but there's a hint in it,
a lesson for you good guys.*

A. Pushkin

PART ONE

THEORY AND PRACTICE

Chapter 1:
ORIGINS, PHILOSOPHY, METHODOLOGY

AN INSIGHT ON THE CONSISTENCY OF THE WORLD

A MODEL OF THE HUMAN AND THE UNIVERSE

Three Aspects of the World

Every formidable system is based on or grows out of certain philosophical assumptions. Zhong Yuan Qigong is no exception. However, while being the oldest of the known systems for the development of people, it at the same time represents a philosophical conception of the structure and evolution of the Universe, of the development of Life and Mind.

Here we'll study the practice of Stage III of the part of ZYQ labeled "developmental." In Stage I we spoke in more detail about this classification. Practice of this part assumes your mastery of the methods of self-regulation for the purpose of your development as a human being, as a representative of a certain biological type. This development is supposed to transform you in such a way that you'll be able to move to a qualitatively different level of life.

The second section—Image Medicine (or Image Therapy)—is meant to correct defects in a person, again with the aim of creating for him an opportunity to develop. This part includes a number of philosophical aspects that are beyond our grasp, since they lie outside the perimeter of our perception of the world. Only after receiving some personal experience with practice and enduring certain phenomena do we begin to realize that, alas, the world may not be what we're used to seeing and that its material part, open to our sense organs, is only one of its components. Life in this viewable world to which we're accustomed is only one of many forms, some of which may seem simply improbable.

Therefore, depending on your intuition, convictions, potential, and level of practice, you can accept or reject all of the following descriptions. You can consider all to be fantasies or fiction, but at the same time remember that *our attitude toward information doesn't alter the information itself.*

So, in Image Medicine—the second section of ZYQ—*the entire Universe is divided into twenty-seven different levels of worlds and the structure of a human and the Universe is identical.*

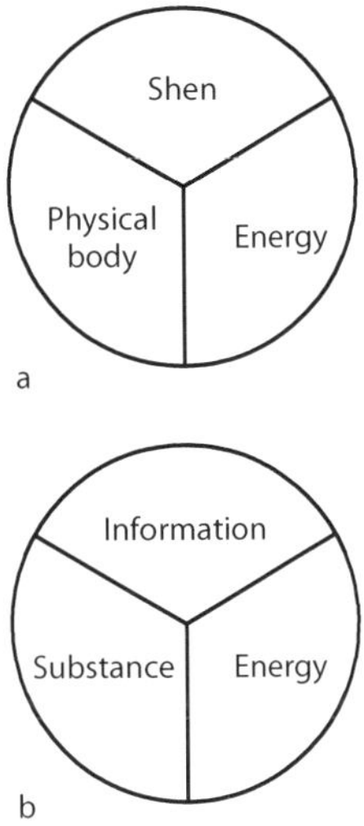

Picture 1: Three Components (a) of a Human, (b) of Universe

Where does this number come from and what kind of worlds are these?

Human has three constituent parts, or three components, or three aspects: a physical body, an energy system, and *a system of information* or *soul* (Picture 1a).

Three aspects can also be noted throughout the Universe: a physical world of substance, energy, and information (Picture 1b).

This can be represented by a model that is the foundation for an explanation of the structure of the Universe. Let's consider this model.

Characteristics of Space

We live in a three-dimensional world where our body, and all the objects around us, consists of matter, physical substance that occupies space.

Do you remember Archimedes' Law: "A body immersed in fluid..."? We're used to representing volumetric bodies in a system of the coordinates x, y, z and to describing them with these three coordinates—x, y, and z. This is the world to which we're accustomed (Picture 2a).

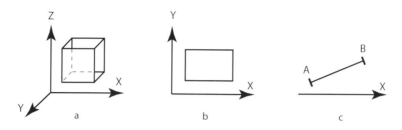

Picture 2: Graphical Images of Different Worlds (a) Three-dimensional World, (b) Two-dimensional World, (c) One-dimensional World

What does the two-dimensional world look like? This, of course, is a plane, and any flat figure is depicted by only two coordinates, x and y (Picture 2b).

When we look into a mirror, we see in it, on a plane, a reflection of our three-dimensional world of volumetric bodies. We're accustomed to orientating ourselves conveniently in this flat image: we straighten out our volumetric clothing and fix our hairdo; sometimes, with the help of mirrors, we try to create a sense of spaciousness in our home's interior; in the calm and smooth surface of water we can see a reflection of the Moon, stars, entire worlds and galaxies. And, of course, the majority of us don't give thought to the fact that we view the events and life of our volumetric world on a flat cinema or television screen.

Naturally, we understand that the one-dimensional world has only one coordinate and is represented by a line on a plane (Picture 2c). In fact, line, plane, and volume are the traits or levels of space. And it's this we have in mind when we speak of, for example, the "three-dimensional world," or the "world of three dimensions."

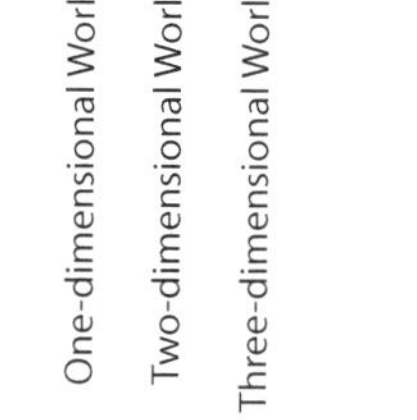

For purposes of illustration, we can "turn" these levels and represent them on an "axis of Space" in the following manner: (1) one-dimensional world, (2) two-dimensional world, and (3) three-dimensional, or physical, world (Picture 3).

Picture 3: Graphical Image of Physical, or Space Aspect

The following trait, characteristic of the human being and the Universe, is the energy component. This energy is known as *subtle energy* to distinguish it from terms accepted in physics (such as electrical, magnetic, and nuclear).

Levels of Energy

For the purpose of understanding Qi well, it's customarily divided in the ZYQ system into three levels—or three types, three qualities, or three parts. The first level is *Qi of fog,* the second is *Qi of light*, and the third is *transcendental Qi.*

The first level is called *Qi of fog*, or the energy of fog, because it looks like fog. The energy of fog is inextricably connected with our health. it's always flowing through our energy channels. Movement, or flowing, is its characteristic. If it flows improperly in a place, if its movement is obstructed anywhere, then there we feel pain, heaviness, or numbness. When we use methods of energy healing, such symptoms can very easily be eliminated, which we learned in the preceding stages.

The second level is known as *Qi of light*, or the energy of light, because during meditation and the state of Quietness you can see flashes or light around the body (a so-called **aura**) or light emitted by internal organs. This is all the energy of light. There's also an aura around each cell. With the Third Eye, we can see light in every part of a body. Every organ, every part of the body, has its own color of light. If in a given part of the body the color isn't what it should be, then we can say with certainty that something is wrong there or that at some point illnesses on a physical plane can arise in this place. Light energy is emitted; in contrast to the energy of fog, it doesn't flow.

As early as Stage I, we spoke about the fact that the concept of the Five Fundamental Elements, or Five Processes, is one of the pillars of Traditional Chinese Medicine (TCM) and the ZYQ system. In Stage II we learned how to regulate and synchronize the functions of our internal organs in accordance with the Wu-Xing circle. These five Qi structures are present in our body, on Earth, and in the whole Universe. Moreover, in some parts of space there's more Qi of one type, while in others, another type is prevalent.

The third level of energy is known in Chinese as *Ling-Qi*. This term has no translation; the closest would be *transcendental energy*.

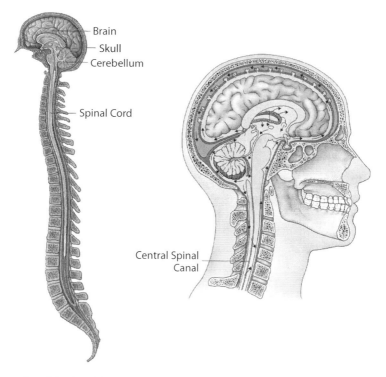

Picture 4: Spinal Cord and the Location of Transcendental Energy Channel

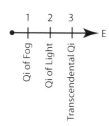

Picture 5: Graphical Image of Energy Aspect

This name is used because this energy lies outside of the perception of our sense organs. We're able to manage it using its natural characteristics.

In our body, transcendental energy is represented only in one place: the spinal-fluid channel, which passes inside of the spinal cord (Picture 4).

For purposes of illustration, we'll draw an axis of energetic direction with these three levels (Picture 5). Later we'll speak in a little more detail about these three energy structures.

Levels of Shen

The third component inherent to the human being and the Universe is information, or Shen. Again we depict an axis, this time informational, and place on it the levels of soul, or Shen. There are also three of these, and we examined them in detail in Stage I: the first level is the soul Yin-Shen; the second, the soul Yuan-Shen; and third, the soul Yang-Shen (Picture 6).

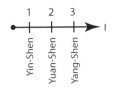

Picture 6: Graphical Image of Informational Aspect

Levels of Worlds

Thus we've created the coordinate axes for Space, Energy, and Information, or Shen (Picture 7). And since there are only three levels on each axis, it turns out that twenty-seven different combinations of space, energy, and Shen can exist: 3 x 3 x 3 = 27 (Picture 8a). And each combination is a certain level of the world. Therefore the levels of worlds can also be twenty-seven in number. But of course on each of these twenty-seven levels there can be many worlds, as there are many stars in our physical world.

Just as we can use three special coordinates—such as height, width, and length—to describe a volume of a three-dimensional object, the level of development of a living being can also be represented by three coordinates, or axis: Space, Energy, and Shen.

Now from this angle we'll see what world, what place, or what "cell" we occupy. In general, the human being is a very complex form of life. We have a physical body; it has volume, like everything consisting of matter. Consequently, from the standpoint of Space, humans are found in the third level and live in a three-dimensional world. This,

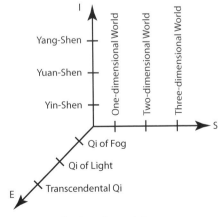

Picture 7: The Coordinate Axis of a Model of Life

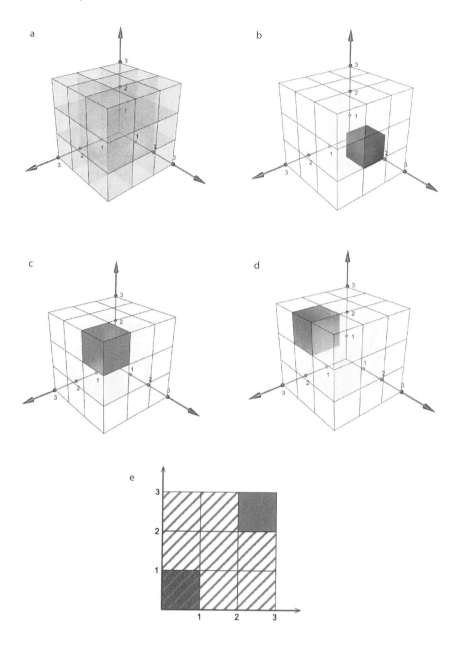

Picture 8: Graphical Model of the Universe in ZYQ
(a) The Worlds of Different Levels of Life,
(b) the World of a Regular Human's Soul After His Death,
(c) the World of Immortals With His Physical Body,
(d)) the World of Immortals Without Physical Body,
(e) The Location of Both: a Regular Human Soul and Immortal.

it would seem, we know. Present in us are all three types of energy: Qi of fog flows through the channels; the organs emit and absorb the energy of light; while transcendental energy passes through the spinal-fluid channel. Unfortunately, however, we have much more energy of the first level—Qi of fog—than of any other.

We're full of the energy of fog; we have very little energy of light; and we have even less transcendental energy. And we have the first level of the soul, Yin-Shen. For our discussion, we divided energy into three levels; however, they don't exist autonomously, that is, independently of one another, but jointly. As we stated in Stage I, a person who doesn't study a special practice has a first-level, Yin-Shen soul.

After death, our Yin-Shen soul continues to exist. Only the Yin energy of fog remains with it. The energy of light and transcendental energy, which are connected with the physical body, disappear. *Following death, the physical body disappears, and you go from living in a three-dimensional world to a two-dimensional one* (Picture 8b). And you leave with all the knowledge you accumulated throughout your life in our three-dimensional world.

Life also exists in the two- and one-dimensional worlds. But life there is of a lower level.

The two-dimensional world is *the world of souls and Yin energy*. In this world, souls, ghosts, and devils—everything not having a physical body—live. With all apparitions and souls of this kind, the level is much lower than with a person. But this doesn't mean that they are unable to harm you. It's like with bacteria: you know that you're on a higher level of development than bacteria, but despite this, they can burden you with many problems.

Levels of Immortals and Their Worlds

Different levels of worlds also exist for immortals. Christian tradition talks about angels; Buddhism refers to the level of Buddha and the immortal Xian. In Taoism, the highest being is the immortal that possesses a physical body (Picture 8c). But immortals not possessing a physical body also exist (Picture 8d). We encounter these terms in literature, and we understand them in a certain way, based on their description and our imagination. But how do they differ?

Master's Story

What's the difference between them: between those not having a physical body and those that do? And what can be said about immortals, a devil, a ghost, spirit, soul, and so on? **They are distinguished by their level of energy.**

The highest world is three-dimensional space—the third level of energy (purely Yang transcendental energy)—and **the soul Yang-Shen with the physical body** *(Picture 8b). This world in Taoism is known as* **Taotian.** *If a person practices correctly and tenaciously, he acquires the abilities to move to other worlds together with his physical body. But it's very, very difficult to get to this world.*

At this stage of development, the physical body is controlled totally by the mind, by consciousness. If from that world you turn up in our world, people will see you as having the same appearance as they—immortals showing up in our world look like people. You can see them with your regular vision, and should you touch them, they will feel like regular people. This signifies that we can perceive them with our human sense organs.

For all intents and purposes, after death the soul of a regular person occupies what can be considered the local two-dimensional world with the first level of energy of fog (Picture 8e, black square), while the soul of an immortal can move at will from its world (Picture 8e, gray square) to any of the worlds (striped part).

Between them is the world with energy of light and the soul Yang-Shen. If beings from this world turn up in our world, they look like immortals with a physical body in our world, but their level of energy is lower. This is why their abilities and opportunities are also lower. People sometimes call beings that live in that world **half immortal.** *In literature, we come across the terms* **"immortal human"** *or* **"earthly immortal."**

They also have **three levels of immortality.** *Where they live differentiates them. If they live on Earth, they are called* **earthly immortals.** *If they live among people, they appear to be "long-lifers," and then are known as* **immortal humans.** *But if they live in a different world, they are called* **celestial immortals,** *and they also have a physical body.*

If they don't have a physical body but have transcendental energy and the Yang-Shen level, then they are also called **immortals.** *However, in contrast to those immortals possessing physical bodies, they must be in a physical object—a tree, picture, or statue—to have the opportunity to associate with us.*

Despite the fact that they don't have a physical body (that is, their level of space occupancy is lower), the level of their soul, of their spirit, is a level higher than that of a person.

*What, then, is the principal difference between a devil, soul, ghost, or immortal that doesn't have a physical body? The level of energy differs, as does the level of spirit. Sometimes, devils or ghosts can possess great force because a very powerful energy of light and transcendental energy are inherent in them. But the level of the development of the soul with them is lower. Thus the **difference still lies in the level of wisdom.***

About Dark Forces

Many stories are told about wars between Buddha, immortals, and a devil. It's often incomprehensible why sometimes the devil and ghosts triumph in battle if their level is lower than immortals'. This occurs because their level of energy is also very high.

In so far as in the Universe there exists such a category as Space, which is uniform for all, and transcendental energy is also found everywhere in the Universe, then any being, no matter where it's located, can utilize this space and this energy. That's why what we consider to be dark forces can also have very strong transcendental energy.

Ghosts and devils live in the two-dimensional world, and their practice aims at moving to the three-dimensional world. For this they must transform themselves in a way that allows obtaining a three-dimensional physical body. For example, if some ghosts have mainly the energy of fog and a first-level, Yin-Shen soul, they practice to acquire a three-dimensional body and to move to a three-dimensional world with the same energy and soul traits. This means that their development transpires along the spatial axis.

But now let's consider *the difference between the human being and animals.* The pig and the human being, for example, live in what world? In accordance with this model, Buddhism asserts that humans and animals have one and the same level. The difference lies only in their structure. After all, they are found in our three-dimensional world and have the same level of energy and level of soul, but their structure is different. *Their level differs only because of form. Within our three-dimensional world, there are also different levels.* The structure of the physical body of animals and plants is the same as ours, but their level of energy and level of spirit are lower.

Where Are These Worlds?

Any teaching has its own model and concept. *But a model isn't reality; it's only a model.* Models exist in every branch of learning. In physics, for example, models for measuring speed exist, but these are principles of measurement and not reality. We have the same thing here.

Sometimes we understand worlds as if each of them is isolated and separate from another world. We're in the habit of thinking this way—this is a problem of our mind and a consequence of logical thinking, but this isn't a real picture of the Universe.

You can't say, for example that in one place there is a three-dimensional world, in another two-dimensional, and in a third place one-dimensional. The fact is, they are located together, as if in one space. This is exactly the same situation inside our body: energy of fog, energy of light, and transcendental energy are all there.

Some beings possess one hundred percent Yin energy, others one hundred percent transcendental Yang energy. Besides this, if we talk about various worlds, then it's very difficult to explain how far they are from each other: how far is our world from the world of souls and how far from our world is the world of immortals? If your mind isn't calm, this world is very far from you. If your mind enters the state of Quietness, these worlds are already here.

Paradise and Hell

If worlds are considered from this angle, then all that are at a level lower than humans are in what we call hell; conversely, all worlds higher than our own are known as paradise (Picture 9).

Consequently, in respect to the twenty-seven levels of worlds, for us there are eighteen levels of hell (all lower worlds) and eight levels of paradise. This is why when a person acts very badly, it's said that he'll be sent to the eighteenth level of hell—to the very worst world.

Why do all teachings state that it's very difficult to get to paradise and very easy to end up in hell? This can be explained in different ways. In general, *after the death of the physical body, people can turn up in various worlds.* If you have a very large amount of Yang energy, you're of light weight; consequently, you rise and are able to go far. But if people don't engage in a special practice, they have a very large amount of Yin energy of fog. This energy is heavy and doesn't allow such people to rise. Thus they go downward.

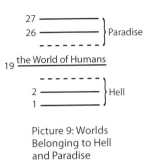

Picture 9: Worlds Belonging to Hell and Paradise

When the soul leaves the physical body and begins traveling around worlds, in the higher ones you feel warmth and bright light. Should you turn up in the lower worlds, you'll sense coolness, heaviness, and darkness.

Qigong is one of the methods that make it possible to acquire the ability to rise higher. However, if you aren't studying any practice but are simply kind and helpful to others by nature, if you perform good deeds, then maybe someone among the higher beings will want to help you and take you higher. Religion is also one of the paths. In any religious current, you're told what you must do to move higher. Prayer often serves to calm the mind and to shift thoughts from worldly concerns to more elevated ones. If you don't engage in Qigong or any special meditation, but every day commit kind acts and help people as part of your routine behavior, this is the best meditation. On the other hand, if every day you practice and meditate for several hours, accumulating in the process tremendous energy, but nevertheless always think incorrectly and try to harm people for selfish reasons, you'll end up in a devil's world.

If during practice you do nothing to distract your mind, you can gain a lot of Yang energy. With this, the soul also develops. But the very last moment is very important. For example, if you do positive things your whole life but suddenly begin acting not quite properly, you can ruin what you already earned.

We spoke about how in ZYQ, as in any system, there are certain principles. One of them is *"don't think about results,"* because your personal result depends on more than just you. It depends on the conditions of the entire Universe. If your mind is intent only on doing good, from this moment you receive an "official place" above from the

Celestial Emperor. After this you receive the chance to become an immortal, Buddha, God. But if your mind and your perception change, if you begin to inflict harm on people, your position will also change: they will place you "in prison"—you'll cross over to the world of a devil.

It's for this reason that *with ZYQ practice they always speak about the need to practice De—good deeds.* In connection with this, in Stage II we studied the practice of the middle Dan Tian and opening the heart. Then kindness and compassion develop, then a person more easily gets rid of negative emotions, and then it's easier to purify the soul for the purpose of ascension.

About the Worlds and Reincarnation

So, in the ZYQ system, the entire Universe is divided into twenty-seven levels. And we already mentioned that we're in the nineteenth world, if we count from the beginning level. There are still eight worlds above us. An analogous picture also exists in other systems. Thus we have the disseminated Buddhist model of a group of six worlds: ours, two higher than ours, and three lower. In this scheme, our world of people is designated by the number three. This means that after death we can be reincarnated in any of these worlds—both in those above us and those below.

Our regeneration in accordance with our karma is controlled by Yama, Emperor of Death and judge. Every soul enters this world many times, and the conditions of its life each time are determined by its actions, behavior, and thoughts—including in previous lives—determined, that is, by so-called **karma**. In our group of worlds, **Yama controls our life cycle.** By life cycle we understand reincarnations in these six worlds, including present-day life in our world. It's possible to be reincarnated many times in one and the same world or in several of these six worlds. Of course, worlds number one and number two (Picture 10) are better than ours, while the other three are much worse.

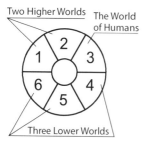

Picture 10: Six Worlds Controlled by Yama, or a Life Circle of a Human

Picture 11: The Depiction of Hell in Buddhism
(Wall Decoration in Buddhist Temple Close to Shaolin)

It's interesting to note that hell in Christianity and Buddhism is depicted in practically the same way, as are the reasons a person ends up there after death (Picture 11), which include malicious gossip, adultery, a disrespectful attitude toward parents, deception, thievery, and more.

Above these six worlds are six more, in which reincarnation doesn't take place. These are the worlds of immortals. They are described in Buddhist literature as a world of bliss, and in Christianity as paradise, or heaven.

Spiritual learning can provide such technique that allows a human to jump beyond the limits of these six worlds and get to the following group of six, thereby breaking free of Yama's control. This is very difficult, since Yama controls these worlds very diligently and manages them in a very just way. Therefore it's important not to inculcate but to eliminate the negative and increase the positive karma.

Master's Story

*Such **spiritual Teachers**[2] as Damo, Lao-tzu, Christ, and immortals wish to help people improve their future and leap past the boundaries of these*

---

2   The capitalization of the word "Teacher" refers to a spiritual Teacher such as Jesus, Buddha, etc., or any living person who can teach high level spiritual knowledge and special abilities.

six worlds. They discuss how we can get to paradise. Of course, if they are in a higher level, beyond the limits of these six worlds, their forces are greater than Yama's. That's why some people have received help from them in going to a higher world.

But the most reliable method is our own practice, which allows us to become aware of and understand ourselves as cosmic beings; strengthen energy; develop our soul and spirit; acquire knowledge about worlds; and prepare ourselves for passing to another level.

For this we open and develop the Zhong-Mai central channel, engage in accumulating and transforming energy, and practice the state of Pause. **The state of Pause is the key that opens the gates to the spiritual development of the practitioner. Without achieving Pause, it is impossible.** *Without the state of Pause, you may call the practice whatever you wish, for example, ZYQ practice for the physical body, the practice of consciousness, of energy, or of the mind—anything you want—but it's not practice of the soul. Without development of the soul, it's impossible to get to higher worlds.*

How the Various Worlds Differ

Light is one of the distinguishing qualities of the different worlds. The lower a world's level, the darker and colder it is. There's no color; it's very difficult to move around. Yet those beings living there are full of desires they can't realize, and this causes great suffering among them.

In worlds of a higher level, there's a lot of light; the color is much brighter and clearer than in our world. These worlds are light, transparent, and pure. And there's no source of light there, as with us on Earth. It seems that light is present everywhere and comes out of nowhere. Moving around in higher levels is very easy. For the inhabitants in those worlds, body, consciousness, and energy are all joined together. For this reason, all desires there are realized in accordance with imagination and mind.

In worlds that correspond in level to our physical world, all structures are built on the surface, and they lean against firm ground. Houses are "built" on clouds. And a house moves together with a cloud.

In the lower worlds, beings constantly experience hunger and cold; they suffer from not being able to satisfy their physical desires.

For example, they want to eat but there's no food. They're always hungry. They want to drink but there's no water for quenching their thirst. In addition, they're always feeling bodily pain, and no one can help them put an end to this pain.

When we first take up practice, we get the opportunity to see various worlds with the Third Eye. Later, in the state of Pause, we're able to look at various worlds and travel around them. And then, on the basis of our personal experience, we can gain an impression as to which world is worse or better, what their distinguishing factor is, and which we wish to get to later.

Why must we purify the body? Why must we transform energy? Because we desire to get to a higher-level world. This is the goal of our practice. But desire is one thing; opportunities and circumstances are something else.

Master's Story

If a person commits suicide or dies in a way unnatural for his physical body, there's no place for his soul in any of the worlds until the time comes when his body would have died a natural death. Those who pass away before the expiration of their allotted term end up in a **world intermediate** *between ours and some other world, which is always lower than ours. There's no more space for them anywhere.*

When I departed for the first time, the first thing I felt was freedom; I was no longer restricted to a physical body. The feeling of freedom and the opportunity to realize anything you so desire were things I had never sensed while in my body. I was able to move immediately to wherever I wanted and to see right away everything I wanted: for example, when I wanted to see lotus flowers, I instantaneously found myself in a place where there were many of them, and I was able to look at them. When for the first time you show up in a different world, you don't at first understand what this is. Seeing its buildings, beings, and nature, you can't figure out where you are and what this is all about.

When I turned up in one of these worlds, I saw that it also had people of different races and nationalities. I also saw a world inhabited by beings radically different from earthlings. In that world they look like people, but their bodies shine and are transparent. And they don't wear any clothing, but walk around just like that. When in motion, they shine. This world is higher than ours. It's a fine one, without suffering and illnesses.

You absolutely must try getting such experience. As for other worlds, much can be said, but it's still early. Only after you have your own experience of the soul going out and traveling, only after you, yourself, are able to talk about this will it make sense to discuss this theme.

My first Teachers left this world one after another. They didn't have time to change their physical bodies. I'm sure about this because they left their physical body in this world. The one I consider my last Teacher used to take me away to practice in the mountains of Henan Province. I would sit down to practice, my soul would go out, and we would head there.

*He had an official position in a higher world. To have an official position in another world means that before your death, you'll know where you're heading later. My Teacher knew this and showed me, so I know where I'll be later. I also have an "official residence permit" there. Sometimes we refer to this as **"getting fruit,"** that is, a certain position in another, higher world that is determined after exiting from this world. This world is beyond the reach of Yama's worlds, and this signifies that you're jumping out of the cycle of regenerations.*

My Teacher didn't take his body with him to that world, because this isn't so easy. Very few have done this. Damo took his body with him, as did Lao-tzu and Lu Dongbin. Damo showed this to his students, demonstrating the opportunities of a person involved in a certain practice. When he was dying, his students placed him in something resembling a coffin. After a few days had passed, someone said that they had seen Damo and conversed with him. When they then opened the coffin, they found only one of his shoes. There was no body.

The same thing happened with Zhang Sanfeng. After gathering his students, he told them his time had come to depart for another world. The students prepared a huge coffin and placed his body there. There's a special way to seal a coffin, and they did this in keeping with Chinese custom. A week after this event, several other students came to the Wudang Mountains and said that their Teacher, Zhang Sanfeng, had ordered that they be summoned. But the first group didn't believe this, since they had seen him dead and participated in his burial. In a word, a dispute broke out between these groups. At this point someone got the idea to open the coffin. They all went together to do this and discovered that the coffin was empty.

Concerning Lao-tzu, there's another story. Upon finishing his book Tao Te Ching, *he said that he would head to the West. He mounted a buffalo and took a little boy with him. And so, on the buffalo, he took off for the heavens, where you can see him.*

There's a similar story concerning Jesus. Crucified, his body after death was placed in a tomb. A few days later his body wasn't to be found there.

Therefore Taoism considers that a person who departs for another world with the physical body is at the highest level of development. Those attaining such a level are called **golden immortals with the physical body.** *Those attaining a previous level are also called* **golden immortals,** *but these are* **without a physical body.** *Such stories have been known in all lands and take place in all times.*

In 1994 in Beijing, I saw one such woman. (I discussed this in detail in Stage I.) She had practiced ZYQ throughout her life. Before dying, she gathered all her children and grandchildren and spoke with each of them, informing them what they should do and in what they should believe. Then she said that her time to leave this world had come. None of her children believed her, since she had always been healthy. But she brought up something interesting. She said that at exactly 1:00 a.m., a light would be visible in a section of the sky—that very place to which she was preparing to go. She stated that they would be able to see this light. And, in fact, all family members saw such a light at exactly the time indicated, as if a lamp had lit up a segment of the sky. I knew her son and grandson and was in her room many days after her death. She looked like she was sleeping in her bed. But by this time the body had dried up. Grease had oozed out from the skin.

Scientists from the Chinese Academy of Sciences' Institute for the Study of Man confirmed that this was really a death, but an unusual one. They conducted constant observations and research. Over the first two weeks, the body preserved warmth, although the heart didn't beat and the lungs didn't function. After several weeks, her body began to dry up, as if mummifying. In Buddhism they would say that she had attained the **level of metal** *and would never die but would live eternally because her physical body would be in that state practically always. It had become a mummy. I was told that a few years ago a monastery took her body and covered it in gold, stating that she had achieved a very high level.*

Her soul can return to the body at any moment, of course; this means that she could live eternally. Even if her soul returned not to her physical body but to some stone body, for example, a statue, then this statue would be able to move. If a soul comes to a statue, even one made from metal, then following a certain ceremony this statue can move and fly. If a soul is in a statue, the eyes and mouth move, and the head turns.

On seeing this for the first time, I was amazed beyond words and decided that I had a vision problem. I saw how the eyes moved and stared at me, how the mouth spoke, and I even heard what it was uttering. Later I frequently encountered similar situations, but the first time was awesome.

For the majority of you, all of this is ahead.

DEVELOPMENT IN THE THREE ASPECTS OF THE WORLD

DEVELOPMENT IN INFORMATIONAL ASPECT, OR THE LEVELS OF THE SOUL AND SPIRIT

The Soul and Spirit

As we read books on spiritual topics, psychology, healing, philosophy, sports, and so on, we usually run across terms such as *"Soul"* and *"Spirit"*. The essence of these terms isn't always clear. For example, let us examine the term **soul**. What do we mean by this term? You hear about the soul or spirit of a company, or the Olympic spirit. You also hear about a certain individual being the soul of a group of people or the soul of a society. People also talk about the spirit that led to victory in competition or battle. Spirit is an abstract concept, and it's very difficult to really imagine what it represents. Therefore what we understand by a term very often depends on our views, philosophy, and simply the language of discourse. In the ZYQ system, however, these terms have a very deep meaning that is connected with our life.

In ZYQ, the soul is a substance found in the human body that turns up there before the birth of a child or during birth. When a person leaves this world, the soul abandons the body and once again departs. So this is *the informational-energy system that we can call soul*. From this standpoint, we know that all people are different.

In ZYQ, *Shen* indicates the soul and spirit. Practice of Shen involves three levels, of which we first spoke in Stage I, at the very beginning of becoming familiar with ZYQ. Now, however, having acquired some practice experience and approaching in earnest the methods and exercises for the development of the soul, we can more deeply and broadly touch on certain aspects of this theme.

First Level: Yin-Shen

So, the *first level is Yin-Shen*, or *Yin-Soul*, which corresponds to our concept "the soul." It's assumed that the soul's level is for all intents and purposes lower than the spirit's. In psychology, this is sometimes called *the second character*. All of us have Yin-Shen, and it's closely connected with the physical body. Each person has only one Yin-Soul. An individual dies, and the soul departs. For where—it's not known! But during life, Yin-Shen can also sometimes go out without any practice. This happens during sleep; a serious illness; an altered state of consciousness as a result of narcosis, narcotics, or alcohol consumption; and so on.

It can be said that Yin-Shen is naturally present in every person and represents Shen without any development. This type of soul possesses no specific or special abilities and is subject to the laws of nature, to the laws governing cause-and-effect connections.

Among many practitioners, the feeling that they already met a person whom they were actually seeing for the first time periodically arises. It seems to you that earlier you were all acquainted. And there might also be a sensation of having visited upper worlds where you associated with God or one of the saints. At this stage, practitioners can very often see pictures of Jesus, Buddha, and other worlds; but such visions, as a rule, are formed by their brains: they are echoes of information a person got from books, films, temple or church visits, stories, and so forth. Therefore often such information that you supposedly get from upper or lower worlds isn't trustworthy. As a rule, this information is present in your brain and undergoes transformation in accordance with your own consciousness. This is simply one of the stages of practice.

If you continue to practice sufficiently well, your Yin-Shen will develop and begin to leave the body. When Yin-Shen goes out, it takes in a large amount of information and knowledge. It can study and bring this knowledge back. But it can go out only if it's in the state of Pause. That's why we say that *a human receives wisdom from a Pause state.*

In this instance, it's not so much you studying as it's your Yin-Shen studying and returning with the knowledge.

With such experience under your belt, you'll definitely believe that *consciousness is a function of our Yin-Shen* and not of our brain. A while after such practice, you'll begin to discover that a lot of knowledge concerning your body—your very self—that you had prior to this turns out to be incorrect.

Second Level: Yuan-Shen

After a while, your Yin-Shen experiences changes, and in a moment you'll suddenly be able to feel that another soul, one qualitatively different, is sprouting in you. At this level, changes transpire within you, under which you begin to be connected with the surrounding world by a multitude of additional channels.

We call this *soul of the second level Yuan-Shen*, and it can divide into a multitude of souls. With this the Third Eye also begins to "divide up", giving you many Third Eyes. Thus, the function of Yuan-Shen is to divide up. And at a certain moment you discover that many souls can come out of you, but their level is higher than Yin-Shen.

There can be many Yuan-Shen in the physical body. Yuan-Shen can be said to be present everywhere: *Yuan-Shen can be as enormous as the Cosmos as a whole, and it can be so small that inside of it there will be nothing.* This soul of the second level also can simultaneously help many different people and for separate purposes.

Master's Story

When you reach the level of practice at which Yuan-Shen appears in you, simultaneously many people during practice or during dreams will be able to see you. And this, in fact, will be your Yuan-Shen.

I demonstrated this type of Yuan-Shen on numerous occasions, and at seminars in many cities: Moscow, Petersburg, Kiev, Donetsk, Ternopol, Tyumen, and Odessa. At these seminars, multiple Yuan-Shen performed a massage, experienced as simultaneous contact made with many people.

For example, at some seminars I spoke about how seventy-two people would feel as if they were being massaged while doing homework on that same evening. My Yuan-Shen performed it. Many people could not see such Yuan-

Shen, but some succeeded. All, however, sensed it as if my own hands were doing the massaging. Different cities witnessed different outcomes. I remember that in Donetsk and Kiev there were thirty-six Yuan-Shen. But since each one was supposed to help two people, I stated that seventy-two people would experience a massage sensation. And I knew this precisely because, after finishing their work, each Yuan-Shen declared on returning what it had actually done. At the following lesson, I checked on this by questioning the seminar attendees and comparing the numbers.

The Yin-Shen and Yuan-Shen practice that I've developed in no way differs from what is described in ancient Chinese books. Now I continue to practice in order to prove the truthfulness of the Yang-Shen concept.

*We stated that while practicing we do a lot to develop our spirit. To understand what our soul is, what our spirit is, we must enter the state of deep calm. In Stage III, we call this **the state of Pause.** During the state of deep calm, Pause, a change takes place in our physical body, and our soul is able to go out beyond the body's confines. Then we can understand exactly what the physical body is, what energy is, and what the spirit is. Even at the level of Yin-Shen, when it begins to leave the body, everything becomes very interesting for us because it's able to visit various worlds.*

*At the same time we must live simply and provide for ourselves and our family members. Besides our life necessities, there's much that is very interesting. With each day, as your involvement in practice deepens, you begin to become more and more convinced that **the most interesting thing for investigation is our spirit.** We must develop our spirit by a special method. We practiced the lower Dan Tian to get a concentrated energy ball there. Then we moved this ball upward and downward along the central channel to open this channel. In Stage II, we open the segment between the lower and middle Dan Tian, and in Stage III we'll continue opening the channel up to the upper Dan Tian. After this channel is completely opened, the soul will be able to go out at a certain moment. This moment corresponds to the state of Pause, which we must learn to enter through the exercises of Stage III.*

When I began Yuan-Shen practice, I understood why monasteries contain many images of spiritual Teachers with many heads, many arms and eyes (Picture 12). Such sculptures and drawings represent one of the methods of instruction: from them we learn of the opportunities we have in the process of practicing. For example, sometimes you feel that you have not one head but many.

Picture 12: Images and Sculptures in Chinese Temples Demonstrating the Various Levels of Practice

24

Picture 12: Images and Sculptures in Chinese Temples Demonstrating
the Various Levels of Practice (Continued)

Picture 12: Images and Sculptures in Chinese Temples Demonstrating the Various Levels of Practice (Continued)

Until I had reached this level, I would look at such images in monasteries as a tourist would: they were merely interesting and unusual to me. When I attained this level, I understood that these images convey knowledge.

In the Shaolin Monastery is a hall devoted to my ancestor. There, on one of his statues, the exiting of the soul is depicted: the body is here on earth, while the soul, similar to the man, is in the sky, on a cloud (a more detailed discussion of this is in the book on Stage I), with two cords leading to it. One cord stretches from the central channel and exits at the Baihui point; the other exits from the back of the head, from the center of transcendental energy (Picture 13a). It supports the life of the soul at its departure from the body. This became comprehensible to students only after their practice of transcendental energy.

In many systems, they practice Yin-Shen in such a way that it would be able to go out and return. But in these systems, they don't practice Yuan-Shen. In the ZYQ system, we practice Yin-Shen with the aim of rising to the next level. If we practice well, Yin-Shen will go out and return, and *we will be able to control our own death and regeneration.*

But Yin-Shen is only one in number, while Yuan-Shen are many. It can be said that *Yuan-Shen, like the wind and light, are present everywhere.* In Taoist systems you can see drawings depicting a human with several souls departing from his or her head, and then from them, in turn, several more, and so on (Picture 13b). This is a demonstration of how Yuan-Shen goes out and divides; they can be many in number and each one can carry out its own work. Such Yuan-Shen can obtain information from different worlds. However, it can't bring about changes in the world; the Yuan-Shen level can't create a world. Having attained the Yuan-Shen level, a person

Picture 13: The Energy Connection between the Body and Soul at Its Departure (a, b) refer to Yin-Shen, (c) refer to Yuan-Shen

already understands everything concerning both his or her immediate surrounding world and the Cosmos as a whole. *Yuan-Shen is also the stage of enlightenment.*

But this isn't the ultimate goal of the soul's development.

Third Level: Yang-Shen

The next level is *the achieving of Yang-Shen,* where there's almost no Yin in the soul, but exclusively Yang. Sometimes Yang-Shen is called **spirit**. But **Yang-Shen and spirit** are different things. The second level, Yuan-Shen, can be called spirit, but the third level, Yang-Shen, is something still stronger.

Yang-Shen is also present everywhere. It can be inside the physical body, but it is a rather dense substance. So it can go out and exist independent of and unconnected to the body. When a practitioner moves toward the Yang-Shen level, one day he may find himself in another world, with the feeling of being in a physical body.

This is the sequence and technology of our practice: at the beginning, *Yin-Shen,* then *Yuan-Shen,* and then *Yang-Shen.* But if you don't practice, if you don't feel this and see, then naturally you won't be able to believe in this. When you practice the higher levels of Qigong, many interesting things transpire in which it's practically impossible for an average person—not involved in his or her own spiritual development—to believe.

If Yin-Shen leaves the body during sleep or an illness, a person can see many pictures or dreams connected with the life and existence of people. But these are events occurring in our world. On the second level, Yuan-Shen, everything is different. Yuan-Shen can turn up at one and the same time in the lower worlds—that is, in hell—in our world, and in paradise, being able to take in information and interact with these worlds simultaneously—if we divide up the Cosmos into three worlds: Earth, Sky, and Human, or our world (world of people), lower worlds (hell), and upper worlds (paradise). But most of the information Yuan-Shen receives is usually about our world, and only extremely rarely does it go down to the lower worlds—to hell, the worlds of the devil.

Yang-Shen can move around all worlds; it has no limitations. If Yang-Shen moves to the upper worlds, it feels the way you feel moving to a different room. On seeing unfamiliar beings in the different world, it begins to get acquainted exactly like a person does with different people. This third Shen level is very difficult to attain, especially if the soul is just beginning to work out its first level.

When shifting from the first level, Yin-Shen, to the second level, to Yuan-Shen, the practitioner feels very big changes. Externally, nothing changes; there are no alterations in the body, face, clothes, and so on. All the changes occur internally and are felt with movement from the second to the third level, Yang-Shen . In this case the practitioner is able to sense each moment and understand the various worlds, with the feeling emerging of having come to this world simply as a guest—and to the other world as well.

Having reached the Yang-Shen level, a human is able to live without his physical body.

The Stages of the Soul's Development

When following a certain preparation and Yin-Shen goes out for the first time, it doesn't go far or for long. At first you see your physical body off to the side. This exiting and returning of the soul takes place many times until the practitioner—more accurately his or her soul—acquires certain skills.

While the Yin-Shen level is low, it possesses consciousness but doesn't sense the body. As the Yin-Shen goes out and returns more and more, it begins to grow and strengthen. After a few times, you begin to sense it better, and finally you begin sensing it as you would your own physical body. You feel the same as you do in your physical body, but perhaps only on smaller dimensions.

After your soul travels to many worlds and acquires knowledge about these other worlds, it will return to your body for a long time. What happens is simply this: following a routine return of the soul, you receive information that your soul will not go out once again, but will continue its practice inside of your body. A certain secret is the key to understanding when the soul must return back: **when you're able** to sense your Yin-Shen in the same way that you sense your physical body, this is the time when it must return inside and remain in your body. This is a symptom or phenomenon that indicates you have completed Yin-Shen practice.

Thus, your soul carries out practice inside your body. After a while, it becomes transformed and rises to the next level of its development. This transformation, this change, requires time. The time of transition from level to level in the soul's practice we discussed in detail in Stage I. There's no specific theory as to why this happens. Simply, at one of the stages of practice, it suddenly becomes clear that your soul can divide, thereby leaving you with several. Should you continue to practice, this dividing process will continue, and the quantity of such Yuan-Shen will increase. And at this point not Yin-Shen, but Yuan-Shen can already go out.

A person can have very many Yuan-Shen—hundreds and thousands. **In the ZYQ system, you usually practice until the dividing process results in eighty-one Yuan-Shen,** in contrast to other Buddhist systems. When this amount of Yuan-Shen is reached, there arises in the practitioner an inner understanding that it's necessary to gather them together so that they continue to practice further inside the body, thereby making continued development and ascension to the next level possible.

But other possibilities exist too. If you don't wish to move up a step, you can continue practicing Yuan-Shen. Then their dividing will continue, and you'll increase the number of your Yuan-Shen. You'll be able to get several hundred and even several thousand of them. But this means that you're preparing to stay at this level of development. For further development, obtain only eighty-one Yuan-Shen—the exact quantity needed to move to the next level. If you decide to go further up in your spiritual development, all Yuan-Shen will once again come to your body and unite with it—dissolve in it—for further practice.

After this procedure, *subsequent practice begins to change the physical body qualitatively.* At this moment the development of the Yang-Shen level commences. By this time, energy, consciousness, and the physical body itself have already become strong. And consciousness gets the opportunity to exercise complete control over your physical body.

Beginning now, and lasting for many years, is the process by which practice gradually transforms the physical body in such a way that it ceases being "normal." As it unites with Yuan-Shen, it starts morphing into something akin to an **energy body**. This again requires more than ten years of practice.

Such a body possesses many new qualities, such as the ability to move instantly. **It can suddenly disappear from one place of space and appear in a completely different one.** That's when practitioners discover that they can suddenly go out from their body or simply change locations. At one and the same time, many energy bodies may exist, and many people simultaneously can see them. Such an energy body can be seen with regular vision; **to your regular eyes, it will look like any other human.**

Master's Story

*An understanding of the levels of spiritual development can give us the ability to grasp what Life is and what the Universe is. We'll be able to understand what the **various levels of Life** represent. This is approximately the same as being able to understand what the life of a single-celled and multicellular being is. In the Universe, however, many levels exist. **A higher level of life can understand what the life of a lower level is. But the lower level of life can't understand life of a higher level.** Besides this, the lower level is always easier to reproduce than a higher level. This law reigns everywhere. On Earth we can observe it among the various populations inhabiting both land and sea. Mice, for example, reproduce much faster than elephants. And the process dolphins and whales undergo to produce offspring is much different from that of regular fish; and their life is longer.*

Our task is to develop the physical body, energy, and spirit in order to attain a higher level of life. Of course, this isn't so easy, but each stage, each level, is very interesting. Students of spiritual Teachers (personal students) tend to know much more about inner secrets than others. A large number of such students experienced their soul departing after a retreat in the Shaolin Monastery. However, very little was said about this at general seminars, because many come for the restoration of their health rather than for the development of their abilities, so it's often difficult for them to understand such results. That's why the ZYQ practiceis are devided in two phases. First, the usual seminars for everyone are conducted. Then, if someone has the desire to study more deeply, he can become a personal student. This situation is similar to when the recipient of a bachelor's degree has the choice to enter graduate school and gain additional knowledge from a specialist.

On the one hand, I teach as a Qigong Master; on the other, I also continue to practice. I've already completed the second level of spiritual practice – the level of Yuan-Shen- and have begun the third.

Yang-Shen can come to you and converse with you. And you can see and hear this with regular vision and regular hearing. Developing the Yang-Shen level requires much more time than the lower levels. We have to practice all of this in order, step by step. Based on my own experience, I can say that such a path of development allows us to realize our goals.

The Properties of Shen

Our soul today is Yin-Shen. Yin-Shen encompasses everything connected with our emotions, our character traits—our human nature in general. The emotions belong to Yin-Shen nature. For example, if you like or dislike something, love or hate someone, then these emotions belong to Yin-Shen. After death, the soul continues to live, and it can continue to hate the same person it hated during life, with the desire to cause this person harm. Our entire nature is contained and preserved in the Yin-Shen soul. Everything that a specific individual represents is his or her Yin-Shen nature. The Yin-Shen soul can enter a concrete physical body from another world. The soul comes to the physical body, unites with it, and with the help of this body, as with the help of an instrument, carries out its function. In our three-dimensional world of material objects with matter, our lives in the body have all three types of energy. While we aren't able to create this energy, we can learn how to accumulate, control, and utilize it.

For transforming our world, we utilize matter and energy. But we can't create matter and energy only with the help of thinking, of consciousness.

As development in the spiritual part proceeds from the Yin-Shen to the Yuan-Shen level, we begin experiencing many more advantages. First and foremost, our wisdom becomes greater, and we begin to understand the laws of the Cosmos more deeply. On the Yuan-Shen level, we still don't have enough force to transform the material world into the world of energy and change our body. But with further development, we gain the ability to use thinking to transform energy into matter.

Master's Story

When the Yuan-Shen level morphs into Yang-Shen, certain phenomena arise. In the beginning, the phenomena may be connected with material objects, happening automatically and without the use of your mind. You pick up a pen and it suddenly disappears. Or you're sitting and something appears in front of you, even though you weren't thinking about it. Everything happens seemingly independent of you. When your Yuan-Shen level approaches the Yang-Shen level, you'll experience changes in the area of consciousness and the heart. You discover that a very strong compassion is revealing itself in you. When you look at people, you feel deeply sad because you sense their suffering. Since you already understand the laws of the Universe at this level, you understand that many people don't know the laws and create problems for one another. This is why they end up manufacturing problems for themselves. And you begin to experience pain for them.

As compassion develops in you, you'll feel a need to help different forms of life. But at this stage your force and consciousness are still not sufficiently strong, so you won't be able to realize all your desires. To this day I have yet to meet a master able to reach a level allowing for the realization of all his desires. But I've seen several Masters who have achieved the level of understanding the laws of the Universe. Their hearts are very peaceful, and when they see something, they immediately see both the cause and how it's supposed to be.

When your level of development reaches Yang-Shen, the possibility of **creating material objects and energy** *emerges, and you manifest yet another advantage:* **you're able to create Life.** *For example, from hair and a piece of meat you can create a living being. You can transform a stick into a tree. You also may have the ability to revive a dead person. At this point, you understand the laws of the Universe very well.*

From the standpoint of interaction, the possibilities of Yang-Shen are limitless. You'll be able to interact freely with any being in any of the twenty-seven worlds. One of my Teachers, my great-grandfather, got to this level. He would occasionally make unexpected nighttime visits to relatives or friends and, after conversing and socializing with them, would just as unexpectedly disappear.

The goal of ZYQ practice is to attain the Yang-Shen level.

The development of Yin-Shen, even to the level of traveling to other worlds, isn't a goal; it's something we must go through as one of the stages of practice. When a practitioner is aiming at the Yang-Shen, he's targeting the level of immortality. Taoism talks about the Eight Immortals, who are revered in China because they left detailed descriptions of methods for the development of humans, methods for our health maintenance and treatment.

When Yin-Shen leaves the body, it can't interact constantly with just any person. It's also capable of interacting only with people in whom the Third Eye functions; with regular people, this is possible only in a dream. Possibilities are also limited with Yuan-Shen. If someone experiences a very strong desire to interact with Yuan-Shen or prays, then Yuan-Shen can feel this and come. However, if a person doesn't have the Third Eye—and Third Ear working for him—he can't see Yuan-Shen or hear it. Therefore such a method of interaction is also incomplete. It's precisely in interacting with live people that the possibilities of Yuan-Shen are limited.

For these reasons, in ZYQ we strive to attain the Yang-Shen level and the level of "**golden immortals**." At first, this all seems improbable, not possible. But with practice, this skeptical attitude usually changes. There's a change in your perception of the world, and your horizons and understanding of human possibilities broaden. Most people don't even believe in the existence of Qi until they sense it themselves. A very small number believe in the reality of seeing with the Third Eye. Only after a certain period of practice and some basic experience do people begin to accept a reality that they had earlier been unaccustomed to.

About Soul Travels

In general, Qigong practice offers people not only benefits but also much that's interesting and pleasant. Those reaching Stage III already have something to talk about. But most interesting of all is the departure and traveling of the soul. The soul can visit various worlds on our nineteenth level (for example, physical three-dimensional worlds and various planets) and can turn up in other, adjacent worlds. These travels involve completely different sensations than what we experience when traveling on Earth. If you see some cities or landscapes on TV and then find yourself in those very places, the sensation is completely different. In the same way, viewing other worlds with the Third Eye in the practice process and taking a real trip of the soul are completely different.

Here the natural question arises: how and with what can we see other worlds? After all, eyes belong to our physical body, and the body remains in place during departures of the soul. For purposes of explanation, the various channels of perception, or sense organs, are illustrated in Picture 14. Inside are the soul's five organs of perception. Any soul possesses them, even when no practice is being pursued. After a person's death, the soul leaves the body. Because these five types of perception are inherent to the soul, it can see, hear, and feel; and it has consciousness. The difference is that, while the soul is in the body, you can feel pain and discomfort connected with the condition of your physical body, but after the soul's departure, you experience a sensation of freedom.

Leaving the body, the soul can see it from the side, so you see yourself. The body doesn't see the soul. It's the reverse: the soul sees the body. Independent of whether or not a given person's Third Eye is working, his soul can see when it leaves the body.

Such sight is one of the five internal sense organs. Belonging to **Yin-feelings**, these organs are inherent to the soul. When we practice, we acquire additional abilities that broaden our perception with our regular sense organs. These **Yang-feelings** are inherent to the physical body, since they are connected to the work of the physical organs. For this reason, both our five usual sense organs and those like the Third Eye and Third Ear belong to Yang-feelings, although the latter can also be called extrasensory feelings. Therefore a person possesses fifteen channels of perception and can additionally open a Second Heart.

If we don't practice, we have five regular sense organs. So what we know

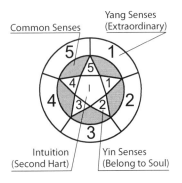

Picture 14: A Model of Perceptional Channels

and understand about ourselves, the world, and nature constitutes less than 30 percent of reality, and perhaps only 10 percent. But because organs and channels of perception are qualitatively—not quantitatively— different, we can't compare them. That's why it's necessary to make every effort to learn how to get the state of Pause, in which our soul is able to leave the body. And only after this are we able to more broadly and deeply understand the surrounding world and our lives. No matter how we try, the five regular sense organs are insufficient for deep understanding.

The soul can hear various sounds and distinguish voices. Souls hear one another just as we do, because everyone has Yin-Shen, which is capable of supplying us with information that's inaccessible to the regular sense organs. We try to achieve the state of Pause so that our Yin-Shen can go out.

When the soul leaves the body, its connection to the latter is maintained. Usually an energy tie exists between the soul and body similar to the energy cord. If this tie is ruined, the soul can't return to the body. If the tie is suddenly broken, another soul can enter. But this concerns only those cases when the soul goes far and for a long time and doesn't see its body. At the beginning stages, when the departures are brief, this danger doesn't exist.

During its travels, the soul can go far, covering great distances. But to return, it doesn't need time and doesn't have to repeat the trip in reverse. This happens in an instant: the soul returns immediately.

Master's Story

First Story

Once a friend and I took off for the Moon after hearing news that an airplane had supposedly been discovered there. We wanted to fly there to see what this was and what inscriptions were on the plane's side. We agreed to do this together to see whether our impressions coincided.

So, we departed. At first there was a whistle in our ears similar to that caused by a powerful wind. Then we found ourselves on the Moon, where we found much that interested us. And we found the plane. But it was very unusual. Until then we had seen only silver coloring planes, but this one had camouflage paint. We had never before seen this. We couldn't read the inscription, and then it was time to return.

While our impressions of what we had seen matched, we couldn't to-tally believe it because the plane was painted in a bewildering fashion, and most importantly, we couldn't figure out what it was doing on the Moon. Much later I saw a documentary about World War II that had shots of planes similar to the one we'd seen on the Moon. Hidden under trees at the edge of a forest, they had a similar shape and paint-job.

Second Story

Once I went deep under the sea to get a look at a pyramid that had also been written about. And I actually saw it there in the place indicated.

When Yin-Shen leaves the body things get interesting. It can travel where a person can't. It can visit other planets, go deep under the ocean, and fly to other cities—all the while gathering a vast amount of diverse information. Information from such travels is always more precise and verifiable than that seen simply with the Third Eye. After all, with the departure, all five Yin channels are working, and you yourself are present where your soul goes, since to all intents and purposes, this is you. Do you really think it's possible to compare a photo of a scenic place to actually being there?

About Consciousness Travel

Sometimes, however, it's not the soul that departs, but consciousness. How is this determined?

People have dreams—some more often than others. And there are various types of dreams. Certain pictures, certain images, appear in them. Some of these images are created by our brain from information contained in it: events from our life, films we've seen, and books we've read; or emotions, thoughts, and so on.

Another type of dream is in no way connected with what we've thought or seen. Everything that goes on in such a dream is so clear that it seems like reality. As a rule, this is consciousness traveling.

While a soul can also travel in a dream, usually it's the consciousness. During such travels, your consciousness can meet with people and even converse with them. But all events and images of such a dream are very closely connected with the physical body, which always reacts to them. Thus, if in such a dream some very sad events take place, while dreaming about them you cry—and then your body also cries, and you can wake up with tears.

This occurs because you have an informational body. As information changes, there's a corresponding change within your physical body. But often you can see this information and perceive it as an image. Having turned up in your informational structure, such an image impacts your physical body.

It's with the help of information that we affect energy and the physical body for such purposes as treating illnesses. If, at first, only information is changed, after a while the body also begins to change. This is a sign of the departure of consciousness.

There is yet another interesting phenomenon connected with consciousness: not only the soul but also *the consciousness can divide*. But a characteristic and fundamental particularity of the departure of consciousness is that at times you can simultaneously sense yourself being somewhere and understand that you're lying in your own bed.

If the soul departs, the body feels nothing and in no way reacts, because all feelings and emotions depart with the soul.

Questions and Answers

1. How does the soul differ from spirit?

The soul and spirit are simply different levels of one and the same thing. After we practice, our soul morphs into spirit.

2. Where are the soul and the spirit located?

The soul and spirit are inside our body, but they can be separate from it. In general, that which is inside our body we call the soul. And only as a result of special training, the soul morphs into spirit. Spirit can also be constantly inside our body and can go out beyond the limits of our body.

3. Is there a place where the soul of a regular person who doesn't engage in any special practice is found? Many consider this to be the heart. Is this true?

There is no local area. The soul of such a person is united with his body and is of the same size and form.

4. In many other spiritual practices, rejuvenation and the attainment of immortality is looked on as a selfish goal and isn't encouraged. Does this apply in ZYQ?

This is a very good question. Of course, when we practice we should develop ourselves. This is proper. After you acquire the ability to help others, you must do it. Take the sun, for example: it gives heat, light, and life to everything on Earth. But if you wish to work like the sun, right now you don't have such abilities and opportunities. Perhaps you have a good heart and are able to be a fine person, but you lack the abilities and opportunities to render serious help. In this instance, your desires are of no use. We can compare this with the level and human qualities of a medical doctor. For example, everyone says that you're a good doctor, that you treat your patients well, warmly, and with an open heart. But when a difficult patient comes your way, you may have a good heart but you don't have the technology necessary for treatment. In this case, with his good heart, the doctor inflicts harm on the patient. **For this reason, from the very beginning we must develop ourselves in order to have the abilities and opportunities to render help—not just the desire to do so and a good heart.**

Moreover, extrasensory abilities and other "unusual" abilities are often believed to belong to the diabolical world, but of course this isn't the case. Jesus had such abilities, as did Buddha, Guan-yin, and many others. Any real Qigong Master possesses great abilities like these. Why, then, shouldn't we develop such abilities? Why should we be saying that this is only for selfish ends? Only those people who don't themselves possess such abilities, those who don't know how to develop themselves in this direction or have some goals of their own can say that other people shouldn't do this. Consider this proverb: **"The fox wants to eat the grapes, but they're too high for his reach. And then he says that they're very sour and taste badly."**

5. Zhong Yuan Qigong doesn't belong to religious confessions. But some pronouncements and goals are the same, such as with Buddhism and even Christianity. What can be said about this?

A lot can be said. Yes, this type of Qigong doesn't belong to any religion. It pertains neither to Buddhism nor to Taoism. This school appeared thousands of years earlier than the rise of world religions. If it hasn't been forgotten but continues to exist, develop, and be vital, this means that it benefits—and is needed by—people. Otherwise, over thousands of years, it would have been totally forgotten long ago. But by the same token, if religions have existed several thousand years, this means that they also can be of help—that is, useful. Systems that are seemingly very apart from one another can both be useful in the same way.

However, we know that every religion in its own way sets the tone for the surrounding world, the Universe, human possibilities, and the interaction between people and their surrounding world. We know also that there have been many problems in the interaction between different religious currents, as well as between the secular and religious way of life. Religion has been and continues to be the basis for a great many wars, because often religion is employed for achieving political aims.

ZYQ is in no way connected with politics, religion, or a race or nation. *Qigong is an art that helps in the development of a human* through the development of the physical body, energy, and spirit. From this perspective, such an art should be purely for a person and should not serve other purposes, separating "chosen" people or countries. *Qigong is similar to science, which is uniform for different peoples and different countries.* Any person of any nation and race can have or can acquire special abilities by working with himself, with his own consciousness and body. For example, now no one country has a monopoly on a particular sport, as it was over one hundred years ago, when we didn't have TV and Internet, and winter sports were unknown in the equatorial countries. After all, the structure of the body is basically the same for all: each of us has a heart, lungs, brain, extremities. And of course everyone has energy, a soul, and so on.

From the standpoint of Qigong, there's no difference between people. Moreover, there's no difference between people and animals, because this is all Life. Many animals also practice, and they also have a soul.

We must develop ourselves, because otherwise we won't be able to have a deep understanding of this world. And if we don't understand it, how will we be able to live in it properly, to develop it and ourselves, and to help one another?

Qigong can contribute both to the good health and the development of the spirit of any human. This can be likened to the situation wishing to read the Bible: you must first go to school and learn how to read. We must have wide-ranging knowledge and the opportunity to develop our abilities.

6. What happens with a person after death?

After death, the soul leaves the body and goes to live in another world. Your friends know that you have died, but you yourself aren't aware of it. The soul doesn't know this—it's living. Or we could look at it this way: you really don't know that you've died already because your physical body is simply like old, worn-out clothing that should be discarded. Your body died in our physical world, but you—your soul—continue to live. From a certain stage, Qigong practice allows you to take in experience and knowledge of where you'll be later. Those practitioners receiving such experience remove the fear of death.

Master's Story

Have any of you thought about why it is that after death the body becomes hard and stiff? Do you know where that freezing and stiffening start? What place retains warmth longest? What is the very last body segment to be warm? The heart.

The heart dies and quits working. But for a long time, heat is preserved there. I think almost everybody sooner or later has to deal with someone close dying. Physicians in hospitals often encounter such situations. Often the process of dying is repellent to the person present, and this is understandable. For me it's interesting, because I see the entire process, although I'm not observing intentionally. It simply happens. When my great-aunt died in my arms, I saw the whole process from beginning to end. Can you imagine what it's like?

First of all you see the most horrible suffering, including pain. The person can't breathe. You can try feeling this by closing your mouth and holding your nose. At first it's very difficult to face death; it's very unpleasant and painful. But then you feel a parting occurring on your head, as if gates of some kind are opening and your soul is departing through them. After this moment, the soul begins to laugh and rejoice as it experiences profound relief from the torment of dying. The sensations are very pleasant. While my great-aunt's body remained in my arms, I saw how her soul began moving around the room with a sense of relief. It looked like a person, and its sensations were very pleasant. Before seeing this, I cried when someone died, but now I don't grieve.

And really, we shouldn't cry when someone is dying; we should be happy. In general, the tears shed for those passing away aren't connected with the sensations the deceased is experiencing. Rather they are our response to the loss of a person who was very close and dear to us and without whom we'll feel sad.

Later, when you reach the state of Pause, you will encounter sensations of dying. During the first moments when your soul is departing, you will experience pain and sometimes suffering or fear. There may also be sensations that are very strange. However, if your body and consciousness are prepared, the only thing you'll feel is pressure in your head, and neither fear or pain. Later, all sensations vanish.

Having left the body, the soul feels nothing—no sickness, no pain, with everything remaining in the body. This is why in Buddhism they ignore the body, and people practicing Buddhist systems don't pay attention to the state of the physical body. They practice in order that the soul will go out, because illnesses of the physical body remain in the physical body, but the soul experiences relief. And Buddhist adherents practice so that the soul is liberated from the ailing body.

But in ZYQ we don't want to proceed in this way. We want the body to regain a normal state. We must be healthy here. Then, if we so desire, we'll be able to take our physical body with us.

7. Why is it, then, that people who never studied anything end up in paradise?

Qigong is simply one of the methods. But if you're not involved in any practice whatsoever and are simply the kind of good-natured individual who helps others, and if you accomplish good deeds, and stay home and pray, then perhaps someone from among the highest beings will want to help you and take you higher up.

We already stated that Qigong and the various religious currents are simply variations of the ways that prescribe what must be done to move higher. In our everyday life, it's the same: if you engage neither in Qigong nor in a special meditation, but every day perform good deeds and help other people, this is the very best meditation. If every day for ten hours you practice and engage in meditation, accumulating enormous energy, but think incorrectly all the time—such as always wanting to harm people and do something that's not good for them—you'll end up in the world of the devil.

8. If a person studies every day for ten hours and thinks only about how he should practice, then where will he end up later?

If during practice you really practice well, with nothing extraneous occupying your mind, you acquire a lot of transcendental energy. And with this, your soul also can develop. But the most recent moment is very important. We consider eight principles in ZYQ. One of them is, Don't think about results during practice, because your personal result depends not only on you personally but also on the conditions of the entire Universe. If you're a good person, you'll receive from the Celestial Emperor an official place there, up above. And after that you can become an immortal, Buddha, God. But if your perception changes, you'll begin to inflict harm on people, and then your position changes as well. They'll put you in prison, and you'll cross over to the world of the devil.

9. But if we eat animals, does this mean that we can't attain immortality, since we're bringing harm to other beings?

Let's examine this. When we eat meat, someone had to kill an animal, which means that you get negative karma, both those who do the killing and those who do the eating. But if we look at our human world, we see that we cultivate many animals for the purpose of killing them. Just think about poultry factories. If a human being didn't care for chickens, 90 percent of them would perish naturally from various diseases. But since people treat them and give them medicines to prevent diseases, almost all survive. Seen from this angle, we develop positive karma.

So, when the time of reincarnation comes, you will be sent to the world that corresponds to your overall karma, and not to a specific episode. Perhaps in your life you'll do a great many fine things, but at the same time just as many very harmful things. In that case, your karma will be zero. But if in your entire life you did nothing bad, and in fact did some good things, you'll develop positive karma. Who is it that weighs, or measures, your karma? This is the duty of Yama.

10. Where is Yama to be found in this model of the universe?

In the two-dimensional world. Yama lives in the two-dimensional world, but he has a very high level of energy. For example, Pusa is the second level in Buddhism. A person might consider Pusa also to be living in hell, but this doesn't mean that his level is low. Yama lives in a world of a lower level than ours, but this doesn't mean that his level is low. Simply his office is there.

11. How do you earn positive karma?

The aim of our practice is to achieve the level of immortals with a physical body. During practice, you can be subjected to the influence of external factors. This means that your perception or mind can change. If in your consciousness is the thought that you want to become useful to all forms of life, this means that you have a tendency to become Buddha. But if your mind is subjected to some influence that causes you want to start causing others harm, at that moment you turn into a devil. Let's look at this concept in Buddhism.

Master's Story

The Buddha is the enlightened one. Is the devil enlightened or not? What is his level? Were we to define a devil as a being with Yin energy that lives in the two- or one-dimensional world, then we would believe that he is of a very low level. But many religions speak about devils of a very high level. Why?

Buddha signifies an enlightened being who serves all lives, not only himself or a specific form. Buddha helps everything existing in the Universe. And what is a devil? A devil is a being that does something for himself or a small group, and he also can be enlightened. If you aren't enlightened, you can't become a devil either, because you then wouldn't have strength for anything. In that case, how would you be able to become a devil and cause harm to others?

However, it's well known that many devils later become Buddha. Twenty years ago, I asked my spiritual Teacher why, as a result of practice, some people can become Buddha, but some become devils. What is wrong here: an improper method or something not in order with the practitioner? (At that time in China there were widespread discussions about good and bad methods.)

My Teacher explained to me that sometimes the right method can lead to incorrect results. If you practice the Buddhist current, it's possible that at the very last moment you can also become a devil. Jesus had several disciples and one of them betrayed him. But all of them practiced the same method and followed the same teachings. Why did this happen? After all, the method was the same for everyone. We have a number of mafia organizations in our world, and some of their representatives become very big donors. For example, in Hong Kong there's an organization that used to engage in exporting while not paying taxes; in doing this, it took in a great sum of money—shady money. Sometimes it pulled off armed attacks on government and private boats carrying various products, seized the products, and then sold them. So they did many bad things, correct? But then they began using the shady money for research, road and building construction, and so on. In this way their image changed. The concept of "bad" or "good" has meaning only as it applies to a person's apparent behavior.

You can employ knowledge for a multitude of useful things, but some are tempted to utilize it to get benefits for only themselves, neglecting everyone around them. This is the road to the devil. Everything depends on your behavior, that is, on how you use your knowledge.

DEVELOPMENT IN THE ENERGY ASPECT
Levels of Energy

Energy is, of course, a very important aspect of our life. We're constantly talking about the need to increase its level and raise its quality, and we regularly engaged in this in Stages I and II. Naturally a question arises: What do we mean by the term *energy* in Qigong, and what's its source? Let's consider energy to be that which in a certain way we can sense and see. From the standpoint of Qigong, energy is a very definite, concrete concept. In Qigong, we don't operate with definitions, as in physics, but rather speak about energy's manifestations, which the practitioner can feel and see, such as warmth, cold, pressure, or light. Let's review the types of energy.

Energy of Fog
The first level of energy—is the **energy of fog**, or Qi of fog. Its characteristic is to move, or flow. The energy of fog passes or flows through our energy channels inside our body. It's always flowing. If it ceases to flow, this indicates an illness. The energy of fog is present both in the body and everywhere throughout the universe. Sometimes it can be seen with regular vision.

Energy of Light
The second level of energy is the *energy of light*. This kind of energy can be seen sometimes with usual vision, but most often it can

be seen with the Third Eye during meditation. The energy of light is that which you can see around all organs and around the cells throughout the body. In contrast to the energy of fog, the energy of light is emitted like the light of stars. However, when we look at the stars with our regular eyes, we see only white light. With the Third Eye we can see various colors, not only white. That's why we see a great many colors when we look at the Universe with the Third Eye.

Everything living emits light of a different color. We can see various colors among plants and animals. In some places on Earth, Qi of one color dominates, in others, another color. In the human body, for example, around the lungs and in many other places, white is dominant. At the liver and gall bladder, the Qi of the color green prevails; at the kidneys, the Qi of a dark color; at the spleen, yellow; and at the heart, bright red. On a whole, white is dominant in the body. In the very same way, when we look at the Universe, white can be seen most often—in sunlight—but there are other colors also.

This energy—the energy of light—is easy to govern. Our hands and our consciousness possess such ability, and we studied this technique partially in Stages I and II and in more detail in the section "Image Therapy."

Transcendental Energy

The third level of energy is *transcendental energy*. It's called by the ancient name **Ling Qi** in Chinese. **Ling** signifies something that you can't feel and is located beyond the boundaries of your usual perception.

Transcendental energy doesn't resemble the energy of fog, which passes along the big channels. Nor is it like the energy of light, which we can see around organs and cells. We can't see transcendental energy, but when it begins to work—inside of the spine, in the channel of the spinal-cord fluid—a very thin, red line appears.

Transcendental energy has no color. It's impossible to describe how it looks. However, this energy governs us, and it's very difficult to explain how it works. It's everywhere in the Universe. In particular the soul, leaving the body and traveling the Universe, utilizes this energy. This can basically be compared to the flight of birds or an airplane: just as they use air for their flight, the soul utilizes transcendental energy.

And just as they can't fly without air, our soul can't travel without transcendental energy.

It's impossible to define transcendental energy and describe what it is. Something can be said about the energy of fog, because you can see it. It flows through channels. You can say what color it is, and where it's blocked. But transcendental energy can't be seen. For this reason Lao-tzu said, "It seems like something is there, and seems like there's nothing." He revealed that this energy already existed when this world, this Universe, didn't. He could receive such understanding or inner vision that comes to a human during deep meditation. Right now we practice transcendental energy with only one goal: to use it for helping the soul during its travels to different worlds. Then, when the soul leaves the body, this energy follows it, and we have two channels: one for the departure of the soul and another for transcendental energy, which helps our soul. But first let's consider where we get energy from.

Where Energy Comes From

First and foremost, practice provides energy. If you don't study, you'll be unable to receive it. Nobody has the power to supply you with energy constantly. To leave the body, the soul needs the energy of fog and the energy of light, and for traveling transcendental energy is required. These two energies are directly linked to our physical body.

Where Does the Energy of Fog Come From?

First, the energy of fog comes from food. It's present in any vegetable.

Second, we can receive it directly from within by practicing certain exercises. Here we accumulate this energy in the lower Dan Tian. When a lot of energy is stored, it begins to move upward. Then the practitioner feels pressure in the upper part of his or her head. After this, the bones of the skull move apart (here the head is opening up), and the soul goes out.

Where Does Energy of Light Come From?

First, energy of light comes from the environment, from nature. During meditation, it's sometimes possible to see a ray of light that moves like a star. There are many such energy rays in the Universe, and we can especially receive and gather this energy of light.

Second, energy of light can be gotten from energy of fog with the help of our emotions, or more accurately, with the help of consciousness that's connected to the emotions. Various emotions engender various types of light energy. For example, love helps one receive red energy, which is capable of treating illnesses. You've likely heard stories in which a person was healed due to a deep love.

Regarding energy, it's necessary to know one very important thing: *energy of fog is Yin energy*, the basis for further development of our soul. *Energy of light is simultaneously Yin and Yang energy.* Some colors prompt the sensation of warmth, others of cold. *Transcendental energy is pure Yang energy.*

Before the soul leaves the body, energy of light also gathers from the various organs and moves upward. A part of the energy collects in the upper part of the head, and this brings about a simply fantastic phenomenon: out of the Baihui point appears a variegated fountain of Qi that looks like a lotus flower. When the various types of light energy rise to the upper part of the head, at a certain moment you can see the fiery flower protrude and come apart, morphing into a multitude of beautiful flowers, much like fireworks. In Chinese, this is called the Celestial Flower 天花乱坠.

If such a phenomenon occurs, it means your soul is ready to depart from your body. But it's rather difficult to attain this state. Many obstacles block the way, which we'll speak about during the appropriate exercises.

What We Spend Our Energy On

During practice, we collect energy. But how can we utilize it?

First, we use energy for our own personal needs; as our health improves, we become more energetic, active, and fit for work.

Second, energy helps us heighten our sensitivity and the range of perceptions of our usual five sense organs.

Third, energy helps us to develop our spirit. When our soul departs from the body, we can understand more about ourselves and the Universe.

Fourth, we expend energy for work in the field of Qigong. If you master energy and understand what life is, you could become a specialist in the field of Qigong and Medicine Imagery.

But most people study Qigong for their own interests. When we have a lot of energy, we have the strength and ability to create in spheres of human activity, such as in the sciences and the arts. And we're able to achieve the best results while expending less time and energy.

DEVELOPMENT IN THE PHYSICAL, OR SPACE ASPECT

Quantitative Changes of the Physical Body

First, the Space aspect is aspect is connected to our three-dimensional world of matter and our physical body. It's the third aspect of humankind, which in our day is best studied by contemporary science. That's why we won't say much about it.

But precisely because we live in a three-dimensional space, in one of its material and physical worlds, it's very complicated both to explain and to understand what other worlds represent. And while practicing Qigong, it's one of the major difficulties in understanding the Universe. Any language describes our usual material world, but we don't have the words and concepts to describe the spiritual world.

When we speak about the development of the self, we don't always understand what it means, because we must understand all three aspects in relation to each other. But assuming we have figured things out regarding our spirit and energy, how can we develop our body?

Of course, body development involves improving health. We also often connect the development of the body with sports or exercise. But we're not talking about the development of biceps or training for a sport. These are commonly known to be good for us, but they do not represent truly valuable development.

Our physical body consists of matter, substance, and occupies a definite volume in space. It's three-dimensional, and we can measure our body in the three currents. Therefore, in respect to physical development—that is, development of the physical body—we can speak about the change of its spatial characteristics. What must change isn't width or height, but something different.. Therefore, the development of the physical body does not signify only health promotion or the strengthening of muscle tone and power that refer to quantitative characteristics. Development has to lead to a change in quality, to the appearance of a new quality.

Qualitative Changes of the Physical Body

How and where can qualitative changes of the physical body appear? The body can be transformed into a two-dimensional body. And if development continues in this current, it can be transformed into a one-dimensional physical body.

What is a two-dimensional physical body? Let's consider the interesting bodily practice that exists in Tibet, as a result of which some Tibetan monks at the moment of death engage in self-immolation. For a very long time, they studied a certain practice and eventually set their body on fire. The body disappears, though sometimes teeth or hair remains.

Many have no doubt read or heard about how the physical body can suddenly move from one place to another, called teleportation. Have you ever heard that a physical body can also go through walls? How this does happen and why is it possible? Because *the three-dimensional physical body morphs into a two-dimensional*, and the latter senses no resistance passing through three-dimensional objects. *In Qigong, we believe that the physical body can disperse or scatter as it's transformed into Qi, but if Qi is concentrated, it can morph into a physical body.* This is a real route for development of the physical body.

Of course, this kind of development is very difficult, and many years must be spent on it. That's why at first it's necessary to focus on the current for developing energy.

LEARNING TECHNIQUES IN ZYQ

Differences in Training Technique

You already know that at the various stages we utilize different methods of training—both for teaching and for learning. This is very important in practicing Qigong. We talk about this at each stage because the methods of training at each stage are different, and they all depart from the generally accepted and customary methods. But for those who haven't been studying Qigong for long or who are using books and videos without attending seminars, this can be incomprehensible. Information on the level of words is one thing, but personal experience is something completely different.

Thus in our world years and years are spent on perceiving and mastering any knowledge, so that later this knowledge can be employed. But there's a special method of study in the East that hasn't been applied in the West. This method increases and develops abilities of a human; and it places the greatest importance on our understanding of what we do, why we do it, and how we do it. ZYQ is a system for the development of people and their abilities, and it uses this method.

Of course, you should accumulate a certain amount of knowledge, since every person should know what mankind on the whole has taken in during its existence. Moreover, it's important to do investigative work in an area of specialization. At times, however, knowledge itself isn't as important as creative abilities. For example, any physician has to deal with various illnesses and various patients. Even in treating what would seem like a very rudimentary illness, for some patients the method is effective, while for others positive results aren't to be had. You can see how a really good doctor utilizes his knowledge in treating a person as well as his abilities, because knowledge by itself is insufficient in many cases. To cure a patient, it's necessary to figure out where the sources of the problem are.

Practice in the ZYQ system is divided into five stages for the sole purpose of making it possible to better develop the exercises and understand their meaning. *In the first stage*, you listen with your hands in order to improve their function, open bioactive points on your palms, and learn how to feel the various types of energy with your hands. *In the second stage*, you listen with your body. This technique can be used in order to increase the functionality of your skin, body, and internal organs. Furthermore, this allows you to practice and receive energy from the Master

In the third stage, we consider the two sides: both how to practice and by what means information is conveyed by the Master. Consequently, a special method of listening is employed at third-stage seminars. We're talking now about listening not only with your hands and entire body, but also with your consciousness and heart. Here the heart signifies not simply a physical organ. This is the heart itself, the mind and the consciousness—for all intents and purposes, our informational system. From the standpoint of Qigong, this is also connected with our attention. It's very difficult to express this concept in words, so at the third-stage seminar, attendees utilize several communication channels—from the standpoint not only of the physical body but also of the soul and energy.

Perception of Information in Images and Its Verbal Description

One of the tasks of third-stage practice is the development of your Shen in order to better understand the surrounding world. This is why it's necessary to utilize the heart and consciousness, because words alone are insufficient for further training. If you take in information at the seminars only verbally, you'll actually be unable to grasp what's taught. For studying in the higher levels, there are not enough words—they simply don't exist. There are no words with which to express inner sensations and feelings. Very often these inner sensations can be manifested only through *images.*

During certain practice, an image arises in a person that can't be expressed with words—or is very difficult to express—but can easily be shown as an image. For example, when you glance at another person, you get an image that includes not his or her only outer appearance, facial expressions, clothing, and so on. Automatically, certain notions regarding this person emerge, based on your perception. Imagine how you'd explain this to other people. If you try to describe this person to someone who hasn't seen him or her, you start with outer appearance.

You have to employ words to describe facial features, hair color, figure, height, shape, clothes, and more to convey the external image which you saw. From your words, the other person creates his or her own personal image of the person at hand. And if you compare these two images, you'll discover a big difference between them.

This occurs because when you provide a verbal description, you ignore many details: you simply omit them because you take them for granted. But it's precisely because of their absence that sometimes a distortion emerges in the way another person "sees" the described image. After all, every person comprehends your account in accordance with his own notions, founded on his own personality and experiences. This is why we find such a high level of incomprehension and misunderstanding between different people—even the well acquainted. And we're always surprised when another person doesn't understand us.

Sometimes we're not simply bewildered: we grow indignant and angry if we believe another person has made mistakes. We tell him, "I already explained what has to be done and how, so why did you not do it right. It's you who did this incorrectly!" But the person might answer, "No, I did precisely what you said. You definitely asked me to do it this way—I remember it clearly. And right now you're saying just the opposite." So, where's the issue here? In such situations, the problem is neither with you nor with the other person.

The problem is one of communication, of the connection, of the expression of an idea and an understanding of what specifically was meant. Consider this expression: "There's the speaker and there's what's spoken." Therefore the truth can't be conveyed with words.

This is why at the third stage we employ listening with the heart. Then it's possible to perceive directly, to take in the images the Master works with.

Master's Story

When I teach, integrated images take shape in me, and I send them to my seminar attendees. Receiving such an image is much better than hearing a verbal explanation. Therefore, at the third stage you must not only listen, but also try to take in the images by listening with your heart. For this, you mentally tell yourself that you're listening with the heart.

Picture 15: Training of the Second Hart

*If this system of interaction is developed, it leads to the development of the Third Eye, Third Ear, and Second Heart, and then you'll be able to understand each other better. At the first and second stage, when you listened to me with your palms and body, you feel certain sensations. This helped to increase the sensitivity of your hands, to open biologically active points and channels. At the third stage, analogous sensations can be felt in the heart, so you must try to listen with this zone. This is a special kind of training of the **Second Heart** (Picture 15). It's also necessary to listen in the usual manner and to try to guess what more will be said, before the words are spoken.*

This is why at the seminars it's necessary not only to pay attention to words as a verbal means of communication, but also to utilize the deep structure of your body.

We possess a massive amount of information concerning the structure and function of the physical body as a whole, and its separate parts and organs in particular. But we know almost nothing about the structure of energy found in our body. Here, at the third stage, the expression "listen attentively" means developing the structure of your internal energy.

My approach to instruction takes the following form: as you're developing, I raise the level of instruction in accordance with the progress I observe you to be making. For example, if you still don't know how to practice sufficiently well and are unable to sense the difference between the meaning of "to look" and "to see," then we make use of another method, which can be defined by the phrase "it seems it is, it seems it isn't." Then you begin to think.

Later you lose this idea. You stop thinking, and the active work of the brain transfers from the front to the back of your head. Things calm within you, and the frontal part of your brain ceases to function, while the region at the back of the head becomes activated. During many seminar exercises I often use "it seems it is, it seems it isn't[3]."

This principle of practice helps you enter the state of calm and Silence of Mind. In this way, you automatically switch to working the brain in the back

---

3   We discussed this principal in detail in the first and second volumes of Zhong Yuan Qigong, Stages I and II.

*of your head. You begin **not only to look, but also to see.** As in the Forbidden City in Beijing, which has many entrances and many doors, you enter through one door and find yourself in an inner courtyard. But after crossing it, you come to the next entrance. On opening this door, you go further inside; again and again. And each time you see something different, though all of this is located in one small area—in one place, really.*

In seminars, theoretical explanations are based on the knowledge from various fields of learning, technique, and everyday life with which attendees may be familiar. If I were to use terms belonging only to the ZYQ system, you wouldn't understand me. Suppose I say, "Look at your back and see whether a bull is climbing up." Who would understand me? Or this question, without a translation of terms: "Is the Kun and Qian rising, or not?" (Such terminology is used in the Ba Gua system.) Here's another expression: "A tiger and lion have come to you." What are you able to understand from this? Or "Did you receive the flowers from the sky?"

For you to begin understanding, you first have to spend a great amount of time on learning the terms, and this is very difficult without knowledge of the original language. How, then, should you go about learning? Students who practice for many years and with high quality once find themselves directly inside the content of the practice. Then they receive this all as phenomena, and it becomes understandable to them. In such a case, they don't need words at all, so no time is lost, and the length of training is shortened. Moreover, it's not as difficult as it may seem, since a practitioner isn't frightened off by many unfamiliar words and the need to memorize them. And once a person has gotten there—inside—it's possible to converse differently. In the fourth stage, we'll learn a different language—yet another language of interaction.

Therefore the very best method of instruction is direct contact—face-to-face, brain-to-brain, heart-to-heart. Only then can the best results be obtained.

WHAT WE LEARN
IN THE THIRD STAGE AND WHY

GOALS OF THE THIRD STAGE

We already spoke about how the ZYQ system pursues several goals. There are main (or fundamental) and accompanying (or secondary) goals. We'll consider the most important of them. Let's begin with what interests the overwhelming majority of people.

Health Improvement

This goal involves two aspects connected with health: first, the state of our physical body; second, our emotional state, or the state of our spirit.

We often meet with circumstances that cause anxiety and eventually cause problems. Qigong practice breeds stability and strengthens the spirit, so that your reactions to the very same situations change. You begin to understand that your reactions are linked not so much with the external milieu and circumstances surrounding you, but with your inner world, because they depend on your attitude toward the problems. You see, many of your reactions are connected with your internal state of happiness or unhappiness, sadness or joy.

Thus an improvement in health is the first result and also a side effect of ZYQ practice.

Strengthening of the Intellect

We pointed out how, in the ZYQ system, heightening our intellect is connected not with external but with internal factors. In practicing, you acquire additional abilities and possibilities not by reading books or studying information of some sort, but from the accumulation of energy. This energy opens all channels and points in our body. This leads to improved blood circulation, which in turn activates the cells of your brain to a degree greater than before practice. In this way, your intellect is strengthened.

Development of Abilities

All of this amounts to *one of the most important goals of Qigong practice: the development of the human abilities.* To achieve this, it's necessary to know what we have to develop. And this is inextricably linked with your understanding of what a human being is.

In Stages I and II, we stated that humans have a physical body, an energy system, and an informational system, with this last sometimes called the soul or the spirit. Much is known about the physical body, although even now most people view it basically from the standpoint of form. But we'll speak later about some of its other aspects. We also said that if there's no energy, the body is unable to exist; it dies. Therefore, to develop a person, it's necessary to develop all three systems simultaneously: the physical body, the soul, and the energy.

Where does our energy come from? In Stages I and II we stated that energy comes from outside, from the Universe, and we can take it in directly. In Stage I, we received it with our hands from Sky and conducted it to the lower Dan Tian. In Stage II we practiced breathing with the body, the fourth method.

But also within our body is a system for the transformation of energy. For it to be activated, we learned the Yang-Qi exercise in Stage I. This is the practice for transforming Jing into Qi in our body. *In practicing Qigong, we first and foremost develop the system for the transformation of energy within our body and then, with the help of this energy, we develop our physical body and spirit.*

In other words, with the help of certain movements and methods of breathing, we develop our body, energy, and spirit. The side effect of such a practice is a healthy body, strong energy, and a strong spirit. In addition comes the opportunity to understand the world, that is, the entire Cosmos and you as a part of this world.

Self-Development

So, the most important goal of ZYQ practice is self-development, on the one hand, and salvation, on the other.

How can we understand this?

Master's Story

One of mankind's tasks is to care for Earth and not destroy it, for we're very closely connected with our planet. This process of restoration and care has already commenced. But Earth, like any living being, gets sick. Just as a person can come down with the flu, Earth can take sick with something similar. Then the people populating it experience problems. So, for example, if at some location on Earth an excess or shortage of Qi belonging to the element Wood arises, the people in that area are stricken by a liver disease.

But only a person studying at the higher stages can understand the path of development of the planet—how it must develop and what has to be done. Consider why various systems of spiritual practice have experienced very robust growth in different countries of the world in the past ten years. Many people are taking every imaginable course or seminar to be "turned on" to greater spiritual development.

In fact, in recent years a large number of specialists have received and felt certain information about our Earth. Earth is a material world and is of the same material as humankind—that is, it has a life, birth, and death, as well as illnesses. This is why **one of the goals of Qigong is to create an appropriate Qi field around Earth and on the planet itself.**

Beginning with Stage I, we have been practicing the Big Tree exercise, in which the Universe, the Human, and the Earth are united. In this exercise we have that joint practice taking place. This is why we still perform the Big Tree in Stage III.

Many Great Masters are helping Earth. In the process of practicing, they study the state of the planet's field. They also receive from another level of intellect, higher than on Earth, information and knowledge as to what is happening on our planet, how it's happening, and what has to be done. With this information they work here. (This is difficult to explain in words.) People's consciousness is also changing for the better. And now the task is to begin developing ourselves. **If over many thousands of years humans don't develop, all of this is meaningless for humanity.**

Why do we have to develop? Because there are different levels of space, various worlds, in the Universe. We in our world need clothing, food, shelter, medicines, and so on. If all of this were not needed, if there were no illnesses, many troubles and problems would go away.

We need a world in which it's possible to manage without all of these problems. Practicing Stage III allows us to open the central channel and to depart our soul to another world. No longer will any Master be needed to remind us about the need to study. When you see a different world and thereby gain personal experience, you'll understand the shortcomings and merits of our physical world. And then you'll be able to select for yourself the world, the place, that best answers to your inclinations and your needs. But for this, it's necessary to *develop your abilities. That's why **the highest goal of ZYQ is our development.***

At the same time, it's imperative not only to think about our future, but also to work for today. If you study correctly, this is easier to feel and be aware of. We should have a regular, normal life. We should not worry or fret about our future life, but we should do something for our future and for the future of other people and for Life in general. We have to think about the fact that everything we encounter is simply our customary life in the physical world, here and now. And if you have your head on your shoulders, everything is fine, everything is normal.

*However, we must also be happy—not at some time in the future but right now. It's not necessary to suffer now, calculating that later you can be happy. This is why ZYQ exercises are structured so that the practice process can also bring a sensation of happiness and joy, and not suffering. **Zhong Yuan Qigong is a method for practicing happiness.***

There are, of course, other approaches, other philosophies, that say we obtain happiness only after enduring a great amount of suffering. However, I believe we must take joy in life and feel this joy inside right now.

For all of this to become possible, it's necessary to open the central channel in our body—the way for the departure of the soul. This is why the chief goal of Stage III practice is to open the central channel Zhong-Mai. With this we construct in our body the Way for the soul to exit, so that we might understand what the world is, what the soul is, and what Life is.

When we begin to more deeply understand *the essence of Life*, it's much easier for us to get rid of negative emotions and feelings, which often poison our life. Therefore we practice opening the upper Dan Tian and building the central channel.

Entering the State of Pause

Yet *another goal is to learn how to enter the state of Pause.* Pause is a special state of the body. We must enter a state of increasingly deep calm, until suddenly our mind ceases to think. During this state, our consciousness can change; our wisdom can develop. Then we can more deeply understand the essence of life, the essence of all situations. Then we can easily understand other people. Only in a state of

Pause will our soul be able to leave the body and see what the world in which we live is like. Only then is it possible to understand *who we are, where we came from, and for what reason.* In connection to the state of Pause we affirm that this is a key state, without which a large part of practice loses meaning. Our development as human beings is connected with the state of Pause; so many exercises are only a preparation for Pause.

To get the opportunity to reach this state, we must raise and develop the level of our energy.

Freeing Yourself from Yourself

One more important goal of ZYQ practice is Freeing Yourself from Yourself.

What does this mean? When a person is born, he or she is helpless and must be cared for. While children are small, it's the parents who do this. Then the children grow and want some independence, but the parents often don't allow it. So not all desires are realized. As children grow into adults, our concerns begin to pile up. Certain duties fall to us and begin to control us. Now we have to take care of our parents as well as our children. Often this ties us down, preventing us from going somewhere or doing something we might choose. And duties at work often make scheduling time for ourselves impossible. Then old age comes, with its attendant illnesses. Even if those illnesses aren't overwhelming, old age limits our possibilities and forces us to modify our desires. If we experience severely depressed living conditions, the needs of our physical body—for example, a feeling of hunger, control us. This all testifies to the fact that many limitations in our usual life prevent us from being free.

Yet these are not the most important thing, since if the desire is great, we can overcome limitation. *The most complicated limitation, which we must overcome, is ourselves.* Only in freeing ourselves from ourselves will we obtain *Freedom.*

Master's Story

It's very difficult to give an explanation of freedom until you have your own personal experience of it. Think about prisoners in handcuffs and metal collars, bound in chains. This forces them to endure physical suffering and torment.

The chains are very heavy, and moving in them is very difficult. Consequently, the absence of freedom is felt even stronger. But after the passage of time, say two years, the prisoners get used to the conditions and react less strongly.

*We can compare such prisoners with our own situation. After all, we also have adapted to **un**freedom in our physical body. If one day you're freed from your burden, you'll feel how everything suddenly seems incredibly light. You'll be able to feel this state of Buddha only after Stage III, after your soul has learned how to go outside your body. Only then will you feel and understand how light it can be without the heavy clothing of a physical body. That's why one of the goals of ZYQ practice is to free ourselves from ourselves. At least we should try to experience this state.*

In life we experience many events, some favorable for us and some not. We'd use all our strength to avoid some of them, because they threaten our life or might seriously harm it. For this reason, still another goal of ZYQ practice is to learn how to foresee and eliminate trouble. However, if an incident must occur, it's necessary to avoid it, to reduce its impact, or to do something so that it will happen not with you.

For better understanding, let's look at four stories.

First Story

During his studies, a Chinese monk saw a thief with a knife coming toward him. The latter wanted to take the monk's things and was ready to kill if monk tried to stop him. The monk was old and poor, and possessed nothing worth taking. Finishing practice, he gathered everything that was of value to him—an image of Buddha and several books—and took them to another place. He then returned to his room and waited.

It grew dark, and soon the monk heard furtive steps. The thief entered the room. The monk greeted his visitor, turned on a dim lamp, and said that he knew why the visitor had come at such a late hour. He stated that the visitor must take something with which he could buy food, but that he himself had only clothing that was worth almost nothing. The monk expressed his sympathy for the thief.

The thief glanced at the destitute quarters and saw nothing to take. Then he shifted his attention to the clothing and saw that there really was nothing that could bring him money. He began feeling ashamed—ashamed that he had wanted to clean out a monk who was as impoverished as he.

The monk had gotten a hold of a small amount of money that he gave to the thief to buy food for himself. The latter broke into tears and said that he would abandon his occupation and change his life.

These kinds of things can really happen in our own lives. This is an example of how a person who has reached a high level of development should know not only how to avoid a certain situation, but also how to prevent it or how to create changes in it. In this story, the thief ended up stealing nothing from the monk, while the monk protected himself against an unpleasant experience.

In some instances, a situation can be avoided; in others, changed. Here's a story that took place in our own day.

Second Story

A Master was supposed to fly from one city to another. At the airport before checking in, he saw that a great problem would occur with this plane, possibly a crash. What was one to do?

The first thought was to not fly. But they were expecting him in the other city. He couldn't cancel or reschedule the meeting, and there was no other flight. Once again he checked out the situation and saw that a problem might—or might not—arise. In any case, he knew an effort must be made to change the situation.

He did just that, and the flight experienced no problems. But the plane had some unnoticed defects, and on the next flight they manifested themselves.

This example shows how each of us encounters certain situations that can lead to extremely undesirable consequences. The task is to change the situation in such a way that an incident doesn't occur—that it is "cancelled."

Well, if something nevertheless has to happen, everything must be done so that it doesn't happen with you.

Third Story

Once I was on my way in a car to the airport to meet a plane. We were in a hurry. Usually during such rides I consider (one can say mentally or with the Third Eye—take your pick) the highway situation, that is, if there'll be some trouble on the road or not. Then, if I see a possible problem, I do everything within my power to change the situation.

On this occasion I also gave consideration to the road going to the airport. As we went along, I suddenly saw at a narrowing of the road ahead that three cars were going to collide, including the one I was in. I saw clearly how one car (ours) was traveling very fast, but two slower, and that these latter were about to form an obstruction before which the car traveling fast wouldn't have the time to stop. As soon as I saw this, I liquidated the situation.

When we got to that place in the road, I saw those two cars. But since the situation had been eliminated, they were now traveling at a different speed and went their separate ways after having come very close to one another.

Usually we draw upon this ability to solve complicated tasks on which a life may depend, such as checking equipment.

Fourth Story

A very famous Qigong Master in China does work connected with testing complex technical equipment. Fifteen years ago or so, he and I had practiced together. But then we went our separate ways, taking up different work.

During recent decades in China, there has been feverish development in space research. That's why many satellites have been launched. Every launching is a very expensive undertaking. After all, both the satellite and the rocket launcher cost millions. Consequently, every failure and every problem means financial losses and ruined projects that were supposed to make use of certain information from a given satellite.

Among the duties of this master was examining and checking the entire apparatus to find possible problems before the launching. For a long time, scientists could not understand how he finds these problems. But if he informed them of the presence of defects in a given place, a very careful check of that place and part would reveal the problems he indicated.

As far as I know, such specialists are found in a number of countries. Their work involves predicting where there might be major material losses in order to prevent unforeseen situations. Right now, given your current level of practice, it's not worth it to look so far ahead. But it certainly does make sense for you to learn how to foresee incidents that can happen with you in particular.

I offer these examples so that you know about the ability to influence events, at least those affecting you. If you practice a lot, you'll be able to do this. ***And if only once in your life you're able to eliminate a trouble that was supposed to come your way, this will be sufficient in itself.***

Self-Realization

There's *one more goal – to find and realize ourselves*. Everyone has goals, but not everyone has a serious goal, one lasting throughout life or at least for an extended period. In accordance with our goals, we plan our life and our lifestyle. For example, practically everyone has a goal of fulfilling something this week, month, or year. Such goals and desires are usually connected with the material world. Someone is preparing to buy a new TV this week; someone else plans to get a computer in a month; and yet another person wants to purchase a fur coat. Someone is planning in two or three years to buy an apartment or a car or a country home. Someone wants to go on a cruise, while someone else wants to buy tickets for an upcoming football game.

People really have a lot of goals, and the majority of them can be achieved because they involve something here, in our world. All you need is to know how to earn money to acquire this.

But sometimes you don't succeed in realizing your goal in the time allotted, and it becomes increasingly out of reach. You are getting so tired in pursuing it that sometimes you begin to doubt that expending so much strength on attaining the desired end is worth it. And so you begin to adjust the goal in accordance with the emerging circumstances.

Our desires are always changing: today we want one thing, tomorrow another. And in a year we'll want something that we earlier had never even thought of. For this reason, once we achieve this kind of goal, we nevertheless really don't feel happy. At first, of course, we're very satisfied, but after a while we begin to feel we're lacking something. Therefore it's not worth it to take such goals seriously. They're fleeting and connected exclusively to material existence; they're not what we should really be striving for.

However, if you succeed in realizing yourself, you'll feel happy all the time. But for this you must first find yourselves, find your place. You have to understand what your tasks are, and how to fulfill them and why.

Maybe solving a problem that is important to all humankind lies ahead for you. You carry this mission your entire life. However, to do this, you must realize *the most important goal of ZYQ practice: to develop yourself.*

So, having examined the goals of ZYQ practice, we can assert that this main goal incorporates all others. After all, as you move forward in your development, as a natural side effect you'll be able to obtain not one but all of the following: sound health, creative abilities, wisdom and high intellect, enlightenment and a state of happiness, an understanding of the goal of your coming into this world, and self-realization.

WHAT WE LEARN IN STAGE III

In Stage III we'll learn two more preliminary exercises: the seventh and eighth. An approximate translation renders them as Getting the Moon from the Sea and Taking in with the Body the Smells of Different Worlds. We understand that it's impossible to do these practices. But a practice method is one thing; the result itself another. In Stage III we begin practicing what seems impossible for the obtaining of the possible.

And then we'll once again study Big Tree, which is the most interesting exercise. In the fourth stage we'll be studying it again.

In the previous stages, we studied the practice of the lower and middle Dan Tian. In the third stage, we'll develop the upper Dan Tian, which is connected with our spirit, or what we call our informational system. We practice the upper Dan Tian to help our soul travel later in the Universe outside our body. During practice, we employ Emptiness, since the other Cosmos isn't the Cosmos we know: there it's quiet and calm.

So that the soul can go outside the body, we must complete construction of the way along the Zhong-Mai channel inside the body. Therefore we'll continue to open the central channel, which passes through all three Dan Tian, at the segment between the middle and upper Dan Tian.

To develop ourselves, we'll practice the three aspects inside our body jointly: Jing, Qi, and Shen. We have to unite them into a single whole.

In our world we're used to perceiving everything in discrete form—at least material objects, which consist of matter. We understand that everything consists of smaller parts: any mechanism, tool, or building is assembled from smaller parts. The same goes for a human being: we tend to look on a person not as an integrated whole, but as the totality of various organs and tissues. We also know that all substances consist of molecules. That's why it's completely natural that the very method of our thinking and perceiving assumes the possibility of both assembly and disassembly. For example, we know that if we cut a piece of paper, there will be two pieces of smaller format or size; cutting an apple produces simply two halves. In other words, one splits up into two, two into four, and so on. In reality, our world and the Cosmos as a whole are developing today namely according to such laws of division:

$$1 \to 2 \to 4 \to 8 \to \ldots \to n$$

According to this same pattern, cells divide after the conception of life. Thus **this is the natural way of development in the Universe. But the natural way for our world is the way from birth to death.**

In Stage I, we examined in detail the philosophical aspect of the opposite process—the process of going backward toward immortality. We spoke about how a large number must be united to form one, that is, a multitude of parts become a single object.

$$n \to 1$$

From the standpoint of Qigong, what represents multiplicity in reference to us? We have spoken about the three internal and three external Yuan and how we have to unite them. The three Dan Tian, with their varying structures of energy, and the three parts of the humans—the three Jiao—which correspond to the energy of the three

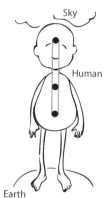

Picture 16: Combine Many into One

Dan Tian, should be understood from the point of view of energy in order to comprehend what Tao (the Path) is. An example of this movement in a reverse direction is the Chanzo exercise: the uniting of Jing, Qi, and Shen—the three internal Yuan, and then also the three external Yuan—Sky, Earth, and Humans (Picture 16). Then we'll be able to return to Tao (the Path) to understand ourselves and the Cosmos.

In Stage III, it's necessary to learn how to enter the state of Pause. A deep state of Quietness can pass over to Pause for a short time. But for an extended state of Pause, there must be a complete cleansing of the body and a temporary halt to all systems, including the heart and lungs. To prepare for an extended state of Pause, we have to have a special method of breathing that helps our body receive oxygen and energy in case our heart and lungs stop. And cleansing the body requires a way of getting nutrients without the usual intake of food. Therefore, in Stage III we'll learn the *Bigu Shiqi* exercise.

Bigu means "without food," and *shiqi* means "taking in only Qi, instead of food." If you want to lose weight, you can practice this exercise. It allows for both achieving optimal weight and returning to your youth, or going from old age back to childhood. Based on the state of your consciousness and your sensations, you'll be able to feel that you've become significantly younger. Those who are fifty can feel like they're twenty again.

Of course, as in the preceding stages, we'll be studying diagnostics, but this time with the help of the Third Eye. We'll develop seeing with the Third Eye. We'll also examine methods of distance diagnostics and treatment. You'll be able to acquire some abilities that will be useful in everyday life, and perhaps they'll be of fundamental help to you in special situations.

This is an overview of the contents of Stage III, which we now take up in more detail.

ABOUT THE STATE OF PAUSE

定 In the first stage, we practiced the state of Relaxation. In the second stage, we can extend and deepen that state, and thereby enter the state of Quietness. Stage III is the extension of the state of Quietness and the transition to the state of Pause. The essence of Stage I practice is Relaxation; Stage II, Quietness; and Stage III, Pause, which can pass over to the state of Stop.

You already became familiar in general terms with these states in Stage II. But in the third stage *the attainment of Pause is the most important goal of practice.* For this reason we'll speak in greater detail about what Pause can give us, how Pause can be achieved, and what obstacles we meet in pursuit of this end.

What Does Pause Signify?

The word for Pause in the Chinese language is **Din.** But the term **Pause** isn't an exact translation, because **Pause isn't quite a complete halt to the processes of all systems of our body.** Pause signifies that everything is regulated or ordered to the highest degree. Pause is a certain harmony with the Universe.

Din is also **Emptiness.** Emptiness is a particular state wherein information comes to us not from this material world, but from another world. This is difficult to understand, and only after reaching such a state in practice do we know what's meant by it. Emptiness is customarily represented by a circle (Picture 17).

Din also signifies a form of movement. It's not possible for this form of movement to be revealed externally. From the outside,

Picture 17: The Image of Emptiness

it looks like total relaxation and immobility. However, internal movement is occurring to allow the harmonization of all systems of our body and bring them into conformity with external streams of energy in the Universe and according to its laws.

Pause doesn't mean that during it you're not thinking about anything. Your consciousness, your thoughts, are concentrating on one thing.

At first, you're thinking about something, and then a halt comes at some point. The energy within your body also moves very slowly, and then everything seems to stop, because everything is put in a certain order. When this takes place, when this order is established, we have achieved Pause.

Master's Story

In China there's a game played on ice (I saw it once on TV in Europe.) A ball is attached to an elastic band. You toss the ball and then pull it back. As you do so, the ball begins to spin very quickly on the ice. The speed of the spinning is so great; it seems that the ball is immobile. But in fact it's rapidly rotating. This is similar to a top: if the rotation speed is great, the top stands and seems to be motionless. This is called **the state of Din.**

When we practice and enter the state of calm and Quietness, a very rapid movement arises inside our consciousness, inside us. In an instant you may feel that you're losing consciousness. And suddenly you sense that your heart is stopping and your lungs are ceasing to function. And you begin to feel that you've lost your body. This looks and feels to you like the absence of motion. We call this state Din, translated as Pause. *When you enter this state, you begin to understand and feel that your soul is totally free and nothing affects it. Then your physical body begins to change, and your soul can go out. Then you pass to the next level, but we'll study that in Stage IV.*

As we study the ZYQ system, we must first learn how *to relax*. Only after achieving complete relaxation can we pass to the practice of **Quietness,** and then **Pause.** When we speak about relaxation we have in mind not only the body itself, including the muscles, but the nervous system as well.

Often we meet nervous people who are always worried about something. Some fret because of their fear of being late for work. Others start freaking out even days before they're supposed to do something important, such as conduct a negotiation, address a conference, or take a test.

Relaxation means there's no situation in which you get nervous. Therefore it's important to learn how to relax your physical body, but *spiritual relaxation* is the most important. Only after you completely relax will you be able to attain the state of calm and Quietness.

In the state of Quietness your physical body is also very calm. But Quietness mainly involves the mind. When you're in this state, you don't experience stress, depression, or anxiety. If you feel anxiety, if you're nervous about something, this indicates that you still haven't attained the state of Quietness. Only after this can one enter the state of Pause.

What Can Be Received in the State of Pause?

The state of Pause is the key to spiritual development. We can say that *Pause is the gateway to the development of a human's potential abilities.* But, again, until a person enters this state, it's difficult for him or her to understand what it is. After all, our mind is used to thinking all the time.

With the state of Pause, spiritual practice commences. Until we achieve this state, no practice can be labeled spiritual practice, and all the exercises with which we become acquainted and which we master are only a preparation for spiritual practice. In the ZYQ, when we speak about spiritual development, we mean the practice in which we understand *what the Human is.*

The state of Pause allows an understanding of two aspects relating to spiritual life: wisdom and understanding of Life.

Wisdom

Wisdom is the ability to solve problems in a way that satisfies everyone. But people often make decisions that have lack of wisdom, or do not have any wisdom at all. In such case they usually cause harm. Often this occurs because people are motivated by their own desires and ignore the wishes of others. But wisdom is the ability to do things in a way that makes winners out of everyone. This pertains to nature, society, and people—everything and everyone that is part of a specific problem.

Understanding of Life

When we talk about Wisdom, we have in mind our understanding of Life. This is written in Chinese: 大智大慧.

These several characters represent the concepts of Knowledge, Wisdom and Great. So, in translation we have Knowledge and Great Wisdom. And Great Wisdom signifies an understanding of Life.

Where Wisdom Comes From

Above all, wisdom comes from our life. How can wisdom be learned? When absorbing knowledge and information, we employ our sense organs. Life wisdom, however, can't be obtained in this way. Our regular sense organs aren't up to the task. Wisdom is acquired when the soul leaves the body and travels. In the process, it takes in knowledge about the Universe and about Life which, on returning, it turns over to us.

Master's Story

Every individual possesses knowledge of some kind. Where is it to be found when the soul goes out from the body? Does all the knowledge possessed by a human being also leave, or does it remain in the body? We possess consciousness; we think. But where is our consciousness, our thinking, located—in the physical body or elsewhere? When the soul abandons the body, consciousness is where? And what happens with our senses: with sight, hearing, and other functions of perception? After all, the sense organs belong to the physical body. Do they remain in the body, or do they leave together with the soul? What happens with all of this when the body dies and the soul abandons it?

In 2002, in the United States, at the First International Conference on Concussion[4] scientists acknowledged consciousness as being an attribute of the soul, not of the brain. However, as long as you haven't separated the soul from the body, your understanding emanates from the brain and heart together, and the knowledge obtained about the external world.

According to Chinese medicine, wisdom is controlled not by the brain but by the heart. Chinese culture and science understand the heart as being not only the physical organ known as the "heart," but the entire nervous system as well. In ZYQ we also maintain that our understanding is connected not so much with the brain as with the heart. And at the aforementioned conference, many scientists recognized **consciousness as being linked to the heart.** *Emotions and desires are connected especially closely to the heart.*

---

4 Tucson Convention Center "Tucson V", April 8-12, 2002

After appropriate training (we'll speak more about this later), the soul will be able to go out for several days and nights to visit other worlds and receive instruction there. This becomes feasible only in the state of Pause. The practice of the soul's departing is also the practice of self-development, or the practice of spiritual development.

The correct way is the way of freedom. *We must be free; nothing should exert an influence on us. You can feel this freedom only when you go into a state of deep Quietness in Qigong. Sometimes in this state you may suddenly feel that you've become as enormous as the Cosmos. And then you may feel that your heart has become as enormous as the Cosmos. You may sense that you've become very kind and that all that exists are your children. Or you may feel suddenly that you're a great mother. You may want to give your love to everyone and everything.*

You may practice various schools. However, as a result of any practice, you have to attain the state of Pause. Without this, it's impossible to develop your wisdom. Without the state of Pause, our bodies can't be cleansed, so we can't get rid of a number of illnesses. Without the state of Pause, we're unable to understand what a human being is. Without the state of Pause, it's impossible to understand what the soul is and why the soul can go beyond the boundaries of the human body.

Therefore practice of Stage III should help us approach the state of Pause, and then the state of Stop. As you enter such a state, you'll be able to reveal that everything is in your heart, and you'll be able to find the correct Way of your development.

So this is why we need Pause.

No one can predict when you'll enter this state. Nor should you even consider aiming for a specific moment in time for this. You'll get no results if you do. Everything must take place naturally.

Phenomena on Entering and Leaving Pause

How do we know when we've come to the state of Pause? When you approach the state of Pause, you begin to sense your body as being very light. With the continuation of practice, you sense in front of you ***not darkness, but bright light***. With the continuation of practice, you begin to feel ***pressure within your body***, and then you lose the ability to move. If you continue practice, you begin to see various ***images*** *and pictures*. Then you begin to enter the state of Pause. You must not think about this state. As soon as you start thinking about having already entered the state of Pause, you immediately leave it. Therefore try to maintain this state as long as possible. Then you'll feel your body changing, and you'll begin to experience some special sensations.

When you practice exercises that can bring you to the state of Pause, in the beginning you'll feel fine and comfortable; you'll breathe easily and be able to experience many pleasant sensations. The body then becomes *light* and feels *transparent and clear. A feeling of Freedom takes hold*. Then this state disappears and doesn't appear for some time, perhaps for a few minutes or thirty minutes or maybe more. Then you'll have Pause once again and departure from it again. Often practitioners begin to wait for Pause. They wait and wait, but still no Pause. Against the background of this waiting, a thought arises: Why is Pause failing to manifest itself? And this emerging impatience hinders the attainment of Pause.

The *halting of breathing* takes place in the following stage. This can last several seconds or several minutes.

In the beginning, we aim at attaining the state of Pause for at least a short time. Such a brief period can continue for several seconds or minutes or even for nearly half an hour. If we more deeply go into this state, the *heart stops*. At first this lasts a short time: from several seconds to several minutes, during which some people are able to have the experience of the soul leaving the body. Then they can see themselves from a distance.

After a certain amount of training, the heart can stop for a very long time without the person dying. Our skin can take in oxygen directly from the air. In Stage II we learn methods for breathing with the skin. During Pause, metabolism lowers sharply, and the body doesn't require the same amount of oxygen as in normal activity. Besides this, the brain doesn't think, thereby seriously reducing its need for oxygen. The practice of breathing and nourishment with the navel, Bigu Shiqi, permits cleansing of the body from "garbage." That's why far less oxygen is needed here.

The circulation of blood continues, but it slows down considerably. According to contemporary medicine, the heart forces the blood to move. This is why we're sure that with the stopping of the heart the flow of blood stops and the person dies. But according to the notions of Chinese medicine, blood is moved by energy, by our Qi. It's been proven that when there's a complete halt of the workings of the heart during Pause, Qi continues to move the blood.

When the soul returns, the first sensation you experience is the beating of your heart. In the first moments of *its renewed function*, the heart begins to beat very intensely. The beats are very powerful and more frequent than usual. They gradually weaken and assume their regular strength and rhythm.

The lungs then begin functioning again. It's easier for them to get going again than for the heart. That's why you feel your heart's powerful beats, while your lungs are harder to sense. There's neither pain nor suffering. However, if there are physical problems, various sensations manifest themselves.

Every time the soul goes out, we expand our knowledge of the world, of the Universe, and of ourselves. But to attain Pause, it's necessary above all to calm down and put a halt to thinking. If we're thinking, Pause is impossible.

About the Frontal and Occipital Parts of the Brain

Everybody knows that the human brain consists of two hemispheres: a left and a right. Common opinion holds that the left hemisphere is responsible more for thinking, logic, and speech, and the right for our emotions and imagination. However, when practicing Qigong, it's necessary to take into account completely different qualities of our brain and other parts of it.

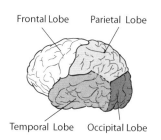

Frontal Lobe   Parietal Lobe

Temporal Lobe   Occipital Lobe

Picture 18: Shares of the Cerebral Hemispheres

In ZYQ, we speak about the frontal part of our brain, which is connected with the thinking process and analysis of information, and the occiput, or the back part of the head, which is responsible for imagination (Picture 18). There's constant interaction between them. When we think, the frontal part of the brain is at work. But if we engage in visualization—when we "look at something" during practice—the back part of the brain is activated, and this helps us enter the state of Pause. Therefore, having learned visualization, you can quickly shift the working of the brain from the frontal part to the back and enter the state of Pause. As long as you think or reason about something, Pause is impossible. During visualization, the thought process ceases, and you can enter Pause and secure a halt to breathing and your heart. Thus we employ visualization, the method of looking at something or feeling something in order to stop thinking.

If you're looking at something, or visualizing, at a certain moment you can forget about this procedure. But then the thought comes to you that you forgot about the visualization and must return to it. This is detrimental, because you're still thinking. You must simply look and forget about what you're doing. Only if you forget about what you're doing can you achieve the state of Pause. *To forget means to enter the state of Pause.*

The process can also unfold in a different way: you think, then you visualize, then you see different pictures in your mind, which follow each other; and then you once again think. At a certain moment, the change of pictures stops, and only one picture stays in your mind. Then you enter the state of Pause. You forget about everything and are able to be absent. The sequence of the process here is the following: You feel what you're thinking, and at a certain moment thoughts give way to images of some kind. They're glimpsed fleetingly as they replace one another. And suddenly your attention dwells on a single image. So at first constant thinking and visualization alternate, then the fleeting glimpses of images stops, and Pause commences. Later we'll talk about how to maintain the state of Pause for an extended period.

If we employ our mind to try to keep it from working, the mind is at work and we'll be unable to get what we're aiming for. That's why we make use of visualization, or that which occurs when we look at something, or feel something, or listen with the hands or body, and so on. *We employ sensations to dispense with thinking.* When we feel, we can stop thinking.

If you constantly engage in analysis, the frontal part of your brain is at work. It's possible to attain wisdom in this way, but it doesn't happen very quickly. We do know about cases involving monks who drew on such a method. Over a period of many years, they devoured book after book and then suddenly, at a certain moment, reached total understanding; both parts of their brain began functioning jointly.

For many years the United States has been the setting for various investigations into the brain activity of humans. One of the findings was that successful people—in the fields of medicine, business, science, art, politics, and others—possessed an active occipital part of the brain. This part of the brain became known as the *"aroused"* part. It's at work in people as they achieve great success, while in others it's asleep.

Our creative abilities are connected precisely with this part of the brain. If the back part of your brain has been aroused, you'll definitely achieve the state of Pause. And if a practitioner has a lot of energy, the "thinking" part of the brain is less active. Consequently, with a sufficient amount of energy in the body, it's easier to attain the state of Pause. For this reason, all methods of accumulating energy are convenient.

This is why, *with proper Qigong practice, every practitioner can achieve the state of Pause for a brief time.* Attaining Pause for a long time is another question.

How to Achieve Pause

There are two ways and many different means or methods for attaining Pause.

Practice of Quiet Qigong

One way is to practice Quiet Qigong, or meditation, as a result of which the physical body relaxes first and then the brain. In the process of meditation, consciousness at first thinks and then comes to a stop. In the beginning, you constantly alternate visualization with thinking because your mind can't quickly visualize. In the process of thinking, you always see pictures in your consciousness. Then, at a certain moment, the fleeting glimpses of pictures come to a halt and your attention focuses on one of them, which is recorded. So when your mind begins dwelling on one picture, the state of Quietness commences. And then everything in general stops, and you enter the state of Pause. For many people this occurs through imagination—through images and pictures. When they see them, everything stops. Then the state of Pause is achieved.

Or, you can simply stand, sit, or lie down, but without any movement, thereby entering a state of complete stasis. After a certain time, the state of very deep Quietness, of profound calm and motionlessness, sets in. Most people employ this method.

Dynamic Practice

The second way to achieve Pause is through dynamic practice, which consists of very quick movements of the physical body. During these movements, the frontal part of the brain ceases to function while the occiput (back part) starts. Sometimes this is called "*the cosmic dance.*" Some people can very quickly enter the state of Pause this way. But this route can trigger serious problems for people who are unable to control themselves completely. This explains why it's not used in the beginning phase of practice.

Let's examine possible methods for entering Pause.

The First Method: Visualization

This can be visualization of a channel or the lower Dan Tian. Relax, feel the lower Dan Tian, and then look at the lower Dan Tian. This isn't only for stimulating Qi, but also for attaining the state of Pause.

The Second Method: Breathing with the Body

Breathing with the body involves the third or fourth way that we practice in Stage II. Usually it's easier to achieve the state of Pause with this method.

These two methods differ in the following way: With visualization, an accumulation of Qi in the lower Dan Tian occurs, while in breathing with the body, the respiratory system develops, which helps to secure a longer-lasting state of Pause. To be in the state of Pause, you need to solve the problem of breathing. If you aren't able to master all these methods and resolve these problems, you won't be able to enter Pause for long.

The Third Method: Feeling the Body

"Feeling" the whole body doesn't involve breathing or visualization. This is sometimes called listening with the hands or with the body. It's also easy with this method to enter the state of Pause. But if you have little energy, it won't produce results. If you already have a great amount of practical experience, then this method works very well; again, it's easier than the other methods. You simply sit down, relax, and enter Pause.

The Fourth Method: Breathing with the Navel

Feel that the navel automatically breathes and receives nutrition from without. This exercise is necessary to secure the state of Pause for a long time. We'll exam it in detail in the section called "Practice."

The Fifth Method: Big Tree Practice

Those who normally have difficulties relaxing and calming down can attain the state of Pause during Big Tree. The protracted practice of Big Tree can help here.

The Sixth Method: Listening to Sounds, including with the Third Ear

When you enter the state of calm during practice, you might hear sounds or music. This lasts for a while, and then suddenly everything stops. You find yourself concentrating on one particular sound. After this, the state of Pause comes. Therefore the state of Pause can also be attained through listening to sounds or music.

Those who have difficulty achieving the state of Pause in class may try other methods. For some people, entering the state of Pause is easy when they watch TV or hear an unfamiliar language, for example.

The Seventh Method: Imagining the Process of Your Own Dying

In the Shaolin Monastery, a special exercise helps to put a stop to the stream of thoughts. The monks practicing there look not at a channel, not at Dan Tian, but at their own bones.

Master's Story

Normally our heart and lungs are working, and our blood, lymphatic system, and thoughts are in motion. All systems are functioning because we are living creatures. Now, if you sit or lie motionlessly and imagine that you're dead and that you have no flesh but only bones—which you can see—then it's easier to enter the state of Quietness. You need to imagine that you've died. A man sits, thinking that he's dying, and he imagines how he is dying. Usually this is a very terrifying practice. You feel that your body is becoming cold, and you really get the feeling that you're dying.

For regular people in a defined social milieu, such an exercise isn't suitable, of course. But in monasteries, the situation is obviously different. There people aren't even supposed to intermingle with everyday problems connected with home, family, and work. Moreover, they can completely cut themselves off from everything for a given period. In a monastery, therefore, you can practice in such a way that the heart "dies": there are no emotions, no anxiety, no concerns or thoughts about loved ones—no thoughts in general. The life of a monk unfolds in isolation from worldly affairs. So, becoming a recluse in an actual monastery for a time or simply renouncing involvement with the surrounding world are both possible.

But we who lead regular lives are linked with other people in innumerable ways. That's why we shouldn't have hearts that are dying. So we practice other exercises for attaining the same state. Moreover, if we try to employ exercises that produce quick results for monks, it will be very, very slow process —much slower than the exercises we study here. That's because our exercises are highly compatible with a normal way of life, while theirs aren't. Ours are good for calming the heart. Also, only after many years of practice, monks work at viewing a channel, a tube. Without this practice (viewing of a channel), it's impossible to achieve a high level. Usually monks are helped by a teacher, who slaps them on the head in the Baihui to help energy open this point and channel. All this takes a very long time, but we do it quickly in Stage IV.

The Eighth Method: Sit Stupidly and Wait Quietly

Another method is simply to meaninglessly sit or walk around— and wait. What for? Simply wait. You'll see what happens.

The Ninth Method: Practicing Calm through Movement

First, simply move around for a while. Then sit or lie down and enter the state of Pause. Prior to becoming familiar with Stage IV, we make very little use of this method. But beginning with that stage, when our body is ready and all channels are open, this is a good method. That's because when we move, we don't employ consciousness. Our body moves automatically. If consciousness isn't used, it calms down. Then the frontal part of the brain calms down, and the occipital part begins to function. The third and fourth preliminary exercises, The Sacred Crane Drinks Water and The Magic Dragon Mixes the Sea, are dynamic, and from these movements you can enter the state of Pause: *the body moves, but consciousness is calm.*

A great amount of movement engenders quietness, while deep quietness engenders movement. If you're very active, a breaking will ensue and you can enter into the state of Quietness. If you're very calm and motionless, internally you'll eventually feel the movement of energy. Therefore there's no need to try to speed up the process, to fret that nothing is yet happening with you. You need only to practice. Many people study for several years and still can't achieve Pause. And if you constantly change methods, you'll delay the realization of Pause significantly.

Prolonged involvement with sports and exercises that demand an intensive working of the physical body lead to fatigue. When fatigued, you can obtain the state of Quietness and Pause easily and quickly. If you're lying or sitting for a long time (an hour or two) without results and can't enter the state of Quietness, participate in a sport or go dancing. Your body will tire out, so when you return to practice, it will be easier to enter Pause.

Be guided by your state when choosing whether to study Quiet Qigong or movement. This is like Yin-Yang: passivity-activity or calm-movement. From Quiet Qigong you can switch to practice with movements, then from movement again to quietness.

The Tenth Method: The Method of Prohibitions

For different people different practice methods are needed. The above-listed, "standard" methods are fine for the majority of practitioners. But for some, methods that are largely different are required. Above all, this concerns those people who have many desires and aren't able to calm down and relax.

In this case, the method of prohibiting is used. The student is prohibited from doing what he loves, wants, and is accustomed to. As soon as he wants to realize specific desires, he recalls that his teacher forbade this.

The Eleventh Method: The Refusal Method

Here the practitioner puts together a list of "no-nos" pertaining to sources of pleasure, such as foods, entertainment, and so on. But this is easier said than done.

The Twelfth Method: The Suffering Method

Sometimes suffering can be provoked by the practitioner himself and/or by his teacher.

Master's Story

Sometimes we employ suffering for separate students, especially some personal students. They are all very nice, very good people who love studying a lot. But these students simply can't enter the state of Quietness, of calming the mind. At that point the teacher adopts an "unkind" attitude toward them. He forces them to perform many jobs that are far from ideal. In such situations the mind, or consciousness, of such a student tires and ceases to think on its own. Immediately, Pause sets in.

Some of my students tell me, "Teacher, I wanted very much to be a good student, but I'm up to my ears in problems. Why? To all intents and purposes, I'm an okay, kind person. But why now do I have more problems? I wanted to do everything but never have enough time for anything. I would like to do something this way but was unable—a problem always arises. I don't know what to do. And then I took sick and was in the hospital for a long time..."

I then ask him, "But what do you know how to do right now?"

He answers, "Right now, I don't remember anything." One student got into a conversation with me about this. As a result of problems that had emerged, he suddenly understood what Life is.

Helping a student reach a high level isn't an easy task for a teacher. He or she must understand the inner world of the particular student and choose the route that is conducive to that student's development. You see, every person has his or her very own soul. When a person grows up after having been under a certain external influence, his or her soul becomes stable and set. Or consider this illustration: Around the soul a very thick layer of dust forms. Through it, light can't reach the soul, and the soul can't be cleansed from the dust. For *this, a **special method of destroying the heart is used: the person must feel pain and experience suffering.** The suffering must be so strong that it seems like the student's heart is covered in blood. And he or she should have many tears.*

In ancient times, another method was used to achieve the state of Pause. For some this resulted in success, but for others it didn't. For an extended period, people ceased eating and drinking, thereby making their bodies suffer. The idea is that they would ruin their body to the point that Yin-Shen would leave the body. Now, we use this method only partially—not in its full form. In Shaolin, when there's a request for it, we sometimes refrain from eating and drinking, although we always eat fruits. This method is suitable and productive for those with a very strong physical body that's a hindrance to their soul departing.

With many people, the soul leaves the body in instances of serious illness, when the body is weakened. Fasting also exhausts the body and facilitates the exiting of the soul.

We've examined a long list of the various methods for achieving Pause for the subsequent departure of the soul. They are designed for practitioners of various levels and personalities. Therefore, should there be difficulties with attaining Pause, first give all of these methods a try; there's no danger whatsoever connected with their employment. But if success is still elusive after a few years, also try the fasting method. But **see to it that your body isn't reduced to a very bad state. Your soul will need somewhere to return to.**

Conditions Required for Achieving Pause

As we've already mentioned on more than one occasion, we must enter the state of Pause for a protracted period. Many people can attain this state for a few minutes, but entering it for an hour or more is far rarer. Some practitioners can achieve the state of Pause for three days. To reach this state and give our soul the opportunity to go outside, we must fulfill several conditions without fail.

- Most important is the need to be healthy. Our physical body must have the opportunity to be in a state of Quietness. This means that we need to be free of any pain or discomfort. You won't be able to achieve Pause if you're in pain; you're tormented by a cough; breathing is difficult; or you can't sit motionless in one position for a long time.

- Breathing with the body must be worked out so that a sufficient amount of oxygen can be had. Breathing with the body is also a preparation, a necessary aspect for entering the state of Pause.
- The body must be capable of receiving nutrition automatically. Consequently, we must develop what we call the second respiratory and digestive system. When we develop breathing and nutrition through the navel (the practice Bigu Shiqi), we thereby develop the second digestive system. If all these conditions are satisfied, it's possible to enter the state of Pause for a long time.
- Besides this, it's necessary to open the central channel and create the Way through which the soul can leave the body.
- The gates through which the soul goes out must be opened.
- We have to have a lot of energy. A lot of Qi in our body helps us to calm down. This is why we have to accumulate energy.

The Obstacles on the Way to Pause

First Obstacle

When we accumulate energy and a sufficient amount of Qi appears in our lower Dan Tian, this Qi gives birth to sexual energy. Men and women produce their respective hormones, which contribute to the formation of seed. During practice, Jing is transformed into Qi. Food, sperm, or the male and female hormones are transformed into Qi. When we have a lot of Qi, it again returns, and begins to produce male and female hormones. When such processes are going on, you always feel a lot of energy.

However, many practitioners complain that they have been studying for many years without any success. Their problem is that when Qi is transformed into Jing, they can't retain it and thus lose energy. This is one of the reasons the Taoist monks practiced in the mountains. Children and teenagers remained in the mountains and practiced until the transformation process was completed and the soul had learned how to leave the body and return. After this, the Teacher permitted them to go down from the mountains and start families.

We already stated that if a person practices correctly and regularly for one hundred days, it's possible to complete this whole process: to reach the state of Pause and the departure of your soul. Now you can analyze why you failed to achieve success. Maybe one of the reasons lies here.

Second Obstacle

No matter where you practice, there's a danger that you might have a dream about a desired woman or man. In the dream, you may get involved in an intimate relationship with this person and lose your energy. Here everything depends on your consciousness: if it's pure, you'll be able to overcome this temptation.

If you're unable to surmount these obstacles, your soul will not be able to leave the body and you won't be able to find out *who you are or what Life is*.

Third Obstacle

The third obstacle is everyday life. Unless we are monks, we can't exist apart from society, family, and interaction with other people. Perhaps the following is going on: you try engaging in quiet meditation but your head is full of thoughts about various matters and problems connected with life, work, family, and so on. These thoughts are a big barrier.

The thought process, then, can be seen as an obstacle because our mind is constantly occupied. Never calm, we often experience some form of anxiety, unease, or fear. When the mind calms down, all these sensations disappear.

Fourth Obstacle

The fourth obstacle is our desires. During practice, you might get new ideas or be moved to satisfy creative urges. Creative ideas can so overwhelm you that you become hyper-excited and can't calm down. Unable to enter the state of Silence of Mind, sometimes you can't even sleep normally. Besides this, desires give birth to an assortment of emotions. All of this obstructs practice.

Fifth Obstacle

The fifth obstacle is our own stupidity. There are many situations in which our mind can't decipher what's good and what's bad, what must be done now and what later. Unable to make good decisions and understand exactly how to behave in a given situation, we get confused. Sometimes our mind works to no purpose, which is also an obstacle.

Now let's examine when it's easier to reach the state of Pause.

What Helps in Achieving Pause

Nobody can think constantly. There are definitely seconds or minutes when the mind doesn't think. They can be called *interruptions in thinking* or *intervals in consciousness*. Our brain works this way. In such moments, it's easier to attain the state of Pause. So thinking is difficult for us when

- we're extremely tired, such as after protracted Big Tree practice;
- oxygen is in short supply (practicing in the mountains is wise since there's little oxygen there);
- the desire to sleep is very strong;
- we're weakened because of an illness and lack the energy to think clearly (staying home and practicing is a good idea here);
- we've just had a filling meal.

Master's Story

Three days in the state of Pause or without a soul isn't dangerous. Therefore, in accordance with Chinese tradition, a person is buried only after having been dead for three days. These three days are based on the condition of the physical body.

I was in the state of Pause for seven days. Departing from the body, the soul travels at a great speed and doesn't feel the passage of time. That's why these seven days seemed to me like twenty minutes.

There's a well-known story about a Buddhist monk whose soul traveled outside of the body for nearly eighteen years, while the body remained in a mountain cave. During these years, which were at the time of the Cultural Revolution, he visited many worlds and learned a lot there. Afterward he wrote a book about his experience and went to Singapore to teach Buddhism and talk about what he had seen in the other worlds.

If our body doesn't change, we don't feel time. Aging during Pause and other bodily processes proceeds very slowly. Therefore practicing Qigong extends your life.

For a practitioner to enter a protracted state of Pause, his body must be prepared. Before achieving Pause for a seven-day period, I practiced constantly and for long periods. And one of the days I didn't want to eat. Out of habit I tried to eat something but ended up vomiting everything. I then understood that I should not be eating. Day and night I practiced with my spiritual Teacher. He taught me a lot in this period. (Earlier I discussed in more detail my experience with my soul's departure and the 108-day fast that preceded it.[5] Ahead of me is the need to find time for a major Pause, perhaps for one to three months, since I've accumulated many questions in the intervening years that must be answered.)

***Special conditions are necessary for a long-lasting Pause,** particularly practice in solitude and an assistant. If several people are to engage in a long Pause, it's best to use several rooms. Sometimes it's necessary to retreat to the mountains or caves to avoid being bothered by anyone and to be able to spend a lot of time in the state of Pause.*

In any case, practicing Qigong should not cut you off from normal life. To this end we need to profess the following philosophical approach: we practice in a very serious way, but we don't devote too much attention to results. If we take practice too seriously and are always thinking about it, then really relaxing is out of the question, and irritability becomes a possibility. It's necessary both to practice and to find time to enjoy life.

Recommendations and Particularities of Individual Practice

***First**, as much as possible, continue practicing skin breathing to saturate your body with oxygen through the skin.

***Second**, practice taking in substances through the navel. And if you feel like not eating on a particular day—don't. This means that

---

5 You can read about this experience in detail in appendix 2 of the first volume: *Zhong Yuan Qigong: First Stage of Ascent: Relaxation.*

you already have enough energy and are able to enter the state of Bigu Shiqi. This can last a week or two, or much longer. During this time, your stomach and intestines get cleaned out. If a person does not take in food for an extended period, it's very easy for him, for her to enter the state of Pause. After this, perhaps, you'll hear a voice or feel that you've got to go somewhere to practice.

Third, don't concentrate on practice excessively. This is different from studying in other branches of learning. Here we're talking about a special state of consciousness; if you concentrate excessively on practice, you train for a long time without getting any results. You can practice every day, but you still won't achieve the state of Pause. To practice well, simply listen to yourself. Then, at a certain moment, you'll suddenly feel the need to learn and will know this is the appropriate time for practice. Teaching the technology or method of this is easy, but conveying this sensation is difficult. It's connected with our physical, energy, and spiritual state simultaneously. That's why it's necessary to practice "it seems it is, it seems it isn't."

Fourth, create a comfortable atmosphere.

Master's Story

Successful practice requires an atmosphere that is good from a psychological point of view. All the practitioners of a group must relate to each other like brothers and sisters, if not even better. All members have to be kind to one another, care for each other, and avoid imparting too much significance to trivial matters. Try forgiving one another; try thinking about others before doing something. Don't do anything that brings you pleasure at the expense of others. A good atmosphere makes practicing easy, especially among personal students. It helps us to reach the state of Pause, without which we'll be unable to grasp what the soul is, what the spirit is. If you're unable to enter the state of Pause, you'll be unable to understand what Life is, what a Human is, and what the Universe is, since there's a huge difference between knowledge and personal experience.

Knowledge you can glean from many sources, but it will differ greatly from your own sensations. For example, if you don't eat an apple, you don't know how they taste, even if you've read many books about them. This is why we must experience things on our own and then, using the knowledge and information of others, do the analyzing and comparing.

It can be said that **Qigong practice is a way to understand Death**[6]. *If we wish to understand what* **Life** *is, we need to understand what* **Death** *is. The state of Pause gives us the sensation of death. Since your lungs and heart cease functioning, this state resembles death. The body's temperature begins decreasing, and if your consciousness is still here, you'll feel coldness.*

While understanding the process of our birth is difficult, we do have the possibility of learning how dying plays itself out. Real death comes with the destruction of the physical body, but in Pause your body remains in a normal state.

Our goal is to know more about Life and the Universe. *For this reason Qigong, and especially* **spiritual practice, must give people freedom.** *Without freedom there can be no spiritual development. That is, a lack of freedom keeps us from meeting personal goals. Furthermore, the restriction of freedom is the means through which selfish goals are achieved. Of course, everywhere there are rules, and freedom does not mean that you can do whatever you wish.* **Freedom allows one to pursuit an understanding of the universal rules and nature's laws.** *In this pursuit, you are uninfluenced by negative factors and in turn are independent. Thus, you are free.*

ABOUT DIFFERENT "I"

We have stated that in ZYQ we deal with the three aspects of the human being: the physical body, energy system, and informational system, or soul. Our practice is directed at balancing and further developing these three. Development is always accompanied by change. On the physical plane, every change is noticeable, but when changes in our energy and informational systems occur, there may not be an external indication of it. But changes in the spiritual state can be noticed, particularly by the practitioner himself.

At a certain moment of practice, you'll be able to feel that **two of you exist.** One of you is inside your body and is being constantly influenced by such external factors as human interaction, social problems,

---

6 The capitalization of the word "Death" means the change of life form for any being in the Universe

and rules and laws. When you direct your attention to something or do something, you have to be aware of the reasons for and possible results of your behavior. Psychologists call this our **consciousness**. So it's our consciousness that tells us what we are and determines our behavior in every concrete situation.

Therefore, your actions and desires are directed by the rules that have been set in place. Often, you are restricted from performing actions that have either been classified as bad or undesirable. This leads you to *consciously make decisions that conform to a certain way of life*. This brings us to our first "I."

Master's Story

*After the complete opening of the central channel, our **second or true** "I"—upon which the physical body doesn't weigh—begins to manifest itself. In Chinese this is called zhin-wo—the true "I." It can be said that our customary "I" is the lower and the true "I" the higher of these two.*

Our first "I" isn't the true "I,"** because we're surrounded by what's known as contemporary knowledge or information of every kind, including that about the physical body. The human is also clothed in various emotions—malice, hurt, and so one. This means that not only the physical body covers the true "I," but the emotional state as well. To the extent that all of this "clothing" is very heavy for your true "I," each of you at certain periods of time feel great fatigue. And **with this your second, true "I" can't move, which is why you often feel uncomfortable.

After certain ZYQ training, you can free our true "I" of all these heavy clothes. And then you'll be able to depart like a bird flies out of a cage. If a bird can leave his abode and return to it, then this can't be called captivity. But if it lives continually in a closed space, in a cage, then after some time passes it simply will forget how to fly. And if it was born in a cage, it simply doesn't know what it means to fly. A comparison can be made with us here.

Since we regularly—in fact, our entire lives—live in the closed space of our body, we can't know what other worlds are like and how to get there. But open the door once and the bird flies out. And at this moment it thinks, "Oh, what a big world." It's the same with us: we're inside all day and don't imagine what a big world it is. Before finally flying out, we receive preliminary information about this other world. This is approximately the same as another bird flying up to a caged one and telling it what's beyond the confines of the cage and room. From these accounts, the first bird understands that there are still other worlds.

*When the Third Eye and central channel open, we also begin to receive information about the surrounding world. However, the information coming from the Third Eye, Third Ear, and Second Heart in this state isn't complete. So, in Stage IV, practicing Zhengong, you'll be able to receive a huge amount of information about the world, but this will not be the work of your **true "I."** Stage IV is only training, preparation for the workings of your true "I."*

Practice of the true "I" is what Stage V is about. After the opening of the channels and the realization of your true "I," you'll be able to receive real and complete information about everything in the Universe.

Right now your first, lower "I"—which you represent in everyday life—and your second, true "I" are approximately the same—divided equally . Therefore, from the point of view of those surrounding you, you're a normal person. At the same time, sometimes your true "I" manifests itself a little more in some situations. When your true "I" begins to grow and becomes activated, you begin to see various pictures or hear voices more often. When your first "I" is active, your true "I" is in what seems like a sleepy or frozen state. It's resting. Even if you can perceive some pictures or voices, you simply pay no attention to them—your first "I" is too active for them to be felt.

But if your customary, first "I" enters the state of Quietness and begins to practice Qigong, your second "I" is activated. In this situation, you begin to hear voices, as well as see images and pictures. You're able to see the Teacher. Then, naturally, you begin to think about this. And if you don't control yourself and listen only to your second, true "I," you'll fall under the control of these phenomena of yours. They'll be able to rule you.

At first everything looks rather harmless: You begin talking at home and to your friends about interesting occurrences. You recall the details and listen for something. Certain parts of your brain may fall into a state of constant excitement. Then you experience insomnia, and your appetite disappears. Therefore be the master of the situation at all times.

If you're able to switch from one state to another as you so desire, then everything you take in when your second "I" is active will not create any problems. But if in a very determined way you pay attention to what you hear or see while in a state of Quietness, and you try to believe in these images and voices, problems will arise: you'll begin to accept reality in a distorted form and your behavior might become wacky. You might fall sway to thoughts that someone is impacting you negatively; you'll talk about this and even—which is more serious— think about it. Then, you'll "get stuck," in this state, and the problems can deepen.

Master's Story

In China I had several students who shifted to the second state and for a long time—a year or two—couldn't return to the first. But once this was accomplished, they switched from one state to another easily.

A lengthy stay in this second state can be the real reason for a person's problems. Sometimes no one can help such people for the simple reason that they like to believe in what they see and hear, and in what happens to them. They believe in this much more than in others. Problems often arise not as a result of practice, but because they already had various problems connected with the physical body and emotional state, or psychological problems, such as instability, stressful situations, or innate or acquired complexes. It's difficult for them to shift back, because they don't want to leave a comfortable state.

Thus practice does not cause new problems to arise. Rather, old and previously hidden problems, such as illnesses and disorders that one had prior to practice, manifest themselves.

Often in China we discussed this question: can a person practice and reach such heights that he would be able to avoid the process of immersing himself in his second "I"—a process that is a sufficiently dangerous and sometimes continues for a lengthy period? For several years we analyzed the work of all currents, of all schools that study similar practices, and we discovered that in all of the currents connected with this type of spiritual development, these problems always arise. There's no system that can avoid them.

A second question we frequently examined was the following: in what instances is it possible to avoid unpleasant situations with the second "I"? It's possible only when you're engaged in the practice of methods designed exclusively to improve your health and with dynamic exercises that have no state of calm and Silence of Mind.

You know that a person consists of a soul, energy, and body. If you engage only in the development of the physical body and changing its state, prob-

lems with consciousness can't arise. You can receive an injury only on a physical level, such as bruises or fractures.

But if you engage not only in the physical body but also the soul, then problems with consciousness, with the psyche, are possible. Therefore have a clear understanding of the possible dangers on the path of your development. That's why I'm always repeating: **we must be our own masters.** *While practicing, we immerse ourselves totally in it. And upon finishing, we shift to our everyday affairs and normal life.*

Chapter 2:
PRACTICE

Our regular, everyday life is the foundation we must have. We practice Qigong to understand how our life should be. Each of us encounters many incomprehensible things and situations over the years, which we try to explain. To solve different tasks and problems during our lifetime, we pursue various routes. Zhong Yuan Qigong is one of them. While we most often utilize this system for health improvement, we can also turn to it for better understanding of the cause-and-effect connections of occurrences and the interaction between separate people, organizations, and entire countries. This means that through practicing Qigong we wish to solve our problems and raise the quality of our lives.

Too often people act wrongly and try to fulfill improper desires. This is precisely why problems, complications, negative emotions, and so on, arise. We have to practice not because this is the essence of life, but because we very often commit errors. If we were to always do everything in accordance with the laws of nature, we would not need practice.

We practice in order to follow nature, to understand it, and to act in accordance with its laws. Therefore Qigong practice isn't the goal of life. ***The goal is to live simply and happily.***

PRELIMINARY EXERCISES

In Stage I, we learned four of the eight preliminary exercises; in Stage II, another two; and in Stage III, as in the second, we'll learn two more preliminary exercises—the seventh and eighth.

海
底
捞
月

Seventh Preliminary Exercise:
ACCEPTING THE MOON FROM THE SEA

The seventh exercise is intended for training the central channel and upper Dan Tian. Translated from the Chinese, its name is To Accept the Moon from the Water or To Accept the Moon from the Sea.

First, you must imagine yourself at the shore of a sea or lake. It is evening, quiet, and without wind. The sky is starry, with a shining and big moon. And all of this is reflected in the calm and smooth surface of the water.

Nothing else is visible, and soon we don't know where the sky is and where the water is—the Moon and stars are equally visible in both directions. And we begin to take into our bodies the Moon from this reservoir, as if our five sense organs are deceiving us.

But we know this isn't possible, because there's no Moon in the sea. There's only one Moon, in the sky, while in the water, there's only a reflection of it. And naturally we can't carry out the task of accepting the Moon in our body. Yet we'll practice using these images.

Why do we have to accept the Moon from the sea? After all, this isn't a reality—this isn't a truth. But if we execute such a practice, we can reveal that we're achieving a certain real result: after the end of practice, with our eyes closed, we see on our internal screen in front of us the Moon. And with eyes closed, we then don't see darkness, as we did earlier, but a bright Moon.

This is a special method in the ZYQ system that offers, *through practice of an untruth, the ability to eventually obtain the truth.* This is completely different from what modern science proposes. In mathematics, we have "proof by contradiction," wherein we proceed from something that seemingly can't be true and, as a result, come up with what must be true. The ZYQ system also employs this principle. We often practice exercises that help us obtain the real from the unreal, or the truth through untruth. The seventh preliminary exercise is one such exercise.

It's best, of course, to perform these exercises in the evening at the seashore or a reservoir, when the Moon is reflected in it. If such an opportunity doesn't exist, we "paint" this picture in our imagination.

As you see or imagine the Moon's reflection in the water, mentally extend your arms outward to grab the Moon. Raise it up and guide it through the Mingtang point to the upper Dan Tian (Picture 19). Then lower it through the central channel to the lower Dan Tian. We'll do this eight times.

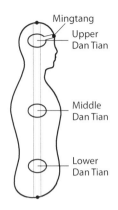

Picture 19: The Path to Place the Moon into Dan Tians

Next, and in the same way, we'll receive the Moon in the upper Dan Tian eight more times; but now we lower it to the middle Dan Tian, again via the central channel. And, finally, another eight times we'll receive the Moon in the upper Dan Tian and leave it there (Picture 20). With this, each successive Moon fuses with the preceding one, like drops of water.

There's usually no special need to link this exercise to breathing. Often this happens automatically during practice. However, if you wish to know this through and through, then note the following: on breathing in we accept the Moon; on holding our breath we lead it inside; on breathing out we lower it.

The Sequence of the Execution of the Exercise

1. Stand straight, with your body as relaxed as possible and your eyes half closed. Imagine a Moon in a lake (the reflection of the Moon).
2. Get the Moon from the lake by raising your arms and spreading them out to the sides. Visualize extending them to the reflection of the Moon, lowering them into the reservoir, and grabbing the Moon from the water with your palms. Inhaling, with these energy arms, scoop up the Moon, imagining it to be the actual, real Moon.
3. Lift the Moon, mentally shrinking it as you do. While lifting, finish inhaling.
4. While holding your breath, bring the Moon through the Mingtang point at the level of your eyebrows (projection of the Third Eye) inside your brain to the upper Dan Tian. When you move

Picture 20: Seventh Preliminary Exercise: Accepting the Moon from the Sea
(a) Into the Lower Dan Tian

the ball of the Moon to the upper Dan Tian, try to feel it going inside your brain.

5. Relax your body and, while exhaling smoothly, lower the Moon along the central channel to the lower Dan Tian, and reduce it to the smallest volume possible (Picture 20a).

At first, when you scoop up the Moon, it's big, like the regular Moon. But when you lead it inside, it shrinks to the size of the diameter of the channel or to the size of the luminous point.

In the process of moving the Moon downward, you can close your eyes and look at it, and then open your eyes. You'll discover that the Moon is still in the water, still reflected in the reservoir. Therefore you must do this procedure once more.

6. Once again mentally extend your arms to the reflection of the Moon. Grab it on inhaling, raise it to your forehead, and as you hold your breath, bring it into the upper Dan Tian. Exhaling, lead it through the central channel down to the lower Dan Tian.

Hence, there are now two Moons in the lower Dan Tian. But when you look, you discover only one Moon. Why? Because they merged together exactly like two drops of water, becoming one drop that is bigger in size.

You can really grasp the process of the movement of the Moon from the upper to the lower Dan Tian.

So we receive the Moon eight times. Each subsequent Moon merges with the preceding one. As a result, all the Moons fuse together and form one large Moon, just as several drops of water come together in one large drop. At the same time, in the lower Dan Tian a white light appears, which becomes brighter from each Moon.

7. Opening your eyes, you once again see the Moon in the lake. Grab it again and, while inhaling, lead it to the upper Dan Tian. Glancing at the Moon with your eyes closed, lower it on exhaling, this time to the middle Dan Tian.

8. On looking at the lake, you see the Moon again. In an analogous way, we accept it in the middle Dan Tian. Once again, mentally extend your arms toward the Moon in the lake, grab

it while inhaling, and raise it to the Mingtang point. Holding your breath, bring it into the upper Dan Tian. While exhaling, lead it through the central channel downward, again to the middle Dan Tian (Picture 20b). Reduce it to the smallest volume possible.

While work with the middle Dan Tian is taking place, the Moon is large as it's being scooped up, like the regular Moon. But, as in the previous case, when it's raised and brought inside to the upper Dan Tian, it shrinks.

This procedure must also be performed eight times.

As in a preceding case, all Moons in the middle Dan Tian dissolve into one large Moon, like earlier in the lower Dan Tian, with the middle Dan Tian made brighter by each successive

Picture 20: Seventh Preliminary Exercise: Accepting the Moon from the Sea: (b) Into the Middle Dan Tian

Moon. Even after this, however, the Moon continues to be reflected in the lake.

9. Begin taking the Moon into the upper Dan Tian. As before, scoop up the Moon on inhaling and lift it. While holding your breath, bring it to the Mingtang point, and while exhaling, place it in the upper Dan Tian (Picture 20c). Again accept eight Moons in the upper Dan Tian. Here also the Moons fuse, and with each successive one, it becomes lighter there.

In this way we receive a total of twenty-four Moons. But when we look at this channel, we see only three Moons, one in each Dan Tian.

Picture 20: Seventh Preliminary Exercise: Accepting the Moon from the Sea
(c) Into the Upper Dan Tian

Meaning and Purpose of the Exercise

First, we know that there are two types of energy: Yin and Yang. Yang energy makes us active; Yin makes us calm. Normally during practice we acquire more Yang. But too much Yang makes it difficult to enter the state of calm.

The Moon is calm, and the energy of the Moon is Yin energy, like the energy of water. And since you receive the Moon from the water, you strengthen the Yin energy. If you receive a lot of Yin energy—the energy of the Moon—then your heart calms down, as does your consciousness: this white energy helps bring your mind to a state of deep calm, and you're able to enter the state of Quietness.

Second, in Stage III, we continue to develop the central channel. As shown, we accept the Moon twenty-four times and place it in our body. Since we lead it through the central channel, we are opening this channel and creating the Way for the departure of the soul.

Third, we open the channel leading from the Mingtang point deep in the brain to the Third Eye.

Fourth, this exercise helps open the Third Eye.

If this exercise is practiced over a few days, it'll be possible to see inside all the Dan Tian a white, luminous ball similar to the Moon. If you practice it regularly, the Moons can occupy the entire channel, merging into one complete, white luminescence.

After that, with your eyes closed, you'll be able to see in front of you a mirror or a screen.

So, the seventh preliminary exercise is intended for the receiving of Yin energy, the opening of the upper Dan Tian, the development of the central channel Zhong-Mai, and the opening of the Third Eye. It also helps you achieve Quietness, in which it's easier to see with the Third Eye. Later, after you've acquired a certain experience, you'll understand this exercise better. It helps in diagnostics, so later we'll begin employing the Moon for some other tasks, in particular, for diagnosing with the Third Eye (see the "Medical Aspects of Qigong" section for more information on the work and development of the Third Eye).

The goals of the seventh preliminary exercise are opening the Third Eye; constructing the Way through the Zhong-Mai channel; and, at the same time, illuminating its three Dan Tian.

Before you begin to execute this or any of the exercises, always have a definite idea of it. In this case, it's the image of a lake or sea in front of you that's reflecting the Moon. With your mind, consciousness, and imagination you must create an image, which is the training of your mind. On receiving the Moon internally, you should feel like you're drinking water: something is entering you that then moves downward through the middle channel. This means that you're really feeling something; there is void.

Master's Story

In the very beginning of practice, you don't have very clear sensations. But they will gain strength after you've practiced for a while. What's important here is that you feel the process of something passing through the channel. With time you'll really be able to feel that the Moon is within you, in the center. In the beginning we don't know what this is: is it really the Moon inside or is this only our imagination? But we're absolutely certain that this isn't the Moon that we see in the sky. However, changes occur in the body with such practice.

*If you practice this exercise regularly for some time, when you enter the state of Quietness, **you'll be able to see the Moon and Sun simultaneously during practice, that is, the combination of Yin and Yang.** You'll see the Moon in one place and the Sun in another. And during practice it will seems that the Moon is shining in one place, while the Sun is shining in another. Sometimes they can simultaneously light up a landscape. This being the case, sometimes you can see them, while other times you can see only the landscape they illuminate, understanding that they are both present at the same time. In this instance, what's to the right and what to the left isn't important: all that's important is that you see such a phenomenon. It's an indicator of your level of progress in Qigong practice.*

At first the Moon is only in your imagination. Later, however, it morphs into something real. From the beginning, our consciousness is primary, while matter is secondary.

This isn't the case in Marxism, which claims that matter is primary and consciousness secondary. That is, everything is the opposite. In our physical world, Marxism is right, but in the other world, this idea no longer holds. But since we sometimes are in two worlds, we can at times see that the first principle is right, while at other times, the second.

Often during practice it's difficult for us to understand what's going on; we think that maybe our sensations are deceiving us. Is this Moon only our imagination, or is there something else in this? After a while, however, the result shows that we are really acquiring something. We can compare this with a question about the emitting of energy: does something really come out from our palms or not, and does a patient really receive something or not? Often what is received isn't felt by outsiders. That's why it's difficult to believe in this and to prove the emitting. But at the same time, patients do get healthy—and this is the result of such outside influense.

仙
香
透
体

Eighth Preliminary Exercise:
RECEIVING AROMAS
OF VARIOUS WORLDS INTO THE BODY

Translated directly from the Chinese, the eighth exercise is called Immortal Smells Enter Your Body or Immortal Aromas Saturate, Soak Your Body.

In the various worlds, smells are different, and they can be felt. We can even see the flowers that give off these aromas. And our entire body is saturated with them with this practice. The energy of these smells helps us "rise" to the next level, to the next world. The smell that comes from another world cleanses and changes our body so that our soul can later depart from it. This exercise allows the body to receive substances from worlds of various levels. It also provides an opportunity to become familiar with sensations that arise in the practitioner at the moment of his or her soul's departure from the body. Thus this exercise is intended to help you prepare for the next flight of your soul.

We've stated frequently that our soul can leave our physical body. And *only after the soul really does leave the physical body can we understand truly what the physical body, spirit, soul, and energy are.*

We practice this exercise, as with all others, eight times, or in eight cycles. In these eight cycles, we become acquainted with eight different levels of worlds. Each cycle consists of one inhalation and one exhalation. While inhaling, imagine that you're receiving and absorbing with your body the aromas of flowers, the Qi of the given world. This means that we'll accept the various smells coming into our body from the surrounding space.

On exhaling, imagine that this energy exits below, moves through your legs and feet, and pushes you upward like a jet stream (Picture 21).

In accordance with Image Medicine, eight worlds are higher than ours, and we'll fly to these higher worlds. Each world has its own aroma, and with the flight to each subsequent world, we absorb these aromas into our body when we inhale.

So, on inhaling you receive in your body the imagined aromas of various flowers, while on exhaling, the air and energy pass downward

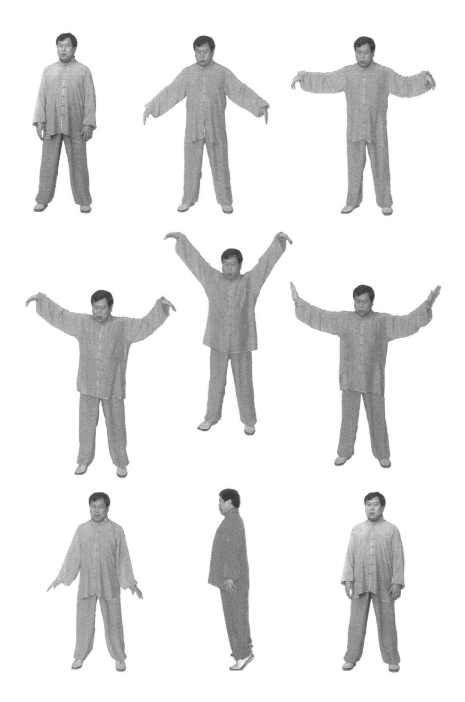

Picture 21: Eighth Preliminary Exercise: Receiving the Flavors
of Various Worlds into the Body

through your feet and legs, and push you upward. Much like a rocket, you shoot up to the next world. With each inhalation and exhalation, you turn up in the next world.

Sequence of Execution of Exercise

1. Stand straight. Relax your body as much as possible and close your eyes partially, as if squinting. Imagine yourself being among flowers.
2. Inhale slowly through the entire surface of your skin as you gracefully raise your arms, like a bird flaps its wings. Imagine that you're absorbing the aromas of the flowers of this world with your entire body, with all your pores.
3. Exhale through your legs. On exhaling, lower your arms/wings, being propelled like a bird by the air. Imagine the energy exiting through your legs and feet, and lifting you off (the floor). As if on a jet stream, take off and fly away to the next world higher than ours. Simultaneously, propelled by your arms/wings, get on your tiptoes.
4. Finish exhaling as you gracefully lower yourself to your heels.
5. Once more, inhale while raising your arms/wings. As you do so, take in with your body the aromas of this next world.

     Again, lowering your arms, push off your body as a bird would, and imagine that the energy exiting through your legs and feet lifts you and carries you to the next world. With this, when you begin inhaling, gracefully get on your tiptoes, and when you finish exhaling, lower yourself slowly onto your heels.

     Do this eight times.

As you execute the eighth exercise, you become a bird that flies from one world to another, with each world higher than the previous one. And you take from these worlds the aromas of the different flowers. From each world, your body absorbs a specific smell, a specific aroma.

According to the model of the Universe accepted in Image Therapy, eight worlds higher than us exist. We want to get to the highest. Therefore, with each inhalation and exhalation we rise one world higher.

When seminar attendees become acquainted with this exercise, they usually raise an interesting question: "We talk about how to fly to other worlds, but we don't discuss or learn how to return. Why don't we practice returning from the eighth world to ours, the first?" Such a question is dictated by logical analysis: after all, if we go somewhere, we have to later return. But in fact this exercise is correct; it seems illogical only from the point of view of popular science and customary logic.

So why is it correct and what does it offer? And why, with this exercise, don't we practice the procedure for returning?

This is simply because you're still in this world. And if you really do fly to another world, then you'll understand how to return back.

In this exercise, it's important to imagine that there are many flowers around you. On raising your arms while inhaling, you must take in the aroma, or energy, of the flowers. Then you lower your arms, like a bird his wings, and raise yourself a little. As you do this exercise you "move" to other worlds. And after the eighth time, you're in another world. But when you open your eyes, you're once again here, in this world. If you even begin sensing that you've moved to another world, when you open your eyes, you'll see that you're still located here and now. Such images of moving to other worlds are natural and normal with this practice.

You know that *one of the goals of Stage III practice is to develop our spirit and acquire the opportunity for our soul to go outside. The goal of this exercise is to prepare the consciousness and body for the subsequent departure of the soul;* to help us understand and feel that moment when our soul goes beyond the limits of our body; and to assist our soul in adjusting to the different worlds and our body in adapting to the sensations that accompany our soul's exit.

When your soul goes beyond your body's boundaries for the first time, you may experience a sense of fear, discomfort, or other unpleasant feelings. This exercise helps us to understand what transpires when our soul leaves, so we aren't fearful.

Phenomena such as loss of balance may sometimes be experienced during this exercise; standing securely in place can be difficult. You may also shake a little. That same sensation makes itself known with the real departure of your soul—the same shaking.

The Meaning and Purpose of the Exercise

First, this is a special exercise for developing the soul. It assists in constructing *the Way for the subsequent departure of your soul.* With this exercise, your soul can't fly off to a different world; this happens later when you engage in *Quiet Qigong*. Such training is necessary for working out certain sensations you encounter during the real departure of the soul. But for this you should have only sitting or lying posture, and succeed here in entering the state of deep Quietness.

If in the process of this exercise you were able to take off, then this exit would occur automatically, as would the return. If your soul really can fly to another world, your body nevertheless will remain here. Your soul is connected to your body and almost immediately returns to it. Without lengthy training, it can't leave for a long time.

When you practice this exercise, simply do it. There's no need to think or to undertake something special in order to return, because your soul remains inside your body. And, again, since the soul doesn't leave the body in the eighth exercise, you need not perform the return procedure.

Second, this is a special method to produce something from nothing. As we do the eighth exercise, we absorb the aromas of flowers— or of what is the same thing: the smells of other, higher worlds. This can be stated differently: here one of the eight principles of ZYQ is realized. It claims that in the beginning there was zero, which then engendered one, or illusion; imagination gave birth to reality. We spoke about this principle during our examination of the seventh preliminary exercise.

Development in the ZYQ system proceeds along two paths or two axes: axis x and axis y. The current along axis x can be called development in our real world, while that along axis y is the visiting of different worlds or movement, with which we go from our world to the next worlds.

The theory and philosophy of Qigong doesn't resemble the theory of contemporary science. This is why phenomena often seem illogical.

Questions and Answers

1. How many times do we guide the Moon into each Dan Tian when performing the seventh preliminary exercise?

Eight times each. Each time you lead the Moon into the upper Dan Tian, but the first eight times you lower it via the central channel to the lower Dan Tian; the next eight you lower it to the central channel; and the final eight you leave it in the upper Dan Tian. Thus each of the Dan Tian will have eight Moons.

2. Can this exercise be carried out for a longer time? How long?

Yes, you can do it for a long time, not eight times but eight hundred. Moreover, you can spend an hour or more on it each time.

3. How often must this exercise be practiced?

Preferably every day.

4. What does the Moon look like?

Like a white sphere or ball.

5. How do you breathe when doing this?

On inhaling, take in the Moon from the water. When exhaling, lower it along the central channel.

6. But why don't we accept the Moon directly from the sky?

If we worked with the real Moon instead of with a reflection, we'd be able to receive it only once, and it would cease to exist. But in the water, the Moon is in the form of a reflection. Of course this could be looked upon as a joke, this untruth. Still, do we or do we not receive the moon? You'll be able to answer this question yourself after practicing for a while.

7. But still, what are the goals in practicing the seventh preliminary exercise? Why is the Moon in a lake and not in the sky?

In a lake, the Moon is visible if the water is very calm. This means that everything has entered the state of calm—there's no wind. Then both sea and lake are calm, and the reflection of the Moon is too. In addition, by bringing in such a calm Moon from a calm reservoir, you calm the area of your Third Eye. This can help bring your heart and consciousness into the state of calm. Therefore this exercise is used for construction of the Way internally and also for entering the state of calm.

8. What does one think about in this exercise?

At first, think about the Moon in the water. And then don't think about anything and try simply to see the Moon.

9. Can we achieve Pause and not think at the same time?

No, there's only the state of Quietness. When you're thinking, Pause hasn't yet been achieved.

10. The moon changes in color and size, depending on how high over the horizon it is, and it has various phases. So, what should one imagine?

You should visualize a white Moon, which is usually the full moon.

11. What's more important: the visualized image or the correctness of the body position? Can you have your feet not parallel to one another and simply imagine this?

This depends on which exercise you're performing. Undoubtedly your consciousness is most important, but having an incorrect pose is not good.

12. Why must the Moon be taken from the sea and not directly from the sky? This is incomprehensible. And then it's the reflection in the sea and not the Moon itself. Why don't we take the reflection instead of talking about the Moon itself?

Again, what we do is an impossible thing. With the help of this impossible thing, we get the possible, and we do something that's different. The goal of the exercise isn't to receive the Moon, which can't be grabbed with the hands from either the sea or the sky. But if you work with the Moon that hangs in the sky, you're working with the truth, and you won't get the result you should from this exercise. This will become understandable only when you practice it and get the result. It's impossible to explain this in any other way. You simply need to do it.

13. Can one practice with eyes closed?

Yes.

14. But please repeat what we can get with the help of this exercise.

With the help of this exercise, we receive three things. The first two are energy of water and energy of the Moon, which are Yin. The third is white light. That's why we receive the Moon from the sea: to receive more Yin Qi.

15. Is it possible for there to be a change in the color of the light that we place in the Dan Tian with the Moon?

Energy changes, and its color can change every day. It could be white or another color.

16. Which preliminary exercises should be practiced, for how long, and in what sequence?

First, and above all, it's necessary to understand the goals of each exercise. Second, you must understand what you need right now. And third, based on this, you select your practice priorities. You'll study mainly those exercises that you most need. There's no prescribed sequence. Practice most what you like most. One person may like the fifth preliminary exercise, another the sixth, and a third Chanzo. One of my teachers liked the fifth and sixth very much. Though he practiced every day, he spent more time on these two exercises.

Regarding each exercise, one and the same thing can be said: if you practice each one more deeply and longer, you'll discover that it can give you much more than you initially thought.

17. How do you know when you've practiced a particular exercise, such as the seventh preliminary, enough?

If you study this practice for a very long time and take into your body a great amount of Yin, you'll feel cold. The Moon will always be present in you, so to speak. If you feel such cold, this means that you have a great amount of Yin. Then there's no need to practice longer; take the Yang of Sun internally.

18. How long can the seventh preliminary be done?

For a long time, as long as you like it. You can do this exercise for thirty minutes straight. It helps to open the Third Eye and to develop the central channel. After such practice, when you close your eyes, you'll no longer see darkness.

19. I began seeing flashes and many sparks after this practice.

Fine. This indicates that the channel leading to the Third Eye is opening.

20. The Moon is big, but what should its ball inside be like?

It should be small. You bring the big Moon in, but before its entering, it shrinks to the size of a dot or a very small ball. Don't define things mathematically. You need to see inside this ball of the Moon. Continue practicing, but with your consciousness you must always reduce the Moon to the size of a very small ball.

21. Okay, but how many Moons should there be inside us?

There should be three Moons, or three balls, with one in each of the three Dan Tian.

22. Why do we bring the Moon inside and not the Sun?

We accept the Moon because the goal of this practice is to calm the frontal part of the brain, that is, the thought processes. If we accept the Sun—and sunlight and the Qi of Sun are excessively active—we won't be able to lead the frontal part of the brain into the state of calm. That's why we accept the Moon: its light in comparison to the Sun's is calming. But if we need to treat patients, we must accept a lot of energy, a lot of sunlight. Sun energy is hot, so when patients are undergoing treatment, they feel heat in the place you're treating.

23. What should we imagine when practicing the eighth exercise?

Imagine that you're accepting into your body the aroma of various flowers; this is what you should be thinking about. When your soul really does go out, you simply know that it must return, and it definitely will. You need not do anything special for this.

24. What will we sense, which smells?

What your sense of smell picks up.

25. I hear noises in my head. What's this about?

Do you have high blood pressure? If so, this sensation may be experienced because you strain a certain group of muscles, and this can trigger tension and bleeding. Therefore, when practicing the eighth preliminary exercise, relax your body as much as possible if you want to have a pleasurable experience.

26. How many times should the eighth exercise be practiced?

Eight times, and then another eight times. Sixteen times is enough.

27. Are the smells of the various worlds repeated each time you practice, or do they change from day to day?

Try it, and you'll find out.

28. After the eighth preliminary exercise, I feel my body vibrating. Is this caused by practicing this exercise or not?

The vibrations that arise during this exercise are connected not so much with the exercise itself as with your nervous system, which is reacting to physical movements with a certain imagination. Also, this can indicate some emerging processes in the nervous system.

29. How should we breathe when doing this eighth exercise?

Breathe in with the whole body, but breathe out through the feet, lifting off as if on a jet stream. When inhaling, bring your arms upward and with your whole body absorb the imagined aromas. Then, thrusting off with your arms, at the same time exhale through your feet.

30. How long can this exercise be performed?

There are no limitations here.

31. How do we move our legs during this exercise?

On exhaling, when you emit Qi through your feet and "thrust off" from the ground, you stand on your tiptoes in your socks. When the exhale has ended and your arms are already lowered, smoothly lower your heels and stand normally.

32. What are the smells we take into our body when doing the eighth preliminary exercise?

These smells are also energy for our body and spirit. From different worlds come different energies. You'll understand this as you practice.

MAIN EXERCISES

大树功

BIG TREE

Here we're already in Stage III, yet Big Tree once again occupies first place among the main exercises. We practice Big Tree in each stage. Many consider it a very difficult exercise, one that's complicated not so much from the standpoint of technique as from the connection with unpleasant accompanying phenomena. It's also difficult to determine in advance how much time a specific practitioner needs to master this exercise. Perhaps you've noticed in the seminars of each stage, especially the first, something that at first glance seems difficult to figure out: for the elderly—and even the very elderly—practicing Big Tree is easier than for young people. Sometimes an athletic-looking youngster, used to dynamic exercises, can no way master a static pose. He can't stand relaxed; his muscles are tight and tire quickly. And what's he thinking? "Let's end this quickly!" Where can there be any pleasure from such a practice? But then there's the case of an elderly woman of frail and unhealthy appearance who, after a few days, stands in the Big Tree pose, feeling no time and experiencing joy.

Master's Story

Even in my childhood, my Teacher always required me to practice Big Tree. Several unpleasant memories of mine are connected with such practicing. One of them pertains to the fact that my fingers would swell up after practicing Big Tree. The second is described in the book on Stage I. I would often practice late in the evening at the home of my Teacher, who would strike me below the knee with a stick to verify that my body had become "stiff as a tree" and had lost all sensitivity. My third memory is about the sensation I experienced then: my legs had really become wooden, and afterward it was difficult for me to move them.

Many practitioners experience painful sensations doing this exercise, especially in Stage I. Of course, our body isn't used to the static pose. Few are the practitioners who succeed in mastering this exercise in a short time. And most people need weeks to adjust to doing this pose for two or more hours. So, of course, Big Tree can be considered the most difficult exercise. This being the case, why do we need to practice it again?

As you already know, the main goal of ZYQ practice is to join together Sky, Human, and Earth. When we unite these three factors, this is akin to uniting with the entire Universe. With this, we gain the strength and abilities for healing. In the quickest possible way, Big Tree allows the accumulation of energy and uniting with Earth and Sky. This is why we continue practicing Big Tree.

You must remember that ZYQ practice consists of two currents: the first is the uniting of Sky, Earth, and Human, or Jing, Qi, and Shen (Picture 16); the second, the separation of Shen from the physical body.

During meditation, while practicing Quiet Qigong, we try to attain the **state of Pause***, and in this state we separate ourselves from Sky and Earth. During the state of Pause, our soul leaves the boundaries of the physical body. Such a separation makes it possible to learn how to understand what Life, Humans, and the Universe are.*

Therefore **unification allows us to achieve harmony and live in harmony, while separation allows us to understand the inner essence of Life.** *Big Tree is the exercise that allows us to merge with Sky and Earth and, besides this, to join together Jing, Qi, and Shen.*

One of the goals of Qigong practice is to receive a great amount of energy: Yin of Earth and Yang of Sky. We also accept energy to increase our own Qi and to activate the internal parts of our body, of our energy system.

Still another goal is the extension of life and good health. Trees live hundreds and thousands of years. Why does Big Tree practice extend life? This is connected with the receiving of certain information. If we associate ourselves with a large healthy, long-living tree (Picture 22), certain information reaches our body and impacts both the body itself and its energy in a concrete way. The experience of many hundreds of generations of practitioners confirms this.

Picture 22: 2,000-Year-Old Tree

In Stage I, Big Tree practice, we concentrate energy in the lower Dan Tian; we stimulate the lower Dan Tian and visualize an energy ball at navel level (Picture 23a). In Stage II, we hold our hands with the energy ball at the level of the middle Dan Tian (Picture 23b) and stimulate the coccyx to facilitate the upward movement of energy. For this we point our feet inward and lower our backside somewhat more than in Stage I. This helps open the channels in the coccyx area for easier energy passage.

One of the goals of Stage III practice is the development of the spirit. For this reason we work with the upper Dan Tian (Picture 23c). Its projection is the Mingtang point at eyebrow level. If it's activated, we sense vibrating in it and then flashes of light. This happens because this point is connected with the Third Eye; opening this point is one of the necessary conditions for the functioning of the Third Eye.

To develop the spirit, it's necessary to work out a whole series of new sensations, including those that arise when the soul leaves the body.

In Stage I, when practicing Big Tree, we not only join together Jing, Qi, and Shen, but also activate the lower Dan Tian.

In Stage II, when practicing Big Tree, we again unite these three factors and now activate the middle Dan Tian. Doing this, we open spiritual power—the power of love.

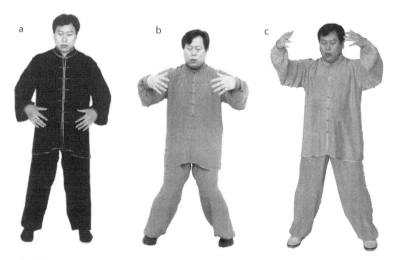

Picture 23: Big Tree Exercise (a) Basic Posture in Stage I, (b) Basic Posture in Stage II, (c) Basic Posture in Stage III

In Stage III, we activate the upper Dan Tian—that zone where our mind is located, in general. As we work with the upper Dan Tian, we open the Mingtang point. At the same time, we experience various sensations.

With the activating of each of the three Dan Tian, we receive defined sensations. Thus correct practice of the lower Dan Tian results in a sensation of warmth and then of heat. And after more practice, the sensation of something like a fire blazes there. Then you can feel how this fire moves upward.

In the middle Dan Tian, you also feel warmth in the beginning, which then becomes heat. After a while, you also begin to feel how the heat moves upward. Many people can at this point experience palpitations. Besides this, our emotional state can change with such practice: deep sadness, malice, irritation, and happiness might all be experienced.

Phenomena Accompanying the Activation of the Upper Dan Tian

Activating the upper Dan Tian engenders many sensations, but of a different character. At first there's pressure at the Mingtang point between the eyebrows. This pressure can sharply increase, and after still more time you may see flashes similar to lightning. In the next phase you'll see light in front of you, but the flashes will be of different colors. With further practice, during meditation or simply in a dark room, you'll see weak illumination, but not darkness. And if you close your eyes, a bright light will appear within you. That's when the *Third Eye* will begin functioning. If not only your body but also your consciousness enters the state of Quietness, you'll be able to see what's very far from you. For this, you must enter the state of calm and Silence of Mind.

At this point, some practitioners begin to see various kinds of pictures, landscapes, and beings from other worlds. We already discussed such phenomena in preceding stages. In these situations, don't try to focus your attention on the pictures or on the phenomena that manifest themselves to you. Continue practicing and then, having attained the next level in practice, you'll be able to move further, actually to worlds of a higher level. For example, if today during an exercise you saw certain pictures, and tomorrow while practicing you want to see the same things or their continuation—if you think about this and get yourself "psyched" over it—this will halt your development. *Instead of advancing further, you'll always be going back to what you've already seen. In the process you'll be chaining yourself to the present.*

The Sequence of the Execution of the Exercise

So, how is Big Tree practiced in Stage III? Again, this exercise is well known to you, and its technique isn't complex (Picture 23d). But in this stage it's very important to use your mind correctly—to know what to think and how to think.

1. The pose of your torso is as described in Stage I: your body is relaxed; your back straight; your head "hanging" from the crown; your tongue raised to your upper palate; your eyes half closed; and your face smiling a bit. Your legs are a little bent at the knees; the positioning of your legs can be the same as in the practice of Stage I or II, in accordance with your desire.
2. Your arms are raised to level of upper Dan Tian. Imagine that you're holding an energy ball between your palms and the upper Dan Tian.

In the beginning of this practice, you can almost immediately feel pressure between your eyebrows at the Mingtang point and inside your head in the upper Dan Tian.

REMEMBER: Those with high blood pressure shouldn't hold their hands opposite the upper Dan Tian and need to practice Big Tree in the position of Stage I or Stage II.

But it makes no difference if you imagine and try to see your second self standing in the same pose and practicing the same Big Tree. With elevated but not very high blood pressure, it's possible to practice opening the Third Eye, for example. However, the pressure must then be lowered by releasing this energy from the upper Dan Tian in order to move downward (in accordance with the method of Stage I, breathe out through the feet or focus attention on the Yongquan points).

3. As in Stage I and II practice, you must imagine that you're Big Tree and that you receive Qi from the Universe and Earth. But as you assume the pose of Stage III Big Tree, you morph into a tree instantaneously, not gradually as in the preceding stages.

4. St the same time, you must imagine and then see that standing in front of you is you, yourself—your *"second you,"* or your *Double*—as if your double is also practicing this exercise. You see yourself as if you've been cloned: from you alone two beings result. In the very beginning of Big Tree practice, you must imagine your Double, standing in front of you and also practicing Big Tree. In the next moment, you immediately are transformed into Big Tree and find yourself in a forest among the same kind of trees.

5. When you seek to see your Double, try to see the face: try to see that your Double, "second you" is looking at you. Actually, during Stage III Big Tree practice you look at each other. Sometimes, however, your Double may have his or her side or back to you.

6. On finishing Big Tree, slowly bring the energy ball to the upper Dan Tian. Then lower it through the Zhong-Mai central channel to the middle Dan Tian. After this, lower it further to the lower Dan Tian. Your Double does the same thing.

7. Having lowered the ball to the lower Dan Tian, immediately— as if leaping—fuse with your Double; take in your second you internally, becoming one person with him or her.

8. Following this, as in Stage I and Stage II, it's necessary to do a complete set of closing exercises (Picture 23e), including rubbing your palms, washing your face, patting your head, and so on.

You can merge with your Double immediately after bringing the energy ball to the upper Dan Tian. Having become a single whole with him or her, lower this ball to the lower Dan Tian. After this, execute the entire set of closing exercises. You may use any of these methods to unite with your Double.

Picture 23: Big Tree Exercise (d) The Sequence of the Execution of the Exercise

Picture 23: Big Tree Exercise (e) Closing Exercises

Accompanying Phenomena

In Stages I and II, you saw various pictures when practicing Big Tree, but not yourself. In Stage III you should see your "second you," your Double, also practicing Big Tree.

The Appearance of a Double

This is a basic phenomenon while practicing this exercise. And your double may not match your present outer appearance. He or she may be younger or older than you, wear different clothes, or have a different hairdo. He or she may wear glasses, though you don't—or the reverse. At the same time, however, your face should be obviously recognizable—clearly yours—and should not arouse any doubts. Your Double also can appear for a brief time and not with every practice. But it can also practice Big Tree for a long time with you, both far away and holding one ball with you. You can't necessarily see yourself while doing Big Tree, but you can when you practice Yang-Qi. The condition you need to be in is Silence of Mind, a state of Quietness.

The Appearance of the Moon and Sun

Yet another phenomenon is the appearance of a picture simultaneously of the Moon and Sun. They could be landscapes illuminated by the Moon and Sun or only the luminaries themselves. They can stand motionless in front of the internal gaze of a practitioner or begin to replace one another, only to later appear together again.

Such a phenomenon can arise with any exercises accompanied by the activation of the upper Dan Tian.

Familiar Phenomena

With Stage III Big Tree practice, the sensations and phenomena you became familiar with during Stages I and II can arise. Since we examined this in Stage II, we won't take it up again.

Master's Story

In Stage III, we not only activate the upper Dan Tian but also develop our soul. What does this mean, and what does the development of the soul actually involve?

Only when your soul really is able to go outside the confines of the physical body can you gain an understanding as to what the physical body and soul are. Of course, while your soul is still unable to depart, imagine it, and then you'll be ready for it. Therefore the Stage III Big Tree exercise is both the practice of Big Tree, as in the preceding stages, and soul practice.

*Only when our soul leaves the body are we able to understand a great many additional things, because **as long as the soul is inside, we ourselves and all our actions are limited by the possibilities of our physical body.** In our usual state, we can get a great amount of information and even believe that there is another world. But we can't move there or see what it's actually like. You can see what another world is like in the state of Silence of Mind. If you continue practicing, you'll achieve the level where you'll be able to really go there and experience it for yourself.*

*Practice of the Stage III Big Tree exercise helps develop sensations similar to those manifesting themselves during the exiting of the soul. **This exercise allows your soul to go outside, but not completely, and for a very short time. This means that it provides an opportunity to practice the soul.** So, as practice of consciousness, or the mind, proceeds, first the aforementioned sensations are developed, and this is training for the soul.*

In Stage III, we must also gain experience of what goes on with the departure of our soul from the body. That's why during Big Tree practice you need to look at your second self standing in front of you while you practice Stage III Big Tree. You may think that you're losing your mind because you're standing in front of yourself. But this is the proper practice.

*At the beginning, of course, you won't see anything, but if you continue to practice and practice, the moment will come when suddenly your Double appears in front of you, also practicing. At first you won't even be able to determine where you are and where he or she is. You stand opposite him or her, although both of you are you yourself, and no one else. And at this time you'll be able to begin understanding **who you are,** or what you represent. And then you'll understand, or it will seem, that the one who appears and stands in front of you is the real you, and the you who from the very beginning stood in the Big Tree pose isn't you, but someone else. You also will not feel naturally yourself; you'll sense your second self as real, as he or she stands in front of you in exactly the same pose and looking exactly the same.*

Don't fear these phenomena; don't get anxious while executing this exercise—just do it. Later, when you're getting deeper into the practice, you'll understand and accept all of this naturally.

In our regular lives, we're used to understanding first and then acting in accordance with our understanding. But everything is the reverse in Qigong practice: often you need to act, and after you do so, you'll begin to understand.

We must study ourselves, *but for this* **we must get to know ourselves.** *After you get to know yourself, you must understand yourself— understand what you represent, what you're preparing to do with yourself and why. Then you must try to understand what is good and what is bad in you, where changes must be made, and what must be changed for you to continue developing.*

In this situation you "extract" yourself from yourself. You check and analyze yourself, after which you're able to develop further. This is a special method for studying oneself. Of course, in our everyday life, we employ different methods of investigation. But in the Qigong system, we use a special method during practice. If this method is united with the usual method, it's **possible to find the Way of your development** *very quickly.*

Questions and Answers

1. Must we imagine or think about how to see our double? Or should we at least know how he or she will look or what he or she will be wearing?

No. You don't have to think about anything. If you enter the state of Quietness, everything will occur automatically. Simply try to enter the state of Quietness.

2. What if my double wasn't standing calmly but was doing some exercises—as if to show me something?

This phenomenon is appropriate, but you need not think about anything or do any analyzing. Simply keep a close watch on things, and that's it. There's no need to repeat the exercises being demonstrated or to try to see something special. This is because, with many exercises in the ZYQ system, the goal isn't always the same as in the real execution of an exercise. We discover and understand it later, under completely different conditions, in another place. In other words, the goal is different, but it's necessary to practice specifically in this way to attain it.

3. I started sensing lots of smells because my double didn't stand calmly but took off for a glade somewhere. Later, there was a marsh there, and the odor was unpleasant. The smells diverted my attention.

You don't need to pay attention to all the accompanying phenomena connected with smells or with someone looking at someone else. Just closely monitor what is going on. The only important thing is whether or not you see yourself, because the goal of this exercise is completely different. All accompanying phenomena are evidence that the exercise is still not being performed properly. When you really see yourself, everything immediately becomes clear, and there will be no questions.

4. In the beginning, my double also seemed to be practicing Tree and held the ball. It even seemed to me that holding up my arms became easier because he was holding the very same ball. But then he began doing exercises, and I began wondering what I should do in this instance: repeat the movements, or try to remember them. When I began thinking this over, my double disappeared and didn't reappear.

Studying in this way is incorrect. During practice you shouldn't be thinking about what you're supposed to do in such situations. You only need to track carefully what's going on—"observing"—and continue practicing.

5. My double was sketched in a picture, and with my consciousness I was able to either keep him motionless or force him to move, whereby he was able even to do acrobatic routines. How should he be conducting himself?

You were seeing incorrectly. You need to see as if you were recalling someone with your eyes closed, and this image would appear in front of you, as on a screen, as if it were real. In general, the way of thinking in the ZYQ systems is completely different from what you just indicated, especially with a change in your state. The very process of practice is a kind of intermediary milieu—a space or measured segment in which there's nothing you can guess, foresee, or predict; you simply practice. However, once you've completed the process of practicing this segment, you begin to understand what happened. You understand after the result is gotten, and when you receive it, you then immediately understand what's going on.

Such a method represents the question and answer without the intermediary procedure. Moreover, we don't examine or analyze how the answer comes.

6. *Is it necessary to hold my palms turned toward my forehead in Big Tree? Can they be lowered toward the ground? And what if I don't have the strength to hold my arms and they go down by themselves?*

Yes, this is necessary. If you lower your palms, this is incorrect; they must be turned toward your forehead. If you do it differently, the energy will go into the ground and your body will get sick. Practicing in such a pose is harmful to your health. If your arms go down, you must nevertheless imagine that your hands are turned toward you and your energy enters you—that is, not the Sky or Earth, but you.

7. *What would you advise if I practice and live in one room with family members who don't practice? Will this have an influence on them, and if so, what kind?*

If you practice and they don't, your energy is stronger and will impact them, especially if they are your parents or children. If they're ill, they'll feel worse, because the Qi will gain strength and start to affect the blocked segments of the channels in their body. Since this doesn't take place as a result of their own practice, the energy may be insufficient for opening the blocked channels completely. For this reason, they may experience discomfort or a flare-up, as this happens with us when "Qi battles illness."

In this instance, practice in the following way: detach the ball from you, expand it to such dimensions that it completely engulfs you, and practice inside the ball. Your energy will not go beyond its limits. It will remain with you in the ball and will not spread outside and fall on surrounding people. You'll be "hidden" in the ball with all your energy.

8. *Could I treat my family members? How?*

Should your family members at home allow you, before beginning practice treat their ailments with the methods learned in Stage I.

9. *I get nauseous when I practice. Why is this?*

If you're having stomach problems, energy entering this area often provokes nausea and vomiting. We examined this symptom when practicing Big Tree in Stage I. Many seminar attendees experience pain in the Third Eye because we conduct imagined depictions of the Moon through this place twenty-four times. If you feel pressure in this area during Big Tree or any other exercises, this means energy has already reached it. In an analogous way, activating the region of the Third Eye often induces pain.

10. I feel constant pulsating there, but no pain.

This is correct and normal. These sensations are also connected with the process of opening the Third Eye.

11. Can I combine Big Tree practice with Breathing with the Body and Small Sky Circle?

If you practice a certain exercise, let's say a Stage III one, then it's necessary to do everything in keeping with what I say. That's because I help those in my seminars practice by forming the structure of energy in a given hall in a certain way. If you do another exercise or do Big Tree in a way that isn't in accordance with this stage, then the structure of the energy will not match what you're doing. The resulting lack of coordination isn't good. Therefore follow my directives, and practice this way and only this way.

12. When I imagine the ball between my hands and the upper Dan Tian, before I try to see my double, the ball disappears somewhere, disperses, and often goes to the middle Dan Tian. Then I discover that my hands aren't above but opposite the middle Dan Tian.

Try to concentrate better on the Stage III pose. If you raised your arms to the upper Dan Tian, the ball should stay there. You need not release it.

13. What about working with children? Is it difference from working with adults?

With children you can begin study immediately with the upper Dan Tian, because they have so much power and energy. With people who are sickly, with the aged and weak, sensitivity in the lower Dan Tian is practically nonexistent because there's no energy there. Therefore people who are under fifty and comparatively cheerful can work with the middle Dan Tian intensively. But those who are older, sickly, or weak must definitely study the lower Dan Tian as much as possible to first refill and then accumulate energy in it.

CHANZO

禅
坐
On several occasions we've mentioned that Qigong practice can help us get rid of bad emotions, while wisdom assists us in avoiding mistakes. If we become sufficiently wise, we'll be able to understand each other and our surrounding world better.

How Can We Develop Wisdom?

It's first necessary to develop the central, or middle, channel Zhong-Mai, which passes through all three Dan Tian and the Baihui and Huiyin points.

As early as Stage I, we've been saying that to join together Humans, Sky, and Earth, it's necessary to practice the three aspects inside the human body: Jing, Qi, and Shen. In Stage I, we practiced the lower Dan Tian and Jing energy; in Stage II, the middle Dan Tian and Qi energy; and in Stage III, the upper Dan Tian and Shen energy. During practice of these three Dan Tian jointly, Jing contributes to the production of Qi, Qi to Shen, and Shen once again to Jing.

What does "to practice Dan Tian" mean? What is our understanding of this expression?

Practice of the lower Dan Tian signifies that it's necessary to learn how to feel this segment (Picture 24a). During the period when we feel the lower Dan Tian well, we have lots of energy, lots of Qi. In Stage II, we practice the middle Dan Tian (Picture 24b). When the middle Dan Tian becomes active, we begin to sense a lot of strength in us. But it's not physical strength that allows us to lift or carry heavy things, for example. Rather it's a state. If in this instance another person looks at you, he'll get the feeling that you have a lot of power. One thing can definitely be said: *if the middle Dan Tian is active, there's a sharp increase in healing abilities.* A human can then offer effective treatment to the sick.

In Stage III, we engage in the development of the upper Dan Tian (Picture 24c). *The upper Dan Tian is connected with wisdom.* It's also linked with *the feeling of compassion and extrasensory feelings.*

The lower Dan Tian is connected with our Qi and the middle one with our spiritual power. This spiritual power can be transformed into the power of love—not customary love, but **Great Love**. This means that every person is be able to feel your love. *Development of the upper Dan Tian leads to an increase in wisdom* and the ability to provide good advice to everyone. People also begin to be aware of your intellect as well as your compassion and tremendous kindness.

We already stated that *one of the goals of Stage III practice is the development of our spirit.* For this it's necessary to understand what the spirit is and what the soul is. In the first chapter we examined these concepts in detail. But we can't totally realize what they mean, because in our everyday life, these three components are joined. The physical body is immediately visible to everyone, and that's why it's been studied so well. We also know a little about our energy and even employ this knowledge for treating others, for example, when we use acupuncture methods or energy healing. But we don't know the location of our soul and what it looks like. To understand what the soul is, we must separate it from the body. That's why we have to prepare the Way for the exiting of the soul. Only then are we able to understand what the physical body, soul, and spirit are.

We have stated that everything has its own Way. But what does the Way of our own soul consist of, and where is it? It's the Zhong-Mai channel, which is similar to a tube. Usually this "tube" is subject to the influence of emotions and different external factors that don't allow our soul to move through it and exit. But after we take the

Picture 24: Activated Dan Tians (a) Lower Dan Tian in Stage I, (b) Middle Dan Tian in Stage II, (c) Upper Dan Tian in Stage III

special steps needed to set up this Way, our soul gets the opportunity to go outside. Only after this are we able to understand what each of our components—physical body, energy, and soul—represent and what the Human is as an holistic being. Therefore *one of the goals of Stage III is the construction of the Way for our soul.*

This exercise is intended for our development, not for health improvement or treatment.

Master's Story

Sometimes we need to practice in order to improve our health. However, each time we should aim for somewhat higher goals. **If your goal is only health improvement, then you won't be able to secure perfect health.** *But if you aim higher, you'll achieve a healthy state as you strive for the higher goal. Therefore, if you don't have any very serious ailments that need immediate treatment, try to establish goals that are much higher. And then, as you approach them, you'll almost certainly be able to achieve perfect health. Try to understand what Human is by investigating yourself.*

We often speak about the spirit and spiritual development. Why, then, do we not try to achieve the state in which our soul can separate from our physical body and go beyond its limits so that we're really be able to understand what the soul is. We do know how to achieve this: **it's necessary to attain the state of Pause.** *We must simply spend time laying the groundwork for entering into this state.*

If you wish to achieve a high level with any practice method, you must go through the state of Pause. Should you not do special exercises that prepare you to stay in the state of Pause, you might experience problems. To prepare our physical body for certain phenomena, we practice breathing with the body in Stage II, and Big Tree and Bigu Shiqi in Stage III. Stage III Big Tree is intended to prepare the mind for an understanding of what the physical body and soul are, while the purpose of Bigu Shiqi is to cleanse the body and make it possible to go without food for a long time.

When all this is done, your physical body will not experience problems with Pause, and your soul will be able to leave the body. However, before this, the preparation of energy for our soul must be done in a special way.

As with practice in Stage II, the exercise known as Chanzo consists of three parts: moving the energy ball between Dan Tian, visualizing the channel, and activating the upper Dan Tian.

Section One:
OPENING THE CENTRAL CHANNEL

In Stage II we began this process: we opened and worked on the Zhong-Mai channel at the segment between the lower and middle Dan Tian. Now we'll continue opening the channel between the middle and upper Dan Tian.

This exercise can be performed in any of the poses described earlier: standing or sitting in a chair; Turkish style; or lotus or half lotus. Most people prefer practicing sitting in a chair (Picture 25), thought the lotus posture is the best (Picture 26). Some people with spine problems feel discomfort or back pain during long periods of sitting, while others easily fall asleep. To prevent problems, stand for Chanzo practice (Picture 27).

The Sequence of the Execution of the Exercise

1. Select a pose that's comfortable for you, and place your hands on your navel as we did in Stage I or II. Relax.
2. Feel the ball inside the lower Dan Tian. Feel this zone (Picture 25a). After getting distinct sensations, begin moving the ball upward (Picture 25b).
3. Mentally move this ball with your hands to the middle Dan Tian. Feel the ball in the middle Dan Tian (Picture 25c). After experiencing distinct sensations, continue to move the ball upward (Picture 25d).
4. Slowly move the ball with your hands upward. Feel the ball in the upper Dan Tian, inside your brain (Picture 25e).
5. Slowly lower it to the middle Dan Tian (Picture 25f). Feel the ball in the middle Dan Tian (Picture 25g).
6. After getting clear sensations, move it to the lower Dan Tian (Picture 25h). Feel the ball in the lower Dan Tian (Picture 25a).
7. Upon sensing the ball or heat from it in the lower Dan Tian, once again move the ball upward to the middle Dan Tian. Then again raise it to the upper Dan Tian. And so constantly move the ball between the Dan Tians.

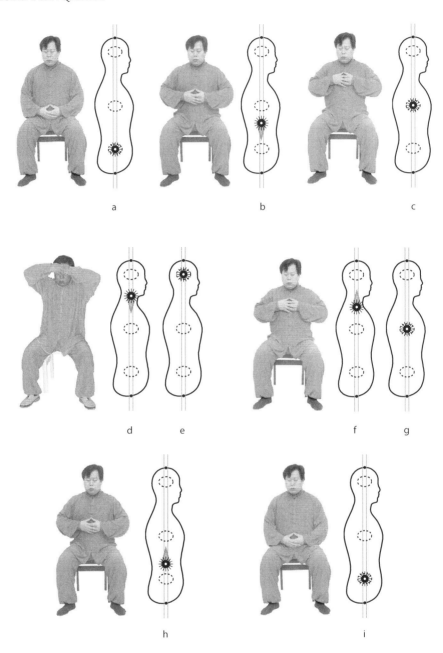

Picture 25: Opening of the Central Channel Sitting on a Chair:
(a) Qi Ball in a Lower Dan Tian, (b) Qi Ball Mowing to a Middle Dan Tian, (c) Qi Ball in a Middle Dan Tian, (d) Qi Ball Mowing to Upper Dan Tian, (e) Qi Ball in an Upper Dan Tian, (f) Qi Ball Mowing to a Middle Dan Tian, (g) Qi Ball in a Middle Dan Tian, (h) Qi Ball Mowing to Lower Dan Tian, (i) Qi Ball in a Lower Dan Tian

8. As you complete the exercise, lower the Qi ball to the lower Dan Tian, and concentrate it there in the smallest possible volume. Relax.

9. After completing the exercise, rub your palms and wash your face with them.

If you practiced for a long time or feel discomfort in your body, consider performing the entire set of Closing Exercises, such as after Big Tree.

The speed of the ball's movement is always up to you and depends on how well you feel the ball. When you feel it clearly in any of the Dan Tian, you may move it further.

With this exercise, we construct the Way for our soul inside us. You don't need to connect this Way with your physical body, because *when you enter the state of deep Quietness, you won't be able to feel your physical body*.

With this method, we open the central channel. And with this method we unite the lower, middle, and upper Dan Tian. For better development of the channel and a more precise sensation of the energy ball, it's possible to activate the ball. For this, you don't simply move the ball, but mentally enlarge and shrink it in each of the Dan Tian.

In Stages I and II, we already practiced the pulsating of the ball for the purpose of activating it. It should be noted that such an energy ball is easier to visualize. With this, its pulsating can be seen.

For visualization we employ *"internal or mind viewing"* (or "looking at"). Understand that the process of visualization requires no effort. Here you don't have to apply physical strength—on the contrary,

Picture 26: Opening of the Central Channel Sitting in Lotus

Picture 27: Opening of the Central Channel Standing

you must try to relax as much as possible and simply "look" at what already exists.

Right now we'll practice what to all intents and purposes is the very same exercise for moving the energy ball, but with the addition of activating the ball and visualizing it (Picture 28). The sequence for moving the ball is the same as above.

1. Assume the pose you've selected and, after relaxing, try to feel the energy ball in the lower Dan Tian.
2. Feel how it gets bigger then returns to its previous size. Once again it will enlarge and shrink (Picture 28a-c).
3. Visualize this ball. Look at this ball. Feel and see how it pulsates in the lower Dan Tian: bigger, smaller, bigger, smaller.
4. After experiencing distinct sensations in the lower Dan Tian, slowly move the ball with your hands upward to the middle Dan Tian. Feel it there and continue visualizing it. And once again the ball pulsates: bigger, smaller, bigger, smaller. Feel the ball; look at the ball (Picture 28d-f).
5. Slowly raise the ball with your hands to the upper Dan Tian, and visualize it in the upper Dan Tian. Once again, mentally enlarge and shrink the ball: bigger, smaller, bigger, smaller (Picture 28g-i).

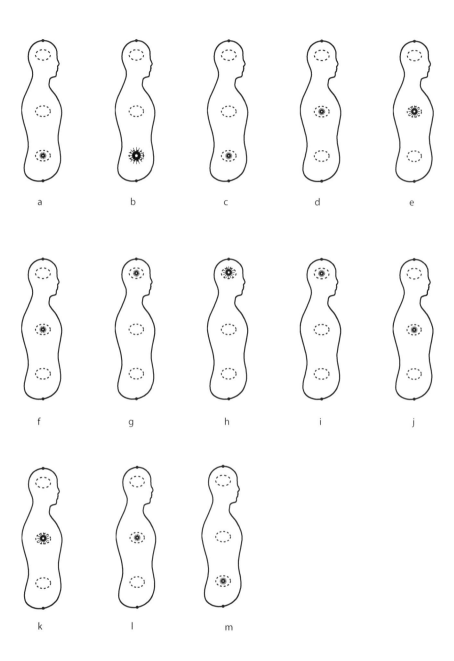

Picture 28: Activating Qi Ball by Pulsation During Its Movement in the Central Channel
(a, b, c) in the Lower Dan Tian, (d, e, f) in the Middle Dan Tian, (g, h, i) in the Upper Dan Tian,
(j, k, l) Again in the Middle Dan Tian, (m) Again in the Lower Dan Tian

6. Slowly move the ball down with your hands to the middle Dan Tian (Picture 28j-l). And again feel this ball and look how it pulsates: bigger, smaller, bigger, smaller.

7. Slowly move the ball to the lower Dan Tian and force the ball in it to pulsate. Feel these pulsations and look how the ball becomes bigger, smaller, bigger, smaller (Picture 28a-c).

8. As before, move the ball upward to the middle Dan Tian. Feel it, visualize it: bigger, smaller, bigger, smaller. Then move it to the upper Dan Tian, bigger, smaller. Then lower it. Do this many times.

9. As you finish the exercise, lower the Qi ball to the lower Dan Tian and concentrate it there. Relax.

10. As in the previous variant, after ending this practice, execute the Closing Exercises.

In the case at hand, the speed of the ball's movement is also up to you and depends on how well you feel it and how quickly you're able to visualize it.

Master's Story

In Stage III, we construct this channel from the lower to the upper Dan Tian. In Stage IV, we open the channel in such a way that uniting with Earth and Sky, or the Cosmos, is possible. In Stage V, we'll open the head. Later you will be able to test the crown of your head. In the region of the Baihui point, cranial joints meet—there's a suture there, so that if this part is exposed, you'll be able to feel soft tissue instead of bone. To avoid harming this area if it opens, you must not press it.

The channel opens and changes gradually as practice is carried out. Changing it immediately isn't possible. Every day it will change a little. The final changes require a long time, possibly several years. For this reason, the technology of practice is subordinate to these patterns.

Earlier we made use of a dangerous method to verify if the central channel was open. If it's open, one could lead a needle or straw through the entire body—from the Baihui point on the head and brain to the Huiyin point and outside the body. If this is done correctly, it brings no harm to a person. In Tibetan systems, this is a test used to check the level of practice. However, if this is tried with a person whose channel or points on it are closed—someone who hasn't mastered this system—that individual will immediately feel sickly.

After certain training, this internal, Zhong-Mai channel opens and stays inside our body in open form. Then all three of our Dan Tian function normally, and we're able to concentrate energy in any of them easily. If in Stage IV an opening of the channel downward to Earth and upward to Sky occurs, we're able to get information directly. At the same time, however, the channel is still not open wide enough. Only after Stage V are we able to feel and accept the energy we need from the surrounding environment. Then we're be able to control the exiting and returning of our soul very well.

Before the central channel is completely opened, the soul can't freely go outside and return back. This could be compared with you being placed in prison. You could live there and do things, but you'd be limited in your interaction with the surrounding world. This is more or less the same for our spirit: when it's inside our body all the time and the part near the Baihui point is closed, this is a prison for the spirit. We study this practice in order to get the opportunity to abandon this prison.

That's why we say that the exercise under consideration is meant not for the health of our physical body, but for the development of our spirit.

Section Two:
VISUALIZATION OF THE CENTRAL CHANELL

Once you've learned how to move the ball between Dan Tian, there's yet another exercise in this block that can be practiced: visualizing the central channel in the form of the figure 1, that is, as a line or luminous tube. What is *"visualization of the central channel?"* Translated from the Chinese, this exercise is called **Retain in Your Consciousness the Central Channel and See It as One.**

Why do we talk about the number one and not simply about a vertical line or tube? What does one signify? In accordance with the theory accepted in the East, everything in the Universe represents *Tao (the Path)*. In Stage I, we stated that Tao produces one. One produces two, or Yin-Yang. Two produces three; this is Heaven, Humans, and Earth. To receive Tao, you must at first receive one.

The practice of Stage IV can be called the return of one to Tao. **The goal of the Chanzo exercise is to unite the three internal Yuan— Jing, Qi and Shen.**

After the ball exercise, which opens this central channel, you see it as a luminous white line, tube, or figure one. Retain it as long as possible. Don't let it go off to the side somewhere or disperse. This is also visualization of the channel.

Similar to visualization of the energy ball in the Dan Tian, here you must also employ internal viewing. Relax as much as possible and simply look at what already exists. No effort is needed. Simply look.

The exercise helps activate the Third Eye and, in addition, helps your soul exit and turn up in the *world of Emptiness.*

Sequence of the Execution of Exercise

This exercise can be practiced sitting or standing. If you practice sitting on a chair, then it's best to straighten your back and not lean against the back of the chair. This said, you must relax your body completely and close your eyes.

In the preceding stages, we practiced the lower Dan Tian and felt the energy ball in it. By placing your hands on your navel, you can strengthen these sensations. Strengthen them even more by activating this ball with pulsation. After getting distinct sensations, concentrate the ball in the smallest possible volume and then begin looking at the channel.

1. Assume your chosen pose. Straighten your back, relaxing as much as possible.
2. Place hands on your navel, and close your eyes. Focus your attention in the lower Dan Tian, and feel the ball in it. When necessary, activate it.
3. Look only at the route between Dan Tians—bright and lighted as a luminous tube that resembles the numeral one. Try to see it. There's no prescribed positioning for your hands now (Picture 29a-b). During visualization of the central channel in broad daylight, other colors might also make themselves known, but this isn't important. What's important is knowledge that the central channel Zhong-Mai resembles the figure one and that you retain it in your consciousness as long as pos-

sible (Picture 29c-d). Look in a relaxed and detached manner. No tensing up.

4. Shift your attention to the lower Dan Tian, and place your hands on your naval, assuming they were not already there. Feel the ball in the lower Dan Tian.

5. Open your eyes, rub your palms together, and wash your face with them.

After practicing for a prolonged period (more than forty minutes), perform a complete set of Closing Exercises.

How to Look at the Channel

When you look at the central channel, your consciousness enters the state of calm. This method allows Jing, Qi, and Shen to united and makes it possible to understand what Tao is.

You can see this luminous tube, this Way, if you enter the state of Quietness. With this exercise, you place your hands only on the lower Dan Tian and look inside to see the white, luminous flow of light from the lower Dan Tian. In other words, you look at *the Way inside you.* After a while, you begin to see the entire channel all at once. As it passes through your entire body, you can see how it goes out above to Heaven and below to Earth (Picture 29d). We will be opening the channel in Stage IV.

Picture 29: Visualization of the Central Channel (a, b) the Position of Hands During Practice, (c) Central Channel at the Beginning of Practice, (d) Completely Opened Channel

Master's Story

If you try to see the Zhong-Mai channel as a real tube, that is, actively attempt to imagine it, then nothing will come of it. It's necessary to relax and enter the state of calm. If you're in the state of Quietness, the tube rises in front of you like a luminous beam. Don't try to see it in parts— from above, in front of you, or below. Don't look from the top down, as if glancing at it. Imagine it appearing in its entirety all at once—from infinity above to infinity below. But you should not be thinking about where the top is and where the bottom is. You need not try to track it from top to bottom. When you enter the state of Quietness, it simply appears without a beginning and end—and always the same. It's like an instant photo and never changes.

Of course, you need not employ regular vision to see it. You must see it with your consciousness, inside of your brain. You should not be thinking about how it may look. You need simply to look at it. Relax as if you're resting, and at the same time look at the central channel.

Your practicing should resemble resting. When you look at the central channel, you should not be tensing-up, but simply looking. Don't think about this all the time, and don't forget about this for a long time. Don't try to see it. Simply look at it. This should be similar to consciousness, which retains the central channel. In this instance, you relax very well. At the same time your body can rest well. But your spirit here changes: changes occur in your consciousness and energy.

Very often seminar attendees ask what the best way to look at the channel is: from top to bottom or from bottom to top. I answer that there's no process for looking at it. If you choose a particular approach, you have to look as indicated by this approach. This means, then, something of an extension in time. Here, on the other hand, there's nothing of the sort: You look and see the entire channel immediately. But until you see, it's hard to understand how it's possible to see simultaneously something that is above and below.

If you look at a lamp that has been turned on and see its light, and then don't move your eyes, the light will hit them all the time. So it happens with the channel: it immediately arises in front of your eyes and is always the same. Then it's possible to approach the state of Pause. Thoughts will continue appearing, but this isn't bad. They appear and disappear, and once again appear for a brief time. But then suddenly they completely disappear. And then Pause comes.

During Pause, major changes occur that are impossible without Pause. Internally, information changes, as do energy and physical matter.

Section Three:
UPPER DAN TIAN PRACTICE

Translated from the Chinese, this exercise is called *To Lead Your Shen to Emptiness.*

In Stage I, we practice the lower Dan Tian, with our hands placed on the navel. This is the method that helps transform Jing into Qi. And we've been calling this exercise *Transforming Qi.* We said that it's necessary to try to feel warmth in the lower Dan Tian and then look at the hot, red ball. We stated that the ball in the lower Dan Tian must be looked at as if it exists but at the same time seems not to exist. Constantly we've been using the expression *"it seems it is, it seems it isn't"*. In other words, we activated the lower Dan Tian and visualized the ball in it.

In Stage II, we activated the middle Dan Tian in the same way. This is the route we take to transform Qi into Shen and the method by which we gain strength and open the heart. The name of this exercise in Chinese consists of two characters. The first means *"to see this ball,"* the second, *"to think about it."* In this exercise you need to understand how to employ your consciousness. If you think about the ball very intensively, you may get a headache. If you don't think about the ball, it will never manifest itself to you. It's best to think about this as we stated in Stage I: "it seems it is, it seems it isn't." It seems you're looking at the ball; it seems you're not looking at it—you must not intensively think about it.

This *middle state* is very difficult to understand. It could be difficult to understand whether you're a good or a bad person, but it could be even more difficult to understand *whether you're good or whether you're not good.* This is the state where it's not day or night but something in the middle, that is, between them. The following could be said: you, it seems, look at the ball in the middle Dan Tian, and it seems not to be there. If you fall into this not completely conscious state, the middle Dan Tian will be activated.

In Stage III, we activate the upper Dan Tian, the Third Eye. The upper Dan Tian is deep in your brain at eyebrow level. The projection of its center is between your eyebrows at the Mingtang point. At this level in the center of the brain is the zone of the Third Eye. If it becomes active, we can feel a light vibration in it.

Sensations Engendered by Activating Dan Tians

Various sensations manifest themselves during work with each of the Dan Tians. With lower Dan Tian practice, you may feel heat in the depths of your body. We don't talk about its exact location. We can only say that it's found a little lower than the navel and somewhere deep. Scientists have discovered that if one practices this area regularly, the quantity of nerve fiber in it increases. After prolonged practice of the zone of the lower Dan Tian, the condition of the lymph system improves. In many countries, people in the medical profession determine age on the basis of the state of a person's lymph system. After such practicing of the lower Dan Tian, a person becomes younger. That's why in the Taoist system this kind of practice is called *longevity practice* or the practice of the *Golden Ball*.

With middle Dan Tian practice, you also may feel heat. As a rule, we experience different sensations when working with the upper Dan Tian: you may feel pressure, but not warmth or heat. Many people experience pressure in this area when practicing Stage III Big Tree. This aria is very sensitive. If you place your finger against it, you'll be able to feel it more distinctly than in any other part.

When you begin the practice of the upper Dan Tian, you may feel strong pressure at eyebrow level, and deeply so. As practice progresses within the brain, a light of a different color will arise in you, and images of every possible type can manifest themselves. Hence, this area is connected with the Third Eye.

Master's Story

*Viewings experienced during work with the upper Dan Tian can be as distinct as those experienced with normal sight. You can turn your attention to these images **only during upper Dan Tian practice**. But then you'll see and feel **Emptiness** inside your brain—**Emptiness in consciousness**. When you feel this emptiness, your soul will be able to abandon the body: it will go to another world known as the **World of Emptiness**.*

Why is it called the World of Emptiness? Because everything that exists here, in this world—clothing, shelter, material blessings—mean nothing in the next world. That's why we can say that everything here is unneeded emptiness. For the soul, everywhere and always, our world is total emptiness because the soul can pass through any material objects: walls, ceiling, and so on. But you understand here that this is you, all the same.

Practice of the Exercise

For the opening and activating of the upper Dan Tian we employ a method similar to opening the middle Dan Tian in Stage II. Here we'll visualize the upper Dan Tian and the ball in it. This must be done in such a way that it would seem like the ball is in the upper Dan Tian and at the same time not. As in previous exercises, don't apply force and don't use your mind. In your imagination, consider the ball to be there already.

With this practice there's no required pose. Just sit in a comfortable way. You can close your eyes, but if you feel that you're going to fall asleep, open them.

1. Assume a comfortable position. Close your eyes and relax. Place your hands over the upper Dan Tian (Picture 30a).
2. Look inside in this area, deep in the interior. Try to see there the white luminous ball. Feel the ball.
   Don't strain, don't use your mind. Consider the ball to be there already. Visualize the ball. What you see at this time is another matter. But you must imagine specifically the white ball, that which you experience when you do the seventh preliminary exercise. It resembles the Moon, which you bring from the water into the upper Dan Tian.
3. Feel the upper Dan Tian. Listen for a sensation in the Third Eye, deep inside. Feel pressure in the upper Dan Tian. Feel the ball pulsating: bigger, smaller (Picture 30b-d).
4. Straighten your back and place your hands with the ball at the lower Dan Tian. Feel how it moves along the central channel from the upper to the lower Dan Tian.
5. Holding your hands over the lower Dan Tian, concentrate the ball in it (Picture 30e). With this, try to see it and feel that it's hot. Open your eyes.
6. After prolonged practice, you can perform the complete set of closing exercises.

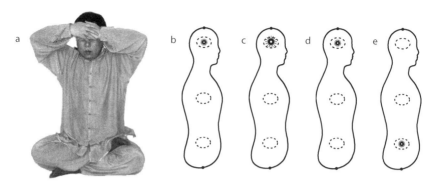

Picture 30: Activating of the Upper Dan Tian (a) Starting Position, (b, c, d) Activating a Qi Ball by Pulsation "Larger, Smaller," (e) The End of the Exercise

ATTENTION: Transference of the mind to the upper Dan Tian can provoke a rise in blood pressure. Therefore those suffering from high blood pressure should practice the upper Dan Tian only for a very short time, keeping tabs on their sensations and how they feel, and then shift their attention to the lower Dan Tian and continue practicing the lower Dan Tian.

Master's Story

You must execute all these exercises in a relaxed state, observing what's happening in a detached manner. On my frequent trips to Europe, I noticed that many people can't relax because of the state of their nervous system. But if they were to maintain a "moderate" or balanced state, the tension would disappear. They would not be aroused or agitated—or so relaxed that they would go to sleep. Our system's name contains the key: Zhong—moderate state.

When you first get into this state, it may seem to you that you're about to fall asleep. But then you become stabilized in this state and find yourself between sleep and a wakeful condition.

If you practice this exercise for a long time, light appears inside the brain. In the beginning, you'll feel pressure in the Third Eye, then flashes—like lightning—following by the appearance of a multicolored light inside the brain. Then it's as if a window is thrown open and you'll be able to see a very wide panorama, often of other worlds. (A more detailed discussion of the work of the Third Eye is found in "Medical Aspects of Qigong.").

In addition, this exercise helps your soul to leave and turn up in the World of Emptiness.

Questions and Answers

1. Please explain the mechanism of visualization, for example, while looking at the central channel. How can one completely relax and then also look?

Visualization means that you look at something but don't recognize anything. When you look in such a way, you use your mind but not your eyes, not your regular vision. When you begin to relax and your physical body enters the state of relaxation, your mind remains very clear. And you can visualize better.

But if your consciousness is relaxed and you relax to such a degree that you fall asleep, this is obviously incorrect. Here you must realize that it's your mind and not your eyes that engages in visualization.

2. What does image mean?

When you look at something, a picture of what you saw takes shape in you. This is one of the different kinds of images. Such images are usual; we constantly receive them. When practicing or diagnosing, the image has a different character. It also represents a picture, but there may be **symbols** in it, or it may consist totally of symbols. In the process of looking at something, not only your regular vision but also your sense organs click in. Together, they create a certain perception.

3. At what depth does the central channel, which we begin to see as a beam, pass, and what are its dimensions?

It's impossible to determine and imagine the distance and depth at which this luminous beam travels. You need to think that it exists and that you simply see it.

4. Where should I be seeing this luminous line, this {figure} one? How deeply from the body's surface does it pass, and how far from the spine?

You can be very specific about everything concerning your physical body. You can pinpoint the place where something's happening. You can specify in centimeters how deep something is or its distance from a zone or organ. But if we're working with this central channel, with this light beam, then you need to understand that this doesn't belong to your physical body and doesn't relate to a concrete part. You must try to imagine that within you there's already this stream of light. As soon as you see it, everything immediately becomes comprehensible.

5. Does it go from top to bottom or from bottom to top? What's its source—the Dan Tian or somewhere else?

It's not important where it originates. And you don't need to think about this. Simply, there's a stream of light, a luminous tube, a luminous beam.

6. Does this light move inside? Does it travel, somehow?

There's no movement. Nothing is moving. The ball can travel, but this is a continuous stream of light; there's nothing there that moves. This stream is also the Way for the movement of your soul. Why don't I ask you to imagine where, specifically, in the body this occurs? Because this already concerns the concept of the soul. At first you can only feel it, but later you'll be able to see it. Practice until you acquire this experience.

7. How should the central channel be looked at?

As you wish: right in front of you, top down, or from the earth upward. It makes no difference. Later it will appear all at once and always the same.

8. How should the fingers be held when moving the ball? In accordance with which stage?

However you find comfortable, following Stage I or II. It's not so important.

9. How long should this exercise be practiced?

It's best to do the majority of exercises for thirty minutes: thirty for the exercise, thirty moving the ball, thirty looking at the channel.

10. Is it necessary to hold on constantly to one and the same image throughout the practice—for example, the color of the ball?

No, this isn't important. It changes. Just do it.

11. While practicing the upper Dan Tian, I begin to sense strong pressure in my head, although I don't have high blood pressure. Should I wait for it to pass and then resume practicing?

Practicing this exercise causes strong pressure, which signals the opening of the corresponding zones. If you don't suffer from high blood pressure, continue practicing until the pressure ceases and the soul departs.

12. With visualization of the channel in the shape of the figure one, should I do this all the time or should I be acting according to the principle "it seems it is, it seems it isn't"?

When I say hold on to something, this really means to retain with your consciousness and not to employ the principle "it seems it is, it seems it isn't."

13. What if there's no line, or if I don't see it?

Then imagine a line there.

14. From what level must one look at the Zhong-Mai channel—eye level or upper Dan Tian level?

There's no need to think about this. At first, practitioners try to think and ask, because nothing is visible. However, with the appearance of light, there's no need to think. When you've already spent some time developing this exercise and have gotten this luminous channel—this figure one—then the level of clarity and precision of your "sight" will rise each time you do the exercise. As soon as you begin executing this exercise, the channel will appear, sometimes as a beam or stream of light and sometimes as a luminous tube. It will be visible not inside your body, but in front of your eyes.

辟
谷
食
气

BIGU SHIQI

Translated from the Chinese, this means that we won't be nourished by regular food, but we can eat energy.

As you know, there are a lot of different organs and systems in our body. The function of many of them has been studied extensively. Since they're necessary for our normal life activity, they're considered indispensable. Often, however, opinions vary regarding some organs. For example, recently scientists recognized the importance of the tonsils and appendix. There was a time when the appendix was considered unnecessary, and in some countries it was removed even in newborns. Typically, tonsils were taken out with little regret when a person had a recurring sore throat. But statistical data over many years showed how such an operation was followed by the onset of chronic pharyngitis, catarrhs of the upper respiratory track, and more frequent catarrhal illnesses, which forced a serious investigation of the functions of the tonsils.

About the Functions of the Navel

So, what are the functions of the navel? What does Western medicine know about it? To what extent is it necessary and useful for a grownup?

Western science holds that after childbirth the navel has no function. After all, in the mind of contemporary people, the navel is the point of contact with the mother; before birth, the child and mother are joined through the umbilical cord, and the embryo is in amniotic

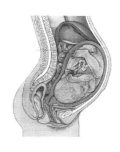

fluid in a suspended state. The child receives and inhales oxygen with his body from that fluid, while he or she gets all the necessary substances and blood from the mother via the umbilical cord (Picture 31). After birth, the umbilical cord is cut, thereby breaking the physical and physiological contact with the mother. From that moment the newborn autonomously performs the functions of diges-

Picture 31: Fetus Before Birth

tion and breathing. Nourishment comes through the oral cavity, while breathing is carried out through the nose and mouth.

However, from the standpoint of Chinese medicine and Qigong, the navel is a very important organ. *The navel is a large channel connecting us with the surrounding world. It's a body part with a specific purpose.* The navel can allow us to live for a very long time—several hundred, even thousands of years. Therefore, in Stage III we learn how it works and how it's used.

Another very important and interesting body part is the coccyx (tailbone). People know its anatomical structure, but only Qigong practitioners understand its meaning from the standpoint of energy and soul. Regarding the human body as a physical object, we know a lot. But when it comes to understanding what *a living human is as a whole being*, we still know very little.

Our body consists of two internal systems: the prenatal, which is already in existence prior to birth, and the postnatal, which begins to sprout and function after birth. The prenatal system secures the growth and development of the body in the womb of the mother while the infant is still connected with her by the umbilical cord and receives through it substances required for growth. Several months after birth, the child starts teething, and his or her food becomes more varied and copious. We consider our normal digestive system to include the oral cavity, esophagus, stomach, and intestines.

Present-day science maintains that after birth a person doesn't need a navel, since it already fulfilled its functions and is no longer active. That it might have special functions is a question about which the medicine community is ignorant. But it wasn't long ago that the same opinion was held regarding the appendix. Of course, our life doesn't depend on these organs, and they don't play as important a role as the heart, without which a person perishes.

In Chinese medicine and Qigong systems, however, the navel is held to be very important to humans. We call the navel the second system of nutrition, although in essence it's the first, being the prenavel system for feeding and digestion. Simply, after birth the navel takes on different functions. *The navel represents those gates that connect us with external energy.* It still receives and absorbs energy and substances from the outside world. But from the moment of his birth the human being functions within a different context, so we lose the earlier, original functions of the navel. If, however, problems arise in the navel area, a person usually experiences health difficulties.

Can we restore these functions totally or partially, and if so, what would occur? Empirical evidence accumulated over many centuries informs us that this is possible and that the navel is a very important instrument for practice. These functions have been revealed again, and we can develop them.

When the navel begins to function, a person starts feeling that he's full and doesn't want to eat—these are characteristic signs of the restoration of the digestive functions of the navel. The method for this became known as *Bigu Shiqi*. We can develop the navel system to receive energy directly from the environment, thereby going without food. Simultaneously, the respiratory system of the navel begins functioning. And this leads to an improvement in the skin's functioning, which becomes fresher and more youthful. The person looks younger. So restoring of functions of the navel is a return to youth. By practicing exercises connected with the development of the navel, we become younger and younger. In Stage III, we study the rebirth and development of the functions of the navel.

After birth the direct connection with our physical mother is broken, but at the same time we pass over to our new Great Mother—Nature. Bigu Shiqi practice makes it possible to receive energy from nature.

The Two Sections of the Exercise

This exercise consists of two sections (it also may be called two exercises): one section involves taking in necessary energy and substances from the surrounding space; the other involves the return to childhood. As translated from the Chinese it's called *Returning to the State of a Child.* We'll imagine ourselves to be a child who hasn't been born yet and is in the womb. In actuality, this is the practice of rejuvenation.

The technique for exercises to restore the digestive functions and the respiratory functions of the navel is identical, and this is why they are practiced simultaneously. Bigu Shiqi embraces breathing and feeding, as well as returning to the state of a child.

When this exercise is performed, changes in the body occur quickly, and you can soon enter the state of Quietness and Pause.

Section One:
BREATHING AND EATING WITH THE NAVEL

In Stage I, we studied breathing through the Laogun, Baihui, and Yongchuan points. In Stage II, we learned methods of skin or body breathing—breathing with the whole body through the entire surface of the skin. In Stage III, we'll learn the method of breathing through the navel. We'll also study the restoration and further development of its functions.

For this practice it's necessary to employ the mind, consciousness, and imagination. We'll imagine that our navel protrudes outward from our body like a tube and opens up like a flower bud. Its petals grow and reach around, surrounding our body from all sides. As they begin to interlock behind our back, we find ourselves inside the navel (Picture 32). In this way you end up inside of your navel. Then you'll be able to feel **the connection between the navel and the external environment**, to feel as if you're imbibing energy through the entire surface and then uniting through it with the surrounding world. You'll sense vibrations in the navel indicating that it's beginning to pulsate and breathe. **Through this navel you're able to sense breathing, and this is similar to taking in food.** When the time comes to eat, you open your navel and take in everything that's needed from the external milieu.

Master's Story

Once, I came across an article in a scientific journal about an interesting phenomenon observed in a certain locality: people there were eating very little and often nothing at all. This observation prompted research into the phenomenon. It was found that the navels of the locals possessed the ability not only to take in air and water molecules from the atmosphear, but also absorb elements dissolved in them—and not only in their preexisting form. The navel can even transform elements into substances the physical body needs. In air and steam water, all of these components are present.

Observe a working air-conditioner, and you'll see how much moisture there is in the air. Everything we need is in air. If we're able to open our navel

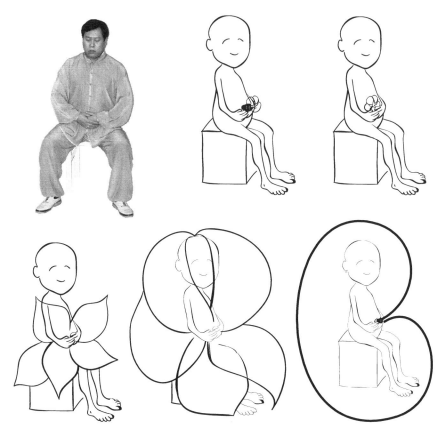

Picture 32: Phases of the Opening of the Navel

outward and make it take in directly from the environment, we can receive all the substances we need to function—carbon, hydrogen, oxygen, and so on. You can simply lie down and your navel will automatically receive from the environment everything needed for the nourishing of the body.

Not long ago, a group of scientists discovered that with a certain practice, the navel, stomach, and intestines function in a way that allows the energy to transform into the substances we need. And then there's the experience of people who, as a result of various incidents, were not able to eat in the usual manner over a long period of many, many days—yet lived. Practically all substances needed by our body to function are found in the air. We require water and carbonate gas, both of which are found in air in large quantities. And our intestines are able to receive and absorb these substances.

I suggest that you try this method; you'll be convinced that we have another digestive system.

We can check to see if this system is continuing to function. Then a question arises: if we continue to develop and support the functions of the navel, in what way can we make use of it for improving our health and for the development of us and our spirit? There's only one way to learn, and that's through our own experience.

What I teach, I went through myself, as did many others. So you can also do this without any problems.

Over several thousand years, practitioners have studied this experience. Therefore such practice can strengthen and develop the functions of the navel in such a way that it gains the ability to take in energy from the environment. This is similar to energy, but what this substance is, in fact, we don't know. Further research is needed in order to answer this question.

All our organs have one characteristic in common: if they are at work, their functions strengthen. And the opposite is true: if an organ isn't at work, its functions weaken and it can atrophy. The navel is no exception.. Because we don't employ this system, it's weakening with each passing generation and is, to all intents and purposes, ceasing to function. If we make the navel work, its functioning begins to strengthen, and we'll be able to sense this.

If you practice diligently, your navel will work in this system automatically. **These functions are the natural, primordial functions of our navel.**

Sequence of the Execution of the Exercise

1. Sit comfortably with your elbows leaning on the back of the chair. Relax your navel area. Unfasten your belt and waistbands. Relax.
2. Rest your hands on your navel, as we did in Stage I. Try to feel it.
3. To begin opening the nave, imagine and feel how your navel increases in size, becoming bigger and bigger, and then begins to move beyond our body's limits.
4. Imagine and feel how your navel begins to open up like a flower bud. Its petals become bigger and bigger. As they continue enlarging, they begin to curve around and eventually envelope

you by linking up from the back (Picture 32). Thus your navel turns inside out, exposing the side that previously had been inside, and it envelops you. Now its internal surface is the external surface of a ball in which you find yourself. This surface is capable of absorbing both energy and nutritional substances from the environment.

You're now inside the ball formed from your navel, and it has direct contact with the environment, with Universe. The needed energy will pass through it to your body.

5. Try to feel how the navel takes in energy and substances from the environment. During breathing, begin to feel the movement of your navel in time with breathing, as if you're breathing through it. Then begin to feel that, through this navel that has been turned inside out, you breathe energy and absorb it—it penetrates your body's interior.

You can feel breathing with your navel when it begins to pulsate, and energy enters you through it and remains inside. It's possible to sense that the energy automatically goes inside while the navel is pulsating, as if it's with the navel that you do your inhalations and exhalations.

6. Feel the navel. Visualize fully the entire navel, the entire ball. Look at yourself inside of this ball. Hold on to this image for a long time. Later you'll feel that you don't want to eat and don't need food.

7. As you complete the exercise, mentally return your navel to its initial state. To do this, imagine all the processes in reverse order. Imagine that the ball becomes unhooked from behind; the petals enveloping you disengage and begin to shrink. As they become smaller and smaller, they gradually curl into a bud, which is then drawn into the navel. Finally, the navel assumes its usual shape. Then, it begins to shrink, hides inside our body, and returns to its normal size and initial state.

8. Place your hands over your navel, and concentrate Qi inside of the lower Dan Tian.

9. Stand and shake yourself a little on your heels to relax your body. If this has been a protracted practice, execute the Closing Exercises in full.

To heighten sensitivity when doing this practice, prepare in this way: Place your hands over your navel and feel how it gets bigger and then smaller, as if pulsating. Feel this breathing and pulsating of the navel—this rhythm: bigger, smaller, bigger, smaller, bigger, smaller. At the same time, try to relax your body and calm your mind as much as possible. Then do numbers three and four above.

Meaning and Purpose of the Exercise

This exercise is very useful for the development of the immune system. Our immune system is connected not only with certain cells in the blood and the lymphatic system, but also with the energy system.

Master's Story

In ancient times, when food was lacking and people sometimes had nothing to eat within a few days after a hunt, their navel was forced to work to compensate for the food shortage until a new supply was secured. This happened everywhere. Now, because many people have enough food, there's no work for the navel. As a consequence, it has become unaccustomed to functioning.

Since we have enough food that can be eaten in the regular way, we don't have to employ the navel—all the more so because our stomach and intestines work much more actively and better. Wherever food is in short supply, the navel works automatically. Notice that in those places where there isn't enough food and people go hungry, they have **very small stomachs, sagging bellies and very large navels.** *Why? Because the navel begins to take in sustenance from outside.*

We have enough food, but many consume it so foolishly and immoderately that they've come down with the so-called **"illnesses of civilization":** *diabetes, heart attack, stroke, obesity, and so on. Navel practice can reduce the likelihood of these illnesses. But how is this possible?*

You've probably noticed that if there's enough oxygen in our body, you feel energetic and active. Now, many illnesses of civilization are linked to a disturbance in blood circulation that causes an oxygen deficiency. If there's a shortage of oxygen in the body, there's a buildup of cholesterol on the walls of the blood vessels, and this leads to disturbances in the circulation of blood.

When you breath with your navel, oxygen directly and immediately gets to your blood. *That's why, when there are cardiovascular* *disturbances, a preinfarction condition, or heart attack, or a stroke, diabetes, high cholesterol, or obesity, the body must be saturated with oxygen. In such instances, breathing with the navel is particularly useful. The practice of Bigu Shiqi provides the chance to restore and strengthen the weakened functioning of the navel, forcing it to work to reduce the likelihood of these illnesses.*

*It's also important to know that **our life expectancy is connected with the function of our navel.** If you're really able to practice Bigu Shiqi over a month or two, your body will completely change.*

You can practice it everywhere, because there's nothing out of the ordinary about it visually. Simply and calmly, sit and work, conjuring up with your consciousness certain images. You'll be able to feel that the frequency of breathing with the navel differs from that of breathing with the lungs, and the same goes for the frequency of heart beats.

If you practice this exercise when you're hungry, the results will be better and quicker. When you go to the supermarket, open up your navel and take in everything you need through it. Since you don't have to pay anything, this makes good economic sense.

This exercise can also be practiced during breakfast, lunch, or dinner. And practice it when going to bed. Open your navel and go to sleep, and your navel will be at work all night.

Practical Recommendations

There are no time limits on the Bigu Shiqi exercise. You can practice it sitting, lying down, standing, walking, and so on. But it's best to practice it in a pose that allows you to relax as much as possible and yield to the sensations, for then the effect will be felt quicker.

You can practice it every day or every night, imagining that you're inside your navel, returning your navel to its initial state when needed. Your navel can be opened before taking a walk outdoors and closed upon returning home. You can open it in the morning and close it in the evening. It's important only that you don't forget about the existence of the two opposites—Yin and Yang. Remember that they replace one another: inhalation and exhalation, sleep and activity, and tension and relaxation. This means that *if you've opened your navel, you must not later forget to close it.*

If you wish to develop the navel's function in the proper way, don't eat for several days, but use only your navel for this purpose. After three days of fasting, you'll see that your navel has started up. The first three days, however, are difficult to deal with because your stomach wants to eat, and it sends you all the signals that it's hungry. Try to bear these three days, after which you'll feel much better and your body will feel much more comfortable.

After this exercise, if you don't feel hungry, don't eat. Maybe you'll succeed in entering the Bigu Shiqi state, during which your body is cleansed and diseases recede. You'll become stronger and your energy will improve. In the state of Bigu Shiqi, a person can really understand and learn a lot.

Master's Story

With correct practice, even if you don't take in food for a month or two or three, it doesn't make a difference, since you'll have enough strength and energy. There won't be any changes in your condition: you won't feel weak, and you won't experience a feeling of hunger.

With Bigu Shiqi, cholesterin will never appear in your blood, since you won't be eating fat. At the same time, your brain is always fresh and works well, not only in the morning after rest, but throughout the day. As a side effect of this practice, your weight will meet what is considered standard. At first a person usually loses weight, but after a month of fasting, the weight stabilizes. And if he or she doesn't eat for a month or two, everything remains as it was.

Everything I'm telling you is not theory but the result of the experience of many people. I also experienced this, since before teaching something I absolutely must know how to do it myself. My Teacher acted similarly.

For example, I fasted for 108 days. During the first month of fasting, I lost five kilograms (eleven pounds). In China, when I started, I weighed seventy kilograms (154 pounds), but my weight stabilized so it was always sixty (143). When I returned to Russia I immediately gained ten kilograms (twenty two pounds): noodles, bread, caviar, lard, and potatoes, which I didn't eat in China, added to my weight.

So, from my very own experience, I can say that after 108 days of fasting as part of Bigu Shiqi practice, I once again felt fine. During a few of the first days I experienced thirst. But if I had drunk water, I would have immediately vomited, because at this point in this practice, the stomach won't accept anything. But if there's a reservoir or a fountain nearby, the steam water and energy can directly saturate your insides. Then you'll immediately begin to sense that you're saturated with water from the environment and no longer wish to drink.

Now, listen to this. When I was engaged in this practice, once I felt that my body was in need of water, but at the same time I had no desire to drink it in the usual manner. I went out for a walk and came upon a fountain. Suddenly I felt the water from the fountain come toward me, and soak my body. After this, my craving for water disappeared.

Now you understand the secret of what used to occur in ancient times and happens now sometimes. In days of old, there were many Taoists and monks who didn't eat. They didn't work and, consequently, were unable to purchase clothing. But they were not concerned with their appearance and went around in ragged clothes. If they needed food, they took it in through the navel. Some people like this exist today.

If we didn't need food, we would be able to work much less, than we do now, because now a part of our working time—and therefore income—goes toward food. If we didn't have to eat, we would be able to save time and money. We wouldn't need to cook or go to restaurants; instead we'd go to a supermarket, stand in front of something desirable, and open our navel. Have you ever tried this? Not yet?

But this might seem uninteresting. After all, we often eat, not because we're hungry, but because we wish to try something, or we simply like the taste and smell.

Thus there's only one key to effective Bigu Shiqi practice: if you don't feel hungry, don't eat out of habit or desire. Don't let your mind get in the way of you following the sensations of your body. Don't let it force you to think that you must eat. If you sense that there's something inside you, that you're full with something internally, don't eat. Don't make use of your "knowledge" in this area; don't think that without food you'll develop problems. If you're in such a state and you don't eat, no problems will arise. Eat only when your stomach tells you that you have to eat and you're really hungry.

Section Two:
THE RETURN TO THE STATE OF A CHILD, OR THE PRACTICE OF REJUVENATION

With each passing day, we age. While we're young, we don't notice or pay attention to this. But during our mature years or old age, we begin recalling how great it was to be young. Then we cast aside these thoughts, since we're well aware that such a dream is unrealizable, although we still like to dream sometimes. We don't want to get old, but that's life.

Beginning with Stage I, we have seen that consciousness controls breathing, breathing controls Qi, Qi controls the blood, and so on. We've also pointed out how Big Tree practice can extend our life and our youth, since we duplicate the pose of a tree, and like a tree, we begin to receive the Qi of Sky and the Qi of Earth. Now, if we imagine ourselves to be a child, an infant, couldn't this return us to the past? Of course not to infancy—this we understand, but still. Perhaps like Big Tree practice, such images could put the brakes on the passage of time for us.

Actually, the empirical experience of many generations has shown that it's possible not simply to slow down for oneself the unrelenting race of time, but to return to one's younger years.

If every day you return in your thoughts backward, eventually you can return to your youth. If you wish to become younger, you can employ the same method, the same technique for opening the navel, but with recourse to a somewhat different mental image. First, you open the navel, and then you should feel it breathing and the taking in energy from without. After this, imagine that you've returned to the state of a three- to six-month-old fetus. (The gender indicators of the fetus form at three months, so it's more convenient to imagine yourself after the differentiation of the corresponding organs has taken place). If this is very difficult for you, imagine that you're an infant who still doesn't know how to sit, crawl, chew, and speak. And it's through the navel that your contact with mother, with the Great Mother—with the entire Cosmo—is realized. With this image you may sleep or practice while sitting.

Sequence of the Execution of the Exercise

The technique of this exercise is analogous to that described above.

1. Execute number one through four. Relax, and straighten your back. Feel the navel. Enlarging it, allowing it to open like a bud, and find yourself in the ball formed by the navel.

2. Imagine that you morph into a fetus of a few months and take in energy through the navel. Try to feel this. Don't think about it, simply feel. This isn't work; this is rest. Feel the navel; feel the waves around it. Feel the movement of energy. Sometimes you can even feel pressure inside the navel. If you're highly sensitive, you might feel the connection between your navel and intestines.

3. Visualize yourself and visualize the ball in which you find yourself. Mentally look at the entire navel and at yourself in it.

4. Continue imagining and holding on to this image: you are an unborn child; you're still a fetus. In this image, the ball-navel is similar to a womb, while your mother is the entire Universe. Maintain this image as long as possible.

As you finish practice, as in the preceding case, mentally put your navel back in place—to its initial state—while you return to the usual state of consciousness.

In the beginning, this is all difficult to imagine, but if you practice regularly, after a while you'll feel completely differently, as if you found yourself in another world.

Accompanying Phenomena

While in the state of Quietness and calm, it's possible to feel the pulsating of the navel like the beating of the heart. Then you begin to feel breathing in the navel, and there emerges in you the sensation that it appears and disappears, that it is and isn't. This breathing is synchronized with the rhythm of the Cosmos, not your own breathing or heartbeat.

Relatively recently, scientific publications were pointing out that the Cosmos isn't stable but pulsates. And the Solar system also pulsates, expanding and contracting.

When you're able to unite with the entire Universe and with it become part of a single Whole during practice of this exercise, you'll feel this pulsation through your own sensations. Then you'll be able to feel that the **rhythms —yours and Cosmos's—coincide; they're identical.**

If you practice this exercise regularly, you'll come in contact with interesting phenomena: *at first your skin will begin to change, then your character.* Your skin will become fresher and tenderer—like that of a child. Your character will also become like that of a child, but there will be no change regarding knowledge and accumulated experience.

Some people need a few months for this to happen, while others require a few years.

Master's Story

When people go to bed in China, even when it's very hot, there's at least one place they cover up—the navel. There the navel reacts most sensitively and acutely to wind and even normal coolness. Therefore this part catches cold very easily. Because of the navel's heightened sensitivity, Chinese people place bandages with herbs (phytotherapy) on it for the treatment of many diseases; when necessary, various ointments and tinctures are applied. The importance of the navel at any age is well known in Chinese medicine. But only in Qigong does it receive great attention.

The exercise of breathing through the navel with the simultaneous taking in of energy from the environment strengthens the immune system. Anybody wishing to reach the higher levels of Qigong must practice this, because he or she will have to eat absolutely nothing for at least two months and take in food and energy only through the navel. At the same time his or her entire body will be cleansed.

If you're able to do procedures of this kind, any illness you might come down with will disappear, because your immune system will be strengthened. This is why Qigong methods are employed in the United States to treat AIDS. Research has shown that practicing this exercise significantly extends the life of those afflicted with the disease. This is the first method that can make the navel active and teach how to take in energy from the environment.

If you do a good job of doing this exercise, you can go many days without eating anything and breathing through the navel in conditions that are unacceptable for a regular person: underwater or while buried in the ground. The oxygen that's dissolved in the water or found in the ground is sufficient for breathing. One of the Chinese Qigong masters demonstrated this ability in Japan: he dived into a sea and remained underwater for fifteen minutes. It wasn't easy for him, because water pushes the body out. If you go down with a stone, it's a lot easier. But he demonstrated this without a stone. Simply put, he sat on the bottom, resisted the pushing and practiced Qigong. After the demonstration of this phenomenon he was named "Unique Man of the Year" in Japan.

Every year in Japan these kinds of demonstrations are held, after which the two "most unique" people of the year are named. These victors end up becoming famous in many countries. Yoga masters demonstrate similar phenomena.

With good, proper practice of breathing with the body and breathing through the navel, you'll be able to do this, but it's better that you don't. Why? Well, this is simply an unjustified waste of energy.

Two years ago I socialized with one of the Tibetan masters, who demonstrated the following. A hole of a meter (forty inches) deep and large enough to accommodate him comfortably was dug in the ground. Then they buried him for an hour. But when they unearthed him, it was clear that the conditions weren't appropriate for this experiment: he began to vomit blood. A film that details all of this is shown frequently in many countries.

A demonstration of these phenomena is simply senseless. For the practitioner, it's simply useless and sometimes even harmful to his or her health. You see, all of these things are only phenomena. All practitioners go through a whole series of phenomena, but if they focus on them to the extent that they're actually practicing the phenomenon, problems with physical health and psyche are unavoidable.

There's a young woman in China who can demonstrate a lot of unique things. For example, she holds chicken eggs in her hands and makes them hardboiled. But what amazes spectators and scientists is that she can return the eggs to their initial, raw state. However, when she begins to demonstrate these phenomena regularly, her health worsens. Demonstrating often is harmful to health.

Therefore **the goal of any practice must be strengthening life forces and increasing intellectual abilities for a normal, active life in society.** *You have to use your intellect, knowledge, and wisdom.*

With regular practice this exercise can be easily mastered. **I can only give you the practice method; it's up to you to work. I can't give you results. They will appear only as a consequence of your work.** *However, though you should know the method, never think about the result.*

What are the results of practicing these two exercises of Bigu Shiqi? What influence can it exert on our body and on our life as a whole? As in the case with most of the exercises, we can point out several aspects that are connected with different sides of our existence.

Health Maintenance, Prevention, Rejuvenation

This practice allows strengthening of the immune characteristics of the body and of the lymph system. It's a defense against contemporary "illnesses of civilization." It permits cleansing the body of "garbage" in its many forms, such as toxins, and restoring its normal function. It also contributes to the rejuvenation of the skin and of the whole body, extending life and youth—we could call it the practice of rejuvenation and longevity. Therefore we can assert that the exercise Bigu Shiqi promotes the fundamental betterment of the quality of our health and, consequently, of our life as a whole.

Developmental Aspects

But purification of the body and improvement of its functions widen our channels of perception, raise our intellect, and consequently expand our understanding. In addition, this practice makes entering the state of Quietness, followed also by that of Pause, rather easy. This means it helps to bring about the departure of the soul. The extended practice of Bigu Shiqi, with its complete cleansing of the body, gives the soul the opportunity to travel far and for a long time and to acquire a great volume of knowledge about different worlds—this helps us understand our own place in this world and mission. Without preparing your physical body with the practice of Bigu Shiqi, realizing such a task is impossible.

Protective Functions

We asserted that when we imagine ourselves as fetuses, we aren't simply in a ball formed from the navel. For us, it's like a womb, while our mother is the entire surrounding world, the whole Universe. The womb protects the developing fetus from unfavorable factors in the external environment, so when we find ourselves inside such a ball, we are residing in a reliable shelter.

Questions and Answers

1. How often should Bigu Shiqi be practiced for rejuvenation and at what time?

If so desired, practice it every evening before sleeping. That's convenient.

2. How should we lie, on our backs or sides?

This isn't important. You need to feel that you're a small child, a fetus a few months old, to sense how the navel is working—how it performs inhalation and exhalation. This method relates to special, higher levels of breathing. When you breathe in this way, you begin to feel breathing in the navel area, and the sensation emerges that it exists, and then it doesn't: this breathing is in sync with the rhythm of the Cosmos. Later you'll be able to feel that the frequency of breathing through your navel differs from that of usual breathing and from the rhythm of your heart.

3. Periodically I have to deal with complicated situations at work and at home. In those times, I don't practice for various periods, but I eventually return to studying. Does this mean that I'm beginning everything from scratch each time I return, because sometimes I don't feel any sensations while practicing? And do emergency situations hinder practice, since they upset a person's balanced state?

If you practice regularly over a given period, you're succeeding in developing something. You're acquiring this. After difficult situation, you may experience the disappearance of sensations of one kind or another, but not the result of what you'd already developed, because this result is connected not only to sensations. It's not influenced by a situation, because it's connected with other factors, not with the passing situations you face.

Emergency situations or incidents of any sort don't exert influence on the result of practice, so they aren't a hindrance to practice. However, if you intentionally commit a bad act or plan to harm someone, this will definitely affect the result of your practice. For example, if someone wishes to kill someone else and as a result of this intention or action ends up in an extreme or stressful situation, this is bad. Some actions are good for everyone—for you and for those surrounding you—and some are good only for you, but have no effect on others. But some actions harm others, and if you do them, you'll be in bad straits.

4. How should we lie when practicing breathing through the navel? By necessity on our backs? Where should the navel be directed?

It's doesn't matter how you lie or in what direction your navel is turned. With this practice it's of no importance. When you practice any exercise, not sleeping is better than sleeping—this is for sure. But whether you sit or lie is irrelevant.

5. Must the frequency of the pulsating of the navel and heart or the frequency of breathing coincide?

This isn't obligatory. If the frequency doesn't coincide, it doesn't matter.

6. Should we always imagine that we're a fetus, independent of our real age? Should this be the same for, let's say, a fifty-year-old and a seventy-year-old? What about a practitioner who is fifteen or twenty?

If you're already "up there"—say fifty—you should imagine yourself as either a fetus or, at most, a month-old child. With proper practice, these images will help divide your age in half; you'll feel twenty-five. When you're twenty, you can imagine that you're a two-year-old.

7. I had been practicing Bigu Shiqi more or less regularly since the last seminar (nearly three months ago) until I stopped not long ago because my navel was getting bigger. Frightened, I turned to my instructor from Stage I. I was told that I had been practicing improperly, since I wasn't closing the navel following practice. Usually I practice before bedtime, and it does happen that I fall asleep while executing an exercise. And in the morning I would think, why close it, since so much time—a whole night—has passed. Sometimes I would simply forget to close it. But my navel really did begin to protrude very noticeably. Can this be a consequence of this, and what should I do now for the navel to go back to its normal positioning?

When practicing any system, you must adhere very strictly to the rules. This means that all exercises absolutely must be practiced with the appropriate image. For example, concerning this exercise, it's performed in the following way: you open the navel, breathe through it, and then close it. In other words, you open to the outside and closed to the inside. Thus a balancing takes place: outside—inside. If you do this, such a practice will not cause any problems.

However, if you change the exercise yourself, difficulties can result. We had such an experience with an elderly seminar attendee who practiced this exercise intensely. He wanted to regain his youth—and quickly. So he used to fall asleep with his navel open, like you, but in the morning would forget to close it, also like you. During the day he would deal with his routine matters and then in the evening open his navel once again. But after a month he saw that his navel had become bigger. You can practice a lot, but you must not forget to close the navel.

To bring your navel to its normal position, you must think more intensely and imagine that it's returning to that position. Very easily, unassumingly, and in a relaxed manner, imagine your navel moving, closing. And after the end of the exercise, more intensely and focused, roll it up with your consciousness. Then everything will return to its initial state.

This example of incorrect practice shows how intensively our consciousness controls the state of our physical body and its energy. That's why it's necessary to learn how to discipline your consciousness and carefully observe the technology of the exercises. No matter what we do, we must maintain balance. And it's namely this result we wish to obtain.

We employ various means and methods to increase Yin or Yang, to decrease Yin or Yang, in order to bring them into a state of equilibrium in our body.

As for our exercises, the very same concept is drawn upon: in the execution of all exercises, balance must be adhered to. Remember the preliminary exercises: in the first, we rotate our hands eight times toward our body and eight times away; in the second, we move our hands, eight times with palms down and eight times with palms up; and so on.

8. When you don't eat for a given number of days because you simply don't want to, is it necessary to do Bigu Shiqi, or only when you want to eat? For me it's difficult to remember that I must open the navel, and then close it. Also is keeping it open safe? What if suddenly too much of something goes inside?

You can open your navel and not close it for twenty-four hours a day while taking in through it nutritious substances. This is safe because your navel will never take in more than your body requires. In the seminars, we usually practice in the following way: we open the navel and over thirty minutes, for example, we practice accepting food and energy through it. Then we close it. But you can open it and for a long time not close it. To each his own.

9. How can breathing with the skin be practiced if we're inside the navel?

Return the navel to its place and then practice breathing with the body. However, if your navel is open, you shouldn't practice breathing with the skin, since the navel takes in not only substances from the environment, but also oxygen.

10. Does the practice Bigu Shiqi mean that we must open the navel three times a day for about thirty minutes, practice eating through the navel instead of the usual way of feeding ourselves, and do this when we don't eat?

You can practice once or ten times a day—whatever pleases you and as often as you wish.

11. Now, with this, is there supposed to be an increase in energy? In general, is it supposed to go somewhere?

No. You simply receive it inside your body. You need not think about and focus on where it's going and how it's being distributed. This exercise allows for entering the state of calm and Quietness very quickly.

12. Must this exercise be performed only at home, or can it be done anywhere, for example, on a bus or at work?

Anywhere, except where there's a bad smell.

13. Is it necessary to go back periodically to the thought that your navel is open?

It's not necessary. At first, when you're just opening it, you need to think. But later, there's no need—it'll already functioning on its own.

14. How should we seize energy?

You don't seize anything. You simply open the navel and surround your body with it. You turn out to be in a ball. And it's through this the ball-navel that you're nourished with energy.

The navel's function resembles that of the lungs. It works automatically. In the beginning, start this work with your consciousness, and everything further will occur automatically. There's no need to think about anything.

15. If I practice regularly, when must the navel be opened and closed?

When you need to work, you should return to your usual state. When you don't need to work, when you practice or are simply relaxed, you can be in an embryo state.

16. Are there any precautionary methods for exiting the state of Bigu Shiqi?

Your body automatically returns to its regular state. On one of the days you suddenly begin to feel hungry and wish to eat. Suddenly you sense a very pleasant aroma from food, which you want to eat. This means you've concluded the state of Bigu Shiqi.

17. With this, can one drink? I tried, but experienced a cold feeling and was afraid to practice further.

Drinking is allowed, and feeling cold is normal. There might be cold and heat. It can continue for one or two days as your body changes.

18. You stated that a person's character changes as a result of practicing rejuvenation. In what way?

You'll notice that you're taking on the characteristics of a child. If you continue this practice over several years, your skin will become like the skin of a child. But you could practice your entire life and your consciousness will not change. Consciousness, thinking, and knowledge, nevertheless, will always remain the same.

19. Will gray hair darken?

Hair changes and turns gray in a way that corresponds to one's age, independent of practice. Here only knowledge is preserved, while the character is like that of a child.

20. How can we cleanse our intestines while practicing Bigu Shiqi? When fasting, we use enemas for forced cleansing.

You don't need to cleanse your intestines in any special way; they will automatically be cleared in the course of practicing. The intestines move very quickly, and after two days are cleansed.

21. Can I eat after this practice immediately, as usual?

You must not eat immediately, and the food will seem tasteless because you forgot how it tasted. The return transpires slowly. Everything depends on how long you're fed through the navel. When I didn't eat for 108 days, I forgot the taste of meat, noodles, and so on. Because of my experience, I can say that your weight will stop decreasing, even if you don't eat.

22. What kind of life did you lead during that 108 days without eating, Bigu Shiqi? Did you go into seclusion during that period? Who helped you—your partner or Teacher?

I didn't go into seclusion. I carried on my usual way of life and worked my usual job as a programmer in the research center of the Academy of Sciences in Beijing. None of my colleagues or acquaintances even harbored suspicions about this practice of mine. Only a few people—those with whom I usually practiced—knew about it. And I went to the cave for the departure of my soul with my friend.

But didn't those around you see how you had lost weight?

Weight loss happens only in the very beginning. With time, there's no change in weight, even if you don't eat for several months. This, of course, pertains only to those who have mastered the Bigu Shiqi method. If, without preparation, you don't eat for such a long time, problems are unavoidable. This is why we study in a certain sequence, step by step.

23. Are there any essential differences between breathing through the navel and taking in food through the navel?

There's no difference. While breathing through the navel, we take in energy, and this energy is food for us. There's no difference between breathing through the navel and eating through the navel. This is simply a matter of somewhat different terms, because both are used depending on what level you're practicing. At first we begin with breathing, and then the accepting of energy kicks in; this energy becomes food. When you've just begun to practice, you should feel the breathing process deeply in your navel. As you continue practicing you'll be able to understand that it's possible to breathe through the navel and that this breathing represents energy, which in turn represents food. You'll understand that it's possible with the navel not only to breathe, but also to receive food through it, because your breathing gives you the sensation that you're actually taking in food.

The exercise is one and the same, but the level is different. If you practice less, you understand less. If you practice more, you begin to understand more. When you do this practice, the processes in your body are the same, but the terms change a bit.

24. How do you know when you've learned Bigu Shiqi thoroughly and are ready for the protracted practice of "not eating?"

When this state comes, you'll know it. If you're fasting, you want to eat. The same happens here: when this state takes shape, you'll know it. If you practice, you'll understand what occurs and all questions will have been answered.

PART TWO

MEDICAL ASPECTS

Chapter 3
DIAGNOSTICS AND TREATMENT

GENERAL APPROACHES AND METHODS

In each stage we examine medical aspects of the ZYQ system, since the longer we practice the more deeply we understand, feel, and are aware of ourselves and the world surrounding us. In the very beginning of our familiarization with the system, as far back as Stage I, we stated that it consists of three units: systems of self-development, Image-medicine, and knowledge transplantation.

In actuality, everything we learn here about the human as a holistic system—the conditions necessary for his normal, healthy function as well as the methods of revealing and eliminating his problems (in other words, diagnostic and treatment methods)—relate to the category of Image Medicine. In general this is very broad and all-encompassing. Image therapy has its own theory. And this theory is based on certain abilities, which can be developed with Qigong practice. At the basis of Image Medicine is the structure of the human being.

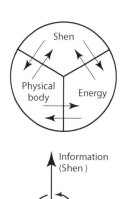

Picture 33: Interaction of Three Aspects of Human

We have stated that the Human is a living being and as such possesses a physical body, energy, and spirit. Consequently all illnesses can be divided up on the basis of these same three currents: we have disorders of the physical body and energy system as well as informational or spiritual illnesses. And, of course, treatment methods are also connected with these three currents: treatment of the body, energy system, and spirit. If we combine all these currents and view them as a whole, then such treatment belongs to Image Medicine. In this kind of medicine these three currents aren't separated, they're united (Picture 33) and interdependent.

Master's Story

Only one, very ancient book on Image Medicine exists. No words are written in it; pictures represent certain philosophical concepts about the evolution of Life and healing. I spent a lot of time trying to understand the meaning of these drawings. And I've succeeded in understanding only about 40 percent of material. The ability to understand what's depicted is closely connected to the level of practice. Until I reach a certain level in practice, I'm not in a position to understand the symbols and pictures in this book. This can be explained as follows: as long as I don't see definite images during my own practice, I can't make sense out of what's depicted in the book. And what is more, I received this very book during practice at Damo's cave (see the Stage I book for a detailed discussion).

It contains a very large number of drawings about the structure of the Universe. The book also talks about twenty-seven levels of worlds. Concerning humans, there are also twenty-seven levels of different systems. The physical body, energy system, and spirit have nine subsystems each: nine subsystems in the physical body, nine in our energy structure, and nine in the current of the development of the spirit. So, adding all of this up, in Humans are twenty-seven various structures or subsystems.

Thus, for example, in the physical body we can pick out the respiratory, digestive, and circulatory subsystems. If we're speaking about our body, then this is the circulation of blood, but if we're examining the energy system, we can speak about the subsystem of the circulation of energy. All in all, nine such subsystems are connected with the energy system. For purposes of examination, we need to divide the entire integrated system into twenty-seven subsystems. However, to utilize the information received and to work with it, we apply the approach to Human as a single, holistic system.

Why We Become Sick

So, why do we regularly experience illness? Why are we constantly sick? There are several reasons for this. Humans are living beings, and our life on Earth is subject to natural laws: from the moment of birth, we grow up and grow older with every day. In old age, the immune system weakens. Research has proved that the work of the immune system is closely linked with our energy: capabilities of the immune system lessen with a decrease in energy. Thus, as a rule, with age both the energy reserve of a person and the capability of his or her body to counter unfavorable influences from outside decrease.

On Earth are many external factors capable of harming our physical body. For example, drastic changes in weather conditions trigger various illnesses. If it's too hot or very cold, if there's a strong wind or high humidity, this can cause sicknesses. Other external factors, such as viruses, bacteria, and poor food and water quality, also provoke illnesses. In addition, there are zones with elevated radiation levels and places that are poisoned by chemicals.

We now understand this because we can decipher unfavorable external factors with the help of modern technology. Owing to centuries of experience, we also know that an increase in our energy results in an increase in a body's resistance power, or using contemporary terminology, the capabilities of the immune system increase. This is why many illnesses disappear with Qigong practice.

However, over the course of our lives, many other problems and sicknesses arise that are in no way connected to the factors above. For many people, the reasons for an illness aren't obvious; but even in ancient times it was known that our external environment isn't a major part of our problems. *We create many problems ourselves.*

EMOTIONS AND DESIRES

About the Reactions of the Body to Excitement and Stress

Most problems are connected with our emotional state. When people experience acute emotional flare-ups, they consume a great amount of energy. Therefore emotional imbalance can lead to loss of energy, as a consequence of which we can become sick. *Stress and nervous tension set off many illnesses.*

The typical reaction of the body to constant emotional agitation and stress is a disease such as stomach ulcers. Nearly 80 percent of patients afflicted with stomach ulcers suffer from emotional or spiritual problems. So ulcers are a disease of the emotions. If an emotional problem is regularly present in your consciousness, if you don't get rid of it, no matter how many pills you take, stomach ulcers will still be present. They can heal up for a few months or for a year, but then they return. If you get rid of the emotional problem, you won't have to take any medications whatsoever, since your stomach has a powerful restorative ability and can revive itself. In this instance, all systems of our body overcome the disorder—possibly within a few weeks. But if the reason continues to affect you, of course you won't be able to cure your stomach and be free of the ulcers.

Very often constant stress grinds a person down to such an extent that the body can no longer deal with it. Sharp emotional upsurges lead to a loss of energy. For this reason, chronic upsetting of emotional balance can trigger very serious—even irreversible—problems. One of them is chronic fatigue syndrome. With this, a person feels constant fatigue, so strongly that he or she is unable to work or to sleep normally. If the illness progresses, the person begins feeling so badly that he or she lacks the strength even to go out for groceries. A careful medical exam won't show a specific problem: everything will be normal with the organs and with analyses, but the person lacks energy and strength to do anything at all. This ailment is most widespread in highly developed countries, such as the United States and western Europe, with around five million people suffering from it. China has almost none, and areas of the former Soviet Union have very little. Such disorders are considered to be beyond any methods of treatment.

Consider, for a moment, electrical lighting. If, for example, the voltage suddenly decreases from 220 to 100 volts, then the illumination is also sharply reduced, so that even though the bulb is fine, the light is dim. It's the same with us—our physical body can be in normal shape, with all our systems and organs in order, but because there's a shortage of energy, they don't function properly. If a body's energy level is low, there can be problems with the power station, with energy production, or with the channels conveying the energy. Physicians can detect problems with the organs if there's a decrease in the energy level because of them.

With Qigong practice, our emotional state stabilizes, and as a result our energy level increases. Therefore those who practice Qigong like it should be practiced aren't afflicted with such a disorder, for by practicing we increase our energy.

Any change in our emotional state is reflected in our face. In general, different emotions affect us in different ways and impact various organs. Let's discuss some of them.

Anxiety

One of the most significant factors is *anxiety*. For example, your children or grandchildren left home and live in a different place—a different city or country. You're getting news from them very irregularly and begin to worry. While you know that everything is fine with them, you still worry about them.

Many people experience problems with work and income. If there's no stability, no assurances about the next day, if financial problems manifest themselves, many people begin to fret—they've been bitten by anxiety.

And then there's the individual who starts feeling pain and, before visiting a doctor, begins ruminating about the reason for the pain by considering possible explanations. If nothing seems convincing, anxious thoughts begin to overwhelm them: Is it cancer or something else very serious?

Anxiety might be connected with family or work situations, relations between you and others, or even a distrustful outlook. When a state of anxiety and worry gets ahold of a person, it may not be manifested constantly. But it's always ready to spring up when that person isn't occupied, when he or she focuses on what's causing the turmoil: pain, the absence of communication with children, work problems, marital difficulties.

Yet another reason for anxiety and worry can be love. Everybody needs love. A human must love and be loved. If you love someone strongly and deeply and sincerely take care of him or her, then when you don't hear anything from this person for several days, you begin to get anxious.

Anxiety reduces the effectiveness of the immune system and leads to sleep disorders and, under certain conditions, depression. *There can be deterioration in the effectiveness of the spleen and pancreatic gland.*

Why do we get anxious? After all, we know that worry, nervousness, and lack of calm can't help. To solve their problem, people need calm and sound sleep to find the optimal solution. But if because of worry or anxiety they can't fall asleep, if insomnia arises, then the body gets worn down, the head can't think clearly, and they make mistakes. If a person stops feeling anxious, the body on the whole and the heart in particular calm down and assume a balanced state. Then solving problems becomes simpler, and many illnesses automatically disappear.

Sorrow

Sometimes situations arise that induce *very strong feelings of sorrow or sadness.* Sorrow can cause great harm: it's capable of sharply lowering the level of our emotions and exerting an *oppressive impact on the immune system.* And a lowering of immunity induces serious problems. In addition, if you're sad a lot, this can *harm the lungs.*

Deep longing can spark **major depression**. In general, if a person's consciousness and spirit aren't sufficiently strong, external factors and emotional states can lead to depression. This is dangerous in that people sometimes commit suicide in a state of depression.

Master's Story

I had many patients whose illness was caused by longing. For example, if an individual who's over fifty loses his beloved wife, very soon afterward he also will pass on. And the opposite occurs: if the husband dies, then very soon afterward the wife, wallowing in deep sadness, also departs. Sadness and melancholy induce a negative emotional state, and this lowers immunity. The person is downcast, doesn't want to be treated, and soon dies. To all intents and purposes, deep sadness can be seen as the reason for this kind of death.

In all of life situations, a person must adhere to emotional balance. This is one of the necessary conditions for the preservation of health. Qigong practice can help us. It assists us in understanding whether or not we're in a state of balance. It allows us to understand how we can overcome everything that's connected with external factors, how we can pass through this inside ourselves—for example, how we can prevail over sadness and pass through happiness. By practicing Qigong, we can triumph over difficulties much easier.

This is connected to the fact that practice gives us an understanding of what can happen. When a problem occurs, we're already prepared for it and can more easily win against it. For example, we know that old people die and are of-

ten ill before this. That's the way life is structured. However, we can understand Life more broadly than before practice. We can understand what will happen with us, with our soul later. Therefore you need not murder yourself over the natural departure from this world of someone close to you. You need not be sad for a long time. You need not allow a feeling of longing and gloom to interfere with your life and cause you to take sick yourself. Of course, a person doesn't remain indifferent in the face of death, but by realizing the interconnectedness of events, we're able to be sad, but not so deeply or for so long.

Fear

Another problem which can upset practice and even our life is *fear*. For example, if you are frightened by something external, this fright affects your kidneys. If you're always being frightened, this can cause problems with your urinary-genital system and kidneys. If someone gets really angry with you, this malice can get to your liver. But if you become very angry with someone, this state from your liver will shift to your brain. You can see this in the expression of the face and of the eyes, and by the ears.

Fear is very often connected with our beliefs. One fear is connected with loss. We're afraid of losing what we have. Sometimes this loss can relate to property and finances, which mostly affects well-to-do people. But people without property have nothing to lose. However, they don't know what tomorrow will bring, and this absence of assurances regarding day-to-day existence can stir up apprehension, anxiety, and fear. Another type of loss is the loss of a loved one, be it the consequence of a grave illness or the absence of relationship. Some people fear losing their own life. There are many reasons for this: an illness, a threat form another person, a dangerous profession, and so on.

So, in any country fear can be encountered among people of different classes, social levels, and material standing.

If you're able to see this world not only in a given moment or given segment of time but over an extended period stretching from the past to the future through the present, you won't have many types of fear—or anxiety. When you adhere to the correct philosophy, you won't have fear.

Grievance

Grievance and feelings of being hurt belong to the category of spiritual maladies and are injurious to a person's health.

Master's Story

I have often encountered patients who constantly go around feeling offended, and their illnesses are of a different sort. Some people feel deeply offended because, in their opinion, their children or friends show a lack of respect toward them. For example, children come over to visit their mom. She feels that they absolutely must bring her something—a gift of some sort or delicious food. They bring nothing and come simply to hang out with their mom. But this offends her. Now, I think this is also an illness. Don't think that someone should do something for you!

And consider this situation: Over a certain period, one of your friends always visited with a gift, flowers, or candy. But he suddenly stopped doing this. At this point, you should find out whether he needs your help and care. It's possible that something happened and he needs your attention. Therefore, in such a situation, there's no need to get offended because of the lack of attention; rather, you should be concerned that perhaps some problems arose and that your aid is really needed.

As we practice Qigong, we begin to understand that we shouldn't create problems for others. On the contrary, we need to try to reduce problems and eliminate their causes.

Anger

If a person is very angry, he can't work normally—the emotions hinder concentration. Malice often leads to a state of excitement. With this, it's difficult to think logically and make sound decisions. Malice that is too strong, or **rage**, harms us. But often we still can't stop being angry, even if we understand that these emotions are harmful. Anger and malice exert a ruinous influence on our liver.

Happiness

Unexpected pleasant news, joy, and happiness can also result in big problems and cause great harm. A person can suffer from a heart attack, and sometimes this can become the reason for an infarct. At times the press or television reveals that a famous individual had suddenly died from a heart attack or a stroke after an evening of celebrating with alcohol.

Why does this happen? Because emotions that are too intense force our body to move, and we can't be calm. These emotions force the heart to beat more rapidly, and this raises our blood pressure. If the vessels are impaired, heart and brain functions can be disturbed. This is why too much happiness, too much joy, can also be deadly.

Our health depends on balance, and if this is upset, problems arise. Many pathologic deviations occur when there's an upsetting of balance. When happiness and sadness aren't in balance with each other and one state is always dominant, problems are unavoidable. This is similar to the Yin-Yang ball, when at all times there's an observable tilt to one side.

Because we often don't know about the very serious problems that can accompany an extended emotional tilt, we don't even try to control our emotional state. But our consciousness, thinking, emotions, and physical body should all be in a state of balance.

Master's Story

Once a patient flew in from Germany for an appointment with me in Seattle. As soon as he appeared, he informed me that he had a very complicated illness, one that nobody was able to treat. He related to me how, in response to constant and exhausting pain, he had undergone two operations on his knee joints that failed to eliminate the pain. Complaining that his whole body was in pain and his emotions were a wreck, he pointed out that he was incapable of thinking about anything, since he suffered from a constant headache, poor health in general, and every problem imaginable. He was very, very bad off.

*I looked at him and said that he had no serious problems and, in general, only one problem: **thinking.***

*According to Chinese medicine, **if a person thinks too much, it disturbs the spleen**. If the spleen is impaired, there's a weakening of the immune system. And this, in turn, leads to a worsening of the state of the lymphatic system. With this, of course, the brain can't function well. In addition, a person feels heaviness in every part of the body. And then even a slight injury can develop into something serious since the body can't deal with it because of its sharply reduced restorative power. In fact, this begins the process of destruction.*

Our thinking, emotions, and physical body are interrelated. If we begin experiencing emotional problems, this may mean that some defects have appeared in our physical body. And the reverse: problems with our physical body may well be a signal of problems in our emotional system.

Consider why, at times, we're in a bad temper but at other times are joyful; why do we feel satisfied and happy, but at other times worried and unhappy; why are we in a state of contentment, but then get angry or depressed? This question can be asked differently: Why is there rain sometimes and wind sometimes? Why do we sometimes feel cold and sometimes hot? Why are there different kinds of weather? Why does the weather change? It's all connected to varying climatic conditions. But why do we have a varying climate? Because this is the climate on our planet. Why is it specifically this kind? We don't know, but just as our varying climates exist, so do varying types of character and different emotional states among humans.

Research has established that different people have different emotions and different levels of emotion. You know that there are people who deal with everything very calmly. They sleep soundly and don't worry about the next day. Then there are those who are constantly fretting and incapable of sleeping soundly. Can we really be free of such negative emotions? Can we replace them with positive ones and become happier?

After a certain amount of Qigong practice, many people undergo a fundamental change in their character. If, before beginning practice, they were easily influenced by external factors—being constantly "stressed out" and in a state of negative emotions—as a result of practice their sleep improved and situations that had earlier caused stress or depression had little impact and ceased exerting such an influence on them.

Master's Story

*But why do such feelings arise in us? Because they represent a natural trait or quality of human nature and relate to **the initial characteristics of a human's inner essence,** to one of the foundations of our life. We have this kind of character, this particular makeup or specific core. Of course a person has many different emotions. Some of them are pleasant as they stimulate and facilitate our life. But some disturb its normal flow. To avoid this, we practice Qigong.*

Qigong practice helps us to **recognize the source of these negative emotions or feelings and to free ourselves of them.**

We normally go to work every day, after which we return home. This is our everyday life. And this is its natural route, because it's correct. If we would wake up at sunrise and engage in work and then at sunset return home, rest, and go to sleep, and if everywhere on Earth everything took place in exactly the same way, then this would be a very peaceful and natural route.

We need a normal, natural life. **We practice Qigong and meditate to understand what our life should be like.** *Over the course of our lives, each of us encounters a great many incomprehensible things and situations that we try to explain. To solve problems confronting us, we search different routes, and Qigong is one of them. Most often we employ it as a means for health maintenance, but also for a better understanding of cause-and-effect connections.*

Generally, our emotional state depends on the conditions of our physical milieu and level of energy. *It's been established that complete control by the consciousness over the emotions is too difficult a task. At times emotions overwhelm us, although we don't want this.*

Then it's logical to pose the question: Why in such a situation do we need to practice? Because we human beings, pass through our life period, from childhood to old age, and eventually die. Sometimes we take sick and suffer, while other times we're joyful and happy. For the majority of people, the sad moments in their lives greatly outnumber the serene.

If you pass through any cemetery, you can see what an enormous number of people have died. And think about all the cemeteries there are. So many people have died during the existence of mankind on Earth! The number of dead during this period is far greater than those presently alive. But this is the natural course of life on Earth: all living beings are born, grow up, get old, and die. **If there were no death, there would be no birth.** *This seems very logical. Generally there are many logical constructs in our life, but much does not occur logically. Living beings with a short lifetime, such as insects, are usually more numerous; their species propagates at a much faster pace and in great numbers than long-live species. As it is with nature, so it is with the essence of life.*

We must practice not because this represents the essence of life, but because we often allow mistakes. *If we always did everything in accordance with the laws of nature, we wouldn't need practice.* **We practice in order to follow nature, to understand it, and to act in harmony with its laws.**

We want to be happy and feel joy; we don't want to experience melancholy and sorrow. But they are present within us whether we want it or not. If there's no suffering, we can't say that we're happy. If there's no comparison, it's impossible to comprehend what *good* means and what *bad* means. Because of the existence of suffering, sorrow, unpleasantness, fear, insults, and so on, we know we need happiness, joy, pleasures, and more.

Nevertheless, some methods allow control of the emotions. One of the most reliable is *to increase our own energy and improve its quality.* This is why we practice certain exercises directed at raising the level of our energy and transforming it, that is, improving it qualitatively. It's then that we acquire the ability to control our emotions. Qigong practice allows our consciousness to control the state of our physical body because of the increase of our energy and improvement in its quality.

Now, changing the emotional state and gaining a high level of energy allows us to be cured of very serious illnesses, since in this instance our mind is capable of controlling the state of the physical body.

Our happiness and our well-being depend not on what we have but on our way of thinking, that is, on *how we relate to everything.*

For this very reason, in many spiritual currents, great attention is given to working with emotions and transforming negative thinking into positive. In speaking about the spiritual development of a person, we're assuming the transformation of his or her qualities and changes in his or her perception of the world. This is very important for the maintenance of health and for normal interactions with the surrounding society.

Loneliness, Helplessness, Hollowness

Various qualities are inherent in humans, and we have both very strong and very weak sides. When we're lonely, we often experience *fear and uncertainty.* But some who feel *ennui,* or emptiness in the heart, as if the Earth were falling from under them. Such a state could be called "*helplessness.*"

In them is the notion that help isn't to be expected from anyone. And this is the very weakest characteristic in the human being. So that such emotions don't dominate, you need to understand the nature of the human and the meaning of existence.

By practicing Qigong, we begin to understand what Life, the soul, emotions, consciousness, and humans are, and this understanding helps us solve emerging problems.

Everyone is *bored* sometimes. While our body and spirit are occupied with realizing goals or desires, we're occupied. However, when we get what we had strived for or begin to understand that we can't attain it, we begin to feel *"empty,"* *defenseless*, or *helpless*.

These are emotions that harm our health.

Master's Story

I had an elderly patient in Belgium who had no family. He lived alone. In tears he came to me and said that he felt fear, helplessness, and loneliness, although he had no material problems and was still physically strong. A necessary component was missing in his life. We feel helpless and lonely if no one occupies our thoughts, if there's nobody in our heart. We need sensations of human **closeness and compassion.**

We also need human contact based on **blood kinship;** *when we do, we are less likely to experience a feeling of loneliness. Yet another type of human relationship rests on spiritual relations and our faith. If people lack faith and family to support them—they may feel fear, loneliness, helplessness, and similar emotions very strongly. At times the sensation of being unneeded and depressed manifests itself.*

Friendship *can also provide support and assistance. But relations based on friendship aren't very strong. Friendship can be destroyed in a moment, but this doesn't happen in the case of blood and spiritual ties: after all, even if you cut off with your relatives, the relationship remains.*

Relations of a spiritual nature aren't as easily established, but if they are already emerging, the sensations of loneliness and hopelessness don't arise. This is because **faith** *is manifesting itself.*

We can feel all of this during Qigong practice. As sensitivity heightens and the abilities for interacting with the surrounding world improve, the practitioner is inevitably faced with the question "Where did we come from?" And at times the sensation that you want to go home also arises. Here, in our routine life, we know very well this feeling. In one place you feel comfortable, such as at home or with a good friend—but in another you're a guest—and maybe not an entirely desired one. The hosts and hostesses may be very polite and kind, but you're still uncomfortable and want to go home. Why are our sensations so different? What's this connected with?

When we're comfortable, spiritual relations are present—a certain energy in which we feel at home.

Love and Hate

These are the strongest emotions of humans. As with the Yin-Yang principle, they possess opposite qualities and are always connected. Under certain conditions, we can turn into the other: if someone doesn't get love, that person may begin experiencing hatred. **Love** is the strongest desire of the physical body, consciousness, and spirit. Hatred is in second place. Thus many great Teachers of humanity and gods have taught that we must love and forgive. They have taught us to give love and that love ought to be higher than the desire to possess things. So it's possible to learn how to forgive and not hate. But following this in practice is very difficult. Such is human nature: we need special knowledge to get rid of our dark, bad sides. That's why it can be said that *our consciousness is closely connected with our heart.*

Love is born out of our desires. And they are dictated, in turn, by our body and our spirit. When the body is in need of something, a certain desire arises. Love is needed by our body and by our spirit, since it mitigates the feeling of loneliness, helplessness, vulnerability, and so on.

Everybody needs love. Moreover, we almost always wish that we had more, for we don't have enough of it. Here **greed** enters the picture. If a person has no sense of moderation and always wants more and more of something he or she received, that person risks losing everything in the end.

As practice continues, our feelings change. Eventually, hatred disappears, leaving only **love, kindness**, and **compassion**. Just as the Sun sends its rays to the whole world, so a person begins to present his or her love to everyone. The concept of Guanyin means "look and listen." But there's another meaning, Great Kindness, because on this level we can understand all people, including their virtues and shortcomings.

About Desires

We all experience many and various desires. They are very different—sometimes specific and sometimes undefined. In accordance with these desires, corresponding thoughts emerge that point the way to the realization of the desires. Desires that engender actions. Desires are the key to all qualities—bad and good.

Master's Story

Love, hatred, and many other qualities arise from desires. If there are no desires, there's no love or hatred. When people don't have desires, the feelings of love and happiness remain stay within us. But while there are desires, we can feel love only from without—from someone, such as spiritual Teachers. What we understand as love at our level of spiritual development can best be labeled emotion, because it is provoked by the desires and needs of our physical body and spirit, above all. Such feelings are natural and are the inner essence of the nature of Humans. But, on a higher spiritual level, such feelings aren't called love.

We love warmth, we need sunlight, but the ability to get sunlight depends on the individual, on his or her understanding. We need love. Everything depends on us, on our level.

*Desires give birth to the various emotions. If there are no desires, our deep nature, our inner essence, will manifest itself. **Desires don't have anything to do with the inner foundations of the human being. Rather, they are the consequence of our upbringing and way of life.** With deep involvement in practice, with deep meditation, it becomes clear that desires don't represent the inner nature of humans.*

However, a lot in our life is set off by our desires, and all too often we nourish improper desires. This is why we commit improper acts. We're not totally aware of all of them, nor can we foresee all the consequences, since there's a lot we don't understand thoroughly. For example, now there are many illnesses connected with improper food consumption.

When and How We Should Eat

When we're hungry, our body lets us know about this it we know that we're supposed to eat. But do we always behave accordingly? In many situations we don't feel hungry but nevertheless eat. For example, when entertaining guests or visiting friends, we sit at the table and continue to eat even after becoming full, because the table still holds a wide-ranging selection of dishes we'd prefer not to leave.

Sometimes we eat automatically when we find ourselves at home with nothing to do and we're aware there's some delicious food around. In such situations, food causes us many problems and triggers so-called *illnesses of civilization*: diabetes; high blood pressure; various cardiac disturbances, including infarct; and so on. From the standpoint of Qigong, such a situation is a *breakdown in the balance between the desires of the body and its capabilities*.

Let's say your body isn't signaling the need to eat; you aren't hungry. But you see in front of you a lot of free, tasty food. Sometimes the desire to eat more arises, as if you need to stock up, so you continue eating. And the food may be a delicacy for you; its smell and taste are so attractive to you that you don't stop. You tell yourself that you'll make tomorrow a light day, but today you'll continue "stuffing your face" beyond any reasonable limit. In this instance you're acting not in accordance with the dictates of your body but in accordance with your thoughts, desires, and mind. And then the problems start.

If food is chronically in short supply, if a person regularly goes hungry, problems will also be inevitable, although of a different sort.

Balance is necessary in everything.

About Problems of Self-Evaluation

Some desires give birth to negative emotions. They are often connected with envy and an inability to soberly evaluate a situation or its possibilities. We can find a number of examples.

Example 1. You go as a guest to the new apartment of a classmate and see furniture that you couldn't even imagine existed. And he, from your point of view, is the most "average Joe" person that ever existed. But it's true that while you excelled in science, he did well in business. You begin experiencing a feeling of discomfort, chagrin, and dissatisfaction: for so many years you worked from morning till night and toiled with great difficulty to defend your dissertation, yet you haven't even earned enough for a decent renovation. And after the visit, you have to hear your wife say, "Well, what use is your work? Your friend didn't graduate from any institutes, and he has everything." Of course you come up with an answer, but the unpleasant taste in your mouth remains for a long time.

Our desires have a tendency to increase. We want more and more, and it becomes difficult to satisfy those desires. Usually people compare themselves, not with people occupying a very high position, but with those like them. If you compare your life and your possibilities with a billionaire, that's an abstract comparison, and you won't feel any disappointment. But if you meet with a classmate who excelled in nothing but suddenly received a huge sum of money, enabling him to buy and furnish a big house while you remained in your apartment, the thoughts of this can begin to poison your life.

But from a larger perspective, this isn't at all a problem. We have to face problems in our life that are far more serious. There are a lot of them, and they're of a very different type.

Example 2. Let's assume you do routine work; you're the person who carries out orders exactly. Someone tells you what has to be done, and you have the opportunity to make sure you understood what's being asked of you. And you execute the directive. Then circumstances clear the way for you to become supervisor. The company is persistent in offering you a position that's tempting both in prestige and compensation. But you don't know this job. You don't know how to manage people, because prior to this someone has always managed you.

You develop a headache and fall into depression, ignited by the fact that you're being asked to do something you're incapable of, although you want to. On the one hand, you're afraid that you won't be able to handle the job; on the other, you don't want to pass up such an alluring opportunity. You decide to give it a shot, and you agree to the offer. All your relatives and acquaintances learn about this, and your reputation with them is strengthened.

But you fail to pull it off. In a month you land in the hospital with a pain in your stomach area. The doctor discovers an ulcer, but medicine doesn't help. Why? Because this problem is a result of stress on the job.

Everyone knows that technical equipment must be used in accordance with certain guidelines. Can it continue to function normally when subjected to constant use? Humans are the same: when we're constantly overloaded with work we can't do, physical problems arise.

Master's Story

Example 3. *Many school children and students in the United States have serious digestion problems.. Many physicians believe it's the result of low-quality food in schools and universities. I tested the food in American schools and discovered that it's much better than what I usually consume. In fact, the problem lies not in the quality of the food but in the stresses. Many students have certain desires, such as to become a millionaire or at least to be a layer. These ideas weigh them down. They want this and plan their lives around it, but they can't achieve it. That's why their consciousness is subject to stresses that result in stomach problems.*

Example 4. *During my many years of working with patients, I've encountered diverse cases. Some of them had illnesses caused not by physical or intellectual problems—they were strong and very intelligent—but because they hadn't found their place in life. In different countries, 10 percent to 20 percent of patients who turn to me have these kinds of problems. I believe that such people can be found everywhere.*

We must work. But many people work in jobs that aren't their cup of tea. A question arises: Why? Why doesn't he like this? For example, he's convinced that he's very handsome or very smart, that he's a college graduate with every imaginable merit, so he believes that what he's doing is simply trivial and way below his abilities. He assumes that he should be working with something on a higher level, and his his job is of no interest to him. But he's working there and not in a place that fits his ideals, because other people have a different opinion—they don't think he's cut out for a different place, a different position. The problem here is one of self-evaluation.

When a person thinks more of himself than others do, the problem is an improper philosophy of life and behavior. With a proper perception of the world and philosophy, you can rise and develop from any level if you have the abilities or talent. This doesn't mean that you have to occupy a special place or position. If that's your attitude, you can achieve success in whatever field you choose, because you can begin from the very lowest positions, from zero, and gradually rise. If you always try to attain what you plan, success will be the hallmark of your efforts, no matter what you do.

Therefore you need not think about where you should be. Simply show others with your actions and work what you're capable of— through actual deeds and not something derived from your own conclusions. With such a philoso-

phy, you won't cause yourself any illnesses. You won't have any problems. But if you're constantly preoccupied with the thought that you don't belong where you are and should be somewhere else— beyond your reach— you'll experience many negative emotions: offense, disappointment, chagrin, sadness, and maybe even malice. Then problems are unavoidable.

*   **Example 5.** *You may experience the following situation at work: You're forced to go there every day and carry out tasks that are unpleasant to you. This continues day after day. You don't want to do anything, but are forced to. After a while, if nothing changes, you take sick. How can this problem be solved if it arises?*

*   *At first glance, you have two options: change jobs or change yourself so that you'll like your job.*

*   *Let's see if there's **a third way**. In any problem, you have to find the key, the reason. For example, why don't you like your work? Maybe your work is right for you and you don't like it simply because you don't know how to approach it or how to do it correctly. And if you change jobs, you might be even less satisfied because the new job isn't "your thing" either.*

*   *We don't have much time in our lives, so whatever we do, we should do it well. If we change something all the time, we aren't able to acquire the experience and skill needed to do something specific really well. Therefore, before arriving at a decision, analyze and understand why you don't like what you're doing now: is it what you're doing that you don't like, or is it your colleagues, supervisor, atmosphere, or something else?*

*   *Therefore **we need to practice because an erroneous understanding of ourselves and of the situations themselves can emerge. We want to know who we are and what we can do—where our path lies, what our trajectory is.***

*   *Practice can help us understand what we should do and how we should do it, so that we experience less chagrin and live happily. It helps us to learn the state of balance between desires and possibilities, because if there's no balance, there's no good health.*

About Energy Balance

It's becoming clear now that our life—be it good or bad—is connected with the state of balance. What does *balance* mean? During the day we're supposed to work and at night to sleep. Sleep and work are two opposite sides, like Yin and Yang. If you work over several days and don't sleep, there may be no tomorrow for you. But you sleep—not work but only sleep, sleep, and sleep—you'll also get sick. Balance is also necessary in regard to food: overeating constantly is a no-no, but if you don't have enough of the right food, good health is out of the question.

In regard to our energy, an **energy balance** must be maintained. What does this mean? There are two types of energy. **One allows us to be very active and to work energetically, while the second type allows us to be in a state of deep calm**. If you have a lot of energy, but only active, you need to work and to expend your energy. The best variant is to be positively involved with your work. However, if you have a very large amount of energy, but no work or anything that interests you, you're likely to create problems for others regularly. When you have an abundance of calming energy, you feel fatigued. The symptoms resemble energy shortage in general, when there's no strength for anything other than what's absolutely necessary.

That's why it's necessary to balance energy and to organize it so that your active life alternates with passive resting. If we don't have enough energy, we need to be in a calm state to enable its level to rise. And if we have a lot of energy, it's incumbent on us to expend it intelligently, to do something useful today and for coming generations.

Sometimes, however, we encounter seemingly incomprehensible illnesses in a person who is totally balanced. The manifestations of the illnesses are obvious, but not the reasons. This is connected with an inadequate perception of the world resulting from some informational disturbances . You can understand what this is from the following story.

Master's Story

I've always remembered a very interesting occurrence in my childhood. To this day I recall it whenever patients come to me with some untypical symptoms.

A new doctor appeared on the scene at a hospital where my father worked as chief surgeon. Since it was a state hospital, everybody received a salary, and nobody was allowed to accept any remuneration—be it money or gifts. After a while, everybody began noticing that patients always brought this new doctor—and him only—a gift of fruits or vegetables that varied in makeup. For a long time, we couldn't understand why. For example, a patient would bring this doctor a bag of apples from his or her garden. Strictly speaking, this wasn't a gift, since the doctor was being treated to a small amount of something that grew in abundance in the patient's garden. The doctor answered, "Thanks, of course, but you don't need to bring me apples. I don't like them. But since you've already brought some today, I won't insult you; I'll eat them. However, don't bring any more, please." And he took them.

It's natural that the patient was interested in what the doctor liked. And the doctor said, as if expressing a dream, "I love khurma very much. Now if this were khurma." Of course, all of this became known among the patients very quickly. And someone brought him khurma. And then the doctor said, "Thank you, but why did you go through the trouble of bringing me this? What a shame, but I have a condition right now affecting my stomach or intestines, for which khurma would not be the answer. If this were only {he'd name another fruit}, then everything would be just fine!"

Soon all the doctors learned about this. They knew that if you gave him garlic, he'd say that onion is better but would nevertheless take the garlic. And then we found out that he'd done the same thing at a previous job.

When I left home to study, he changed hospitals again. This was over twenty years ago. At that time we still had communism. There were different rules then and different laws in many areas of life.

Years later, in different countries, I met similar people among my patients. Constant role-playing whereby a person systematically displays his dissatisfaction with something that he in fact likes leads to imbalance in the body, to the undermining of the balance between the mind, the consciousness, and the demands of the physical body. Then many unpleasant disturbances in the body are inevitable. And they begin in almost identical fashion: at first informational problems, from which develops an inadequate perception of the world, and then the inevitable emergence of physical ailments.

From this we can understand that our body reacts in a very definite way to our emotions, desires, and thoughts. At first glance, this seems invisible, intangible, and therefore insignificant. And this is connected with the fact that, over many centuries in the West, aspects of life like energy and information were not taken into account, while primary significance was allotted to the physical current.

If equal attention is given to all three factors—body, energy, and spirit—our health will be better and our life happier.

Necessary Conditions for Good Health

Let's consider what's needed for good health; how an unfavorable situation can be corrected; and how in general can we be protected from illnesses.

Since ancient times, humans have been gathering knowledge about how to be healthy. If we ignore this basic knowledge, illnesses are inevitable. Every living organism requires specific conditions for normal function, and humans are no exception.

Once again we return to the fact that we consist of three components: a material body, energy, and spirit. We must maintain all three of these elements in a balanced state.

So let's consider what can destroy this balance. What are the conditions that can cause its destruction or, in other words, how is human life connected with the external world? About the factor of the emotions, desires, and thoughts we've already spoken. Therefore, now we'll discuss the material current.

How Humans Are Connected
with the Environment

When we speak about the life of our physical body, we are dealing with specific conditions of its existence in the material realm. For example, we must take in food—this is matter; we have to breathe—air is also matter. Everything that's excreted by our organs is also matter. We use speech and can hear sounds—they are matter. What does disturbing conditions in the material current mean for us?

We receive sounds from without with our ears. If a sound is extremely loud, it disturbs our hearing, and this leads to problems with speech—we're unable to hear our own voice and regulate its sound. Therefore we know that very loud sounds and noise are harmful for us. It's the same concerning light. If it's too bright, or too dim, we feel bad; our body is uncomfortable. And if there's little air or an insufficient amount of oxygen in it, it's difficult for us to breathe, and problems with breathing arise.

Now let's examine which physical ties with the external world are more important for us, even if we don't direct them.

Suppose you find yourself in a noisy place and can't decrease the level of noise. Then you can leave that place. The same goes for light: on a bright, sunny day you can go into the shade or hide from it indoors. We constantly breathe, and if the air isn't good, it can make us uncomfortable or even ill. The same goes for the sensations of our body: if the weather isn't very welcoming, our body adapts—as if reorganizing in harmony with the sensations. However, if weather conditions change abruptly, we don't have enough time to restructure and will take ill. From the standpoint of Chinese medicine, a head cold signifies that the conditions of the external milieu changed but the body didn't succeed in restructuring itself.

Good food and water belong to another category— not the external milieu, such as a change in weather or in noise. We're able to control them independently; with them, we can regulate many aspects of our body's systems. That's why, in the material world, food and drink are most important—all the more so since we're supposed to eat and drink daily. This is written even in ancient Chinese books. Many serious illnesses—cancer, cardiovascular diseases, gall stones, and a number of others—are connected with bad diet. Many problems of the liver, stomach, and small intestine, among others, are caused by a disturbance of balance.

We know about the five primary elements. Within us there must be a balance of the five types of organs connected with these elements. For their energy balance, we learned the Wu-Xing circle in Stage II. And first and foremost, the balance between Yin and Yang, about which we spoke in Stage I, must be supported. Now to maintain this state of balance between Yin and Yang, we must be wide awake and work during the day and sleep at night.

Unfortunately, a certain category of people ignore this rule and don't observe the balance between work and rest, sleep and wakefulness. Often they are passionately involved in something, such as research or business. But when the balance is upset, people most definitely acquire health problems. And when there's no good health, plans and needs change.

Master's Story

*In the first chapter of the Yellow Emperor's treatise, the most revered medical book of ancient China,[7] we find the conditions necessary for good health. As we already stated, in ancient treatises of various peoples, we can find descriptions of the interactions between the health of an individual, his emotional state, his nutrition, and his attitudes toward the surrounding world. Most important is good sleep,and only then all other necessities of our physical body, including food, drink and so on. In Chinese language, only twelve characters are employed to describe these rules. In translation they mean "**sleep well, eat well, and have a good sex life**." If these three aspects aren't balanced in your life, problems are inevitable.*

A Good Night's Sleep and Its Criteria

If a person doesn't sleep well, he or she can't be healthy. This is why, when checking the state of your health, you should first investigate whether or not your sleep is good. What does "good sleep" mean? Some people can sleep twelve, even sixteen hours in a row. Does this mean they sleep well?

It's necessary to take into account how deep and "sound" the sleep is. Here are the criteria:

- On wakening, a person should above all feel rested.
- The norm for good sleep is wide, from five to nine hours.
- Sleep must be uninterrupted. If you wake up often or for a long time, turn from side to side, and have difficulty falling asleep, you can't say you sleep well.
- You should fall asleep right away—within one to three minutes. If you can't fall asleep for a long time, you must seriously consider what the problem is and eliminate it.
- Sleep should be deep and "sound"; external noises or light should not disturb you.

Sleep deprivation was considered the most terrible form of torture in the East. People were awakened by various methods as soon as they began to fall asleep. Some died, while others lost their minds. In Russian folk tales, some heroes were asked a riddle: "What is sweetest

---

7 Familiarize yourself with excerpts from this book in appendix 1(1).

of all on Earth?" Invariably the answer was "sleep." Identical notions about the importance of sleep and other life factors reside in many cultures. Many individuals stricken with cancer don't die from the illness, but from the anxiety that won't allow them to fall asleep. Sleep has always been considered a necessary condition for a successful recovery.

Good Food

What does this mean? Above all, food must be balanced. We need variety in our food.

From the scientific point of view, we require different substances: proteins, vitamins, carbohydrates, and various microelements. And we should eat not more than 70 percent of our capacity, although this is sometimes difficult, especially when we're a guest or in a restaurant. It's very harmful is to go without eating one day and then "pig out" the next. To live long, it's necessary to cleanse your digestive system periodically. This means that sometimes you need to eat nothing and drink only water.

We take in food through the oral cavity, while the waste produced by our life activity is excreted by our body through the anus. "Eating well" also means a balance between inhalation and exhalation, between the devouring of food and expelling of waste products. If you ate a lot, but little was excreted, this signals problems in the body; on the other hand, if you ran to the toilet right after eating, this is also not good. And the type of food is also important.

Good Sex

Our sexuality is connected with our hormonal system. For health, we need three important substances: vitamins, antibiotics, and hormones. Our body contains a great amount of hormones, which affect various aspects of its functioning. If the male and female hormones aren't balanced, your health will definitely begin to suffer. Therefore "good sex" means bringing the hormonal system into balance. Good sex doesn't signify more or less. It means that it's necessary to maintain the needs of our body, that is, the quantity of hormones required by our body.

As we remember from Stage I, some people experience strong sexual desire when practicing Yang-Qi, so they practice Small Sky Circle to direct this energy toward the brain's development. In this way we also balance hormones in our body. In addition, food and various herbs can be employed for regulating the hormonal system. But if hormones from without in their pure form are applied, there will undoubtedly be side effects.

Master's Story

A comfortable family life is an indispensable condition for good health. It places a person in a state of love and intimate relations. Otherwise, illnesses will occur.

In diagnosing patients with cancer of the lungs, breast, ovaries, and prostate, I looked with the Third Eye and examined the patients' past to find the reasons for their illnesses. I discovered that **the reason for disease was in always imbalance.** *Food can also cause oncological illnesses. For example, I know that hormones in chicken or pork trigger certain illnesses in people. Diseases can be caused by fruits, vegetables, and other foods.*

Through my own experience, I came to the conclusion that the reasons for the appearance of the diseases described in the ancient treatise of the Yellow Emperor correspond to our present-day notions. The theory of Chinese traditional medicine and Image Medicine is based on experience set forth by many Great Masters in accordance with their abilities to see, feel, and understand. From the very beginning, there were no theories, only experience. When this experience accumulated in a sufficiently large amount, they summarized it. They discovered that everything is subject to certain patterns as our body interacts with both external and internal factors, including thoughts, desires, and emotions.

Qigong practice helps us to understand each other better, be more tolerant, and respect the opinions of others. Don't always think that such-and-such a person is bad and you can't stand him. Don't be aggressive regarding an opinion different from your own; if you do, you'll feel bad. If you try to understand why a person acts in a particular way and what provokes his remarks, you'll eventually be able to understand his inner world. It'll be clear to you that he has certain defined desires, and in accordance with these desires his thoughts arise, also totally defined, which are directed at the realization of these desires. So it's desires that provoke actions. If you understand a situation, then even in the case of your family members making mistakes, you'll be able to forgive them. And if you understand a situation correctly, the mistakes will be far fewer.

Changing yourself is a lot easier than changing another person, be it your spouse, colleague, and so on. **If you can't change yourself, don't try changing others.**

If you're ready to change yourself, you'll have more happiness than suffering. Of course, it's much easier to discuss things than to act. Very often, if we're asked, we give advice that we ourselves can't carry out (and even if we aren't asked, we give it). For example, a friend approaches you wanting to know how to lose weight. You answer, "Very simple. Don't eat a lot." And then your friend asks you, "Why haven't you gotten rid of some pounds?" You answer that you simply love to eat. Yes, for sure, talking is much easier. But Qigong practice is oriented toward doing, not discussion.

An understanding of these things and dedicated practice allows you to change situations and maintain good health.

DIAGNOSTICS

As far back as Stage I, we spoke about how several methods in Traditional Chinese Medicine and Qigong are employed in diagnosing a patient. A diagnosis is believed to have been established correctly if the same result is obtained by at least four different methods. You already know two methods.

In Stage I, we learned the method of diagnosing with the hands. It's very simple, useful, and easily applied. In Stage II, we considered the methods for diagnosing with the body. In Stage III, we're examining the methods of diagnostics and treatment connected with the work of the Third Eye. This is engendered by the fact that many Stage III exercises contribute to its opening and activating. Therefore, in Stage III the abilities of the Third Eye in diagnostics and treatment are developed.

If a person has the ability to see with the Third Eye, the healing work will come much easier. But if the Third Eye doesn't work, sometimes even a huge store of knowledge can't guarantee the right choice for a patient's treatment.

In Eastern medicine, all parts of our body have links with each other. However, since we don't see all these connections with regular vision, we often don't know how to treat illnesses correctly. Some examples very dramatically show how it's possible to harm a person without this ability to see.

Master's Story

A little girl with serious vision problems was brought to me in Seattle. Her mother said that a few months earlier, the seven-year-old's vision had suddenly begun to worsen, with one eye showing strong shortsightedness and the other farsightedness. And the situation had continued to deteriorate. Although they had visited many doctors, no one had been able to find the reason. And no one could help her.

My usual diagnostic method involves my asking the patient to stand away from me—at least a few meters—and I simply look with my Third Eye at what he or she has and where there's a problem. I began looking and saw that bad energy had collected in the girl in the area of her eyes. To establish where it came from and why it appeared in that location, I began to track its movement from her eyes downward. Reaching the liver, I saw that it continued downward and ended in the area of the stomach. At that point I said that her eyes themselves, as organs, were not the problem; her stomach was.

There's interdependence between the eyes and stomach that contemporary Western medicine rejects.

My treatment isn't cheap, so the mother said that she'd have to borrow the money but would pay for the treatment if there was a positive result. I conducted four sessions, but the mother still didn't believe there would be success. After the fourth session, an eye doctor checked the girl's vision, and there had been a 50 percent improvement. After three more sessions, her vision was completely normal.

More than a year has passed, and there are no problems with the girl's vision. In this case, any other mode of treatment would have been ineffective. As a rule, laser treatment is proposed at this point, which of course involves altering the shape of the lens. If the girl had undergone standard treatment, her vision may have been ruined irreversibly. i

Yet everything was very simple: the girl had eaten something she shouldn't have. And as a consequence of this food, some sort of substances that weren't right for her remained inside her, as did the bad energy they produced. As this energy passed in natural fashion through the channels, it rose upward and impacted her vision. All I did was simply trace the path of this bad energy to reveal the reason or sources of her illness.

For this reason we say **there are no standard reasons for illnesses.** *They can be different for each case. While the symptoms can be identical, the reason can vary. A patient can tell you a lot about the assumed reasons for his or* *her illness and the accompanying symptoms, but all of this may not correspond to reality. So you have to know how to find the reason. And despite the medical investigations the patient has undergone—simply analyses or computer diagnostics—you still must know how to diagnose; otherwise harm can be done.*

With the Third Eye, the anatomy of the spirit, or the work of the informational system, can be seen. A person's informational system can also be seen with the Third Eye. If something isn't right with our informational system, the physical body falls under its influence. In our body, organs function and collaborate in pairs. For example, the liver and gall bladder are supposed to work together, as are the kidneys and bladder.

If such pairs don't function properly, problems arise. However, when each of these organs is checked separately, there may be no deviations from the norm. For example, if there's a problem in the joint workings of the kidneys and bladder, this could result in frequent visits to the toilet during the night. For example, the bladder may fail to communicate to the kidneys that, for a given period, they must not take in a lot of fluid from the blood, turn it into urine, and send it to the bladder, because it's time to rest. Of course there are additional reasons for such behavior from the kidneys and bladder, but they can be seen without difficulty when the Third Eye is used properly.

Such lack of coordination can lead to high blood pressure. My observations and experience allow me to say that approximately 30 percent of people with high blood pressure have a disturbance in the joint function of their bladder and kidneys. The kidneys are supposed to absorb urine from the blood quickly to lessen the pressure of the fluid on certain systems of the body and then send it to the bladder. If this happens, blood pressure won't rise. If there's an abundance of fluid in the blood vessels, naturally the pressure will rise. This occurs because of a breakdown in the signal system: the bladder and kidneys aren't coordinating properly.

Generally speaking, diagnosing with the Third Eye isn't complicated. But you have to have a lot of energy for it. If you don't have a sufficient amount of energy, then in a short time—maybe in a few days—you'll stop seeing because of a lack of energy.

THE THIRD EYE

Usually when we speak about the Third Eye, we mean the ability to see and perceive the world in a way broader than normal vision allows. It's necessary to have certain knowledge about it, because the concept itself is fairly general.

What's Necessary for the Third Eye to Work?

For us to see with the Third Eye, the Mingtang point, which is between the eyebrows, must be opened. Extending from it to the depths of the brain is a channel that also has to be opened (Picture 34). The term *Third Eye* was given to a certain part of the brain because, similar to regular eyes, it's from this place that the signal travels to the back part of the brain. If this channel is closed, the back part of the brain doesn't receive signals, and the practitioner doesn't see.

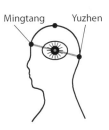

Picture 34: The Third Eye's Channel

After many years of practice, this channel—and many channels from any part of the body—can conduct information to the back part of your brain. Then it's not necessary to look specifically through this area—it's possible to use any part of the body to look in the same way as the Third Eye does: you can look with your hands, toes, or any other part of your body. After certain training, *any part of our body functions as the Third Eye, but the channel from the Mingtang point is the basic one for our goal and the biggest.*

If one part inside your brain is weak, even with all points open, including the Mingtang point and the channel emanating from it, you still won't be able to see. When practicing the seventh preliminary exercise, as we guide the Moon we stimulate both this channel and the back part of the brain to **see**.

Still another indispensable condition for seeing is *Silence of Mind.* Without it, thoughts and information perceived through the regular channels won't allow you to receive subtler signals.

After practicing of the state of Quietness, the mind and the Third Eye begin to function jointly. But if your mind is active, if your thoughts are too strong, the picture disappears. It's necessary that your consciousness, your mind, works not in a relaxed way, but very weakly—then the picture will change but not disappear.

Many people see light or various images during practice. Many experience flashes of light in front of their eyes. This means they have the ability to see with the Third Eye. With almost everyone, the Third Eye can be opened after a certain period of practice. However, this period differs: for some people, five days is enough, while others need five or even twenty years to get results. This depends on many factors.

In the beginning, the Third Eye usually works with eyes closed, because the practitioner's energy isn't strong enough to overpower usual daylight. However, when your energy becomes strong, there's no difference between having your eyes open or closed. If the Third Eye has opened, you can see what exists beyond the limits of regular vision.

If you look with the Third Eye, you see with greater depth and breadth than normal. With regular vision, your visual field is less than 180 degrees, but when the Third Eye begins working, it's much more than that.

If you continue practicing, the functions of the Third Eye expand. Simultaneously you'll be able to see many images from different directions. You'll be able to see scenes, similar to those in a film, that come at you from four and even five directions. In the beginning you see a film coming at you from one direction, then from two, and then four—but never three. As a rule, after you see scenes from two directions, you'll immediately be able to see from four directions: in your brain, it'll be as if four different films are going on. You'll be able to understand what you're seeing and where it's from. You'll understand everything immediately—at one and the same time.

If you look only with the Third Eye at the very beginning of its development, you may see one film that envelopes everything around you. But when you see in four directions, that same effect arises from all sides, not one. It isn't a continual or circular film; completely different images approach from four directions.

Phases in the Opening
of the Third Eye and Its Levels

Many levels of seeing exist with the Third Eye—more than ten. As development of the Third Eye proceeds, the range of its possibilities expands. It passes through completely distinct phases and acquires additional functions. And this is reflected in the changing names of the Third Eye in each of the phases, reflecting its increasing abilities.

First Phase: Heavenly Eye

The first phase of the development of the Third Eye *is Heavenly Eye*. It's characterized by three functions, or three levels.

On the first level, you simply *see the quality of Qi.* You can examine the entire person in sequence and see something dark, unpleasant in some places. This is immediately evident. For example, if there's dirty and dark Qi in the liver, there's a problem there. This is called diagnosing with the help of Qi. A change in the quality of Qi allows you to make a specific determination about an illness, regarding its existence.

The second level arises when more energy comes to the Third Eye. In this instance, you *begin to see bones, joints, and then separate muscles and organs.* With this level of seeing, you can determine specifically where there's a problem and what isn't in order. Here you have an opportunity to diagnose someone and see disturbances in the body and their location clearly. But this is only *"black-and-white seeing"*: at this level of diagnosing, you see Qi and organs in black and white.

The third level is seeing in color. As practice continues, your energy increases and the Third Eye's nourishment improves. Then colors begin to appear. At first you'll feel pressure in the Third Eye, then flashes of light that resemble lightning, followed by multicolored light arising inside your brain. From this phase your diagnosing becomes more precise; for example, if a stone has formed in an organ, you see it in color. And if, while diagnosing, you see color, you can easily determine oncological diseases because its color characteristics differ qualitatively. In the beginning you see simply the varying luminance of the zones by color, but later you'll be able to see that some cancer cells are much more active than others and that in the active zone, internally, movement is present.

In the third level another function of the Heavenly Eye appears: the ability to see what's very far away, such as in other cities and countries (so-called "distance-viewing").

The work of the Third Eye is also connected with our consciousness. Merely *thinking* about wanting to see another city can be enough to have that city immediately in front of you. If you think, "I want to see what was here ten years ago," immediately a picture will appear in front of you, an image of what was there ten years ago.

In this level of the opening of the Third Eye, you're able to see still other worlds. This happens only if you don't think about time and space. During Quiet Qigong you'll experience the sensation that the window flew open, and you're able to see a broad panorama. This is a sensation of looking out the window from a high altitude or seeing a wide-screen film. Often here are pictures of other worlds. Some people can see the worlds of Buddhism, Taoism, or other religions—worlds described in various religious books. This is why this level of development received the name Heavenly Eye.

Second Phase: Intellectual Eye

If you continue to practice, you'll be able to see your past and then your future. And later, you gaze at something, you'll be able mentally to take an interest in the past or future of the place, person, or event, raising mentally a question about it. Then the picture begins to change, and it will become possible to see what will happen in a few days, weeks, or months. This means your *Intellectual Eye* is open.

Third Phase: Eye of Wisdom

If you continue practicing, you'll be able to see the reason for what's happening and why. This phase of seeing is called *Eye of Wisdom* because you see the past and understand what provoked current circumstances and how. You'll be able to see what's connected with karma, and you'll understand how all of this can be changed. You'll also understand how today's actions affect the future . In this period you'll begin to understand and know everything, because when questions arise or there's a problem to solve, the answer comes from inside your heart—automatically and immediately.

Fourth Phase: Eye of Law

The next phase is called Eye of Dharma, which means *Eye of Law or Eye of the Essence of Nature*, because you see the reasons and principles of the Universe, the laws of its development, and the laws of the evolution of Life. You immediately see what's proper and what's not. Moreover, you begin to understand the interconnectedness of everything with everything in the Universe.

Fifth Phase: Eye of Buddha

With further development of the Third Eye, tremendous force manifests itself, and if you look at something and think it isn't right, the Third Eye can change it. This can pertain to the health of a person and to an event. You acquire very strong energy, and if you see something violating the laws of Universe, you can change its direction and change the situation.

If someone asks you a question regarding their problem, you might answer, "I don't see any problem." And this will be the truth, because at that moment the problem is disappearing. This will occur because, just by glancing at a given part at that moment, you'll be able to make correct what's incorrect, and the problem will disappear. Or you see a situation that shouldn't be—it's fraught with negative consequences. And merely by seeing it, you immediately change it automatically. In this way it's possible to avert an event or incident. When you possess the Eye of Law, you see and understand. Early in practice, for correction or treatment, you must spend time and exert yourself, and you won't always be successful. With the Eye of Buddha, you can correct everything with a mere glance.

Lou Tszin Level

There's yet another term for a level of the Third Eye—Lou Tszin—but it's not translatable, and the functions at this level are difficult to explain.[8] This eye has unlimited seeing power in time and space—it's an All-Seeing Eye. Its abilities go way beyond the bound-

---

8   Generally, the mechanisms for perceiving reality lie beyond the limits of the regular sensory organs; since the nineteenth century, scientists have been trying to explain them in. See appendix 2 for a detailed discussion.

aries of our contemporary notions about the structure of the world. Hence, it's impossible to explain them today.

Be aware of the fact that all levels of the Third Eye are connected with the deepest state of Pause: the deeper you go into the state of Pause, the more the Third Eye develops and the higher the levels it is able to reach. And, of course, the levels are connected with our level of energy.

As we already stated, all these names simply distinguish a level of development of the Third Eye that allows carrying out this or that function. But in everyday life, we usually employ the Third Eye for diagnosing—that is, the first phase of its development, Heavenly Eye.

What's Needed for Diagnosing with the Third Eye?

Diagnosing with the Third Eye is very easy if the function is working. However, to practice seeing with the Third Eye and then diagnose, certain abilities are required. Special training is a must, as it is with developing skills for diagnosing with the body.

Normally, when our eyes are closed, you don't see anything; it's dark. This is true for the majority of people. After practicing for a while, a white light emerges when your eyes are closed. This is the beginning of the working of the Third Eye. But at this beginning stage, nothing is visible. Light of a different color will then appear. But even this isn't enough. Only after you learn how to control the movement of this light— radiating it from yourself and receiving it back—will you be able to see objects illuminated by this light. Therefore the first thing you have to learn is how to see the light.

Everyone can diagnose with the Third Eye if he or she has strong energy, because this is the means by which we send energy and receive information. This information helps us to create an image in front of our mental gaze—on an internal "screen." And such an image can provide the answer to our question. For doctors or healers, this function of the Third Eye is simply a necessity.

To acquire these abilities, learn how to enter the state of Quietness very quickly—in one minute—and how not think about anything.

In this state, look at another person very intensively. Here your energy (usually this is the energy of light and fog combined, although the energy of fog is dominant) is emitted and "spots" the patient. Then you can clearly see what you're looking at, what you've tuned in to. For example, if you're looking at the brain, you see the brain with all its vessels—veins, arteries, and capillaries. You'll be able to see everything that you'll need to make a diagnosis.

With this seeing, turn your attention to the color. While you still can't see everything clearly, look at the organ as a whole—for example, that same brain—and try to compare the color in its various parts, noticing whether or not the color is the same throughout the organ. If there's some kind of problem, some disease on a physical plane, you'll be able to see that the color isn't the same: where the disease is, the color will be dark, gray, or intense.

Many people have a working Third Eye, but they don't know the nature of the illness. For example, if you see an X-ray film but haven't been taught to read it, you can't understand what's shown on it; you can't grasp the real nature of the illness. In the beginning stage of seeing, the Third Eye can't work in a discerning way: it sees everything immediately and has difficulty determining an illness. But after training, you develop the ability to disclose the problem.

You need not focus any attention on the healthy parts, in which there's no disease; you see only those places where there are problems. This happens automatically, as with an experienced doctor who immediately notices irregularity on an X-ray.

When diagnosing a healthy person with the Third Eye, there's simply nothing to see, since illnesses and problems aren't present. If an organ isn't healthy, the color of its light changes, making it immediately visible.

General Principles and Methods of Diagnosing with the Third Eye

For this, a very deep state of Quietness isn't needed; the state of calm is sufficient. Closing your eyes isn't required either. You can sit with eyes your open, because the ability and knowledge required to see depends on your energy, not on your eyes. For example, consider looking at your own heart. With your eyes open or closed, you can see an identical picture in front of you. But this picture isn't like one you'd see with regular vision—with two eyes. It's a transparent picture because the Third Eye sees a three-dimensional picture of all of space immediately and of any object. With one eye we see a two-dimensional, flat picture and with two, a three-dimensional picture; but with the Third Eye, we see a transparent, spatial one.

The information you receive at the very first moment is correct. If you begin to think, the picture begins to change, depending on your thoughts. Therefore you think about what you see—a heart or not a heart, you see it or you don't see it. Simply grasp the picture that appears at the first moment and determine what's not right in it. You'll need to learn how to maintain the consciousness of that first picture, because the picture is now connected to our mind, and your mind can affect it and change it.

Usually the Qi field of a healthy organ or its part is more transparent; an unhealthy organ is less transparent. Consequently, there's no need to look everywhere; focus on zones that are distinguished by their color and the density of it. While it's possible that you won't know what illness is there, from a medical point of view, you'll get the feeling that there's a problem in such-and-such a place.

At the beginning phase of diagnosing, you'll be able to "catch" a motionless picture. Then, after training, you'll be able to see a moving picture instead of a static film. Movement signifies that you see the workings of that organ or the part at which you're looking, that is, its functioning.

Master's Story

I'll give you an example of diagnosing. Once, in Shaolin, I was looking at this dynamic picture of a patient with infarct. I saw that the blood, which is supposed to pass through all channels, had stopped in one place; it had reached a certain segment and then returned, as if being thrown back in the opposite direction. In another segment, a similar picture emerged. The blood moved and I followed the course of its flow. But I again saw that it wouldn't pass any further. I began to look at the vessels and saw where they were blocked. I found this very interesting, because an ultrasound also showed that the blood was reaching a certain segment and then turning back. But the ultrasound didn't show the exact location of the blocked segment; you could only see how the blood flowed in the beginning in the proper direction and then returned.

In general, the Third Eye can be opened in many people. But the number of people who can properly diagnose with it is very small, because they don't know some particular characteristics of how it works. Often, simply seeing a picture isn't enough to disclose a specific problem. And the Third Eye can be compared with looking through binoculars. How far you see—the spatial magnitude—depends on your energy and on how you use it.

So, to diagnose an external object with the Third Eye, we must use it as we would binoculars. When diagnosing, if you don't place your energy in the specific place you want to see, but in an arbitrary one—that is, you miss the mark—you won't see anything. To see a specific segment, you must focus the penetration of energy in the body toward the segment in the same way that you adjust binoculars to get the sharpest focus. This is connected with the magnitude and quality of your energy.

Master's Story

First Story

About fifteen years ago, friends of mine seriously took up practice. However, their method was incorrect, and they wanted to achieve everything very quickly, especially one of them. He would often come to me and tell me what he supposedly saw, what he did with the help of his Third Eye, and so on. Since we were friends, I'd ask him how much money I had in my pocket, and he couldn't tell me. He began to get angry, while I began to laugh.

Why not use simple things, with the help of which you can immediately test whether or not your Third Eye is working? When I studied, we first trained using objects, not humans, because it's necessary to pass through this stage. Our Teacher would often squeeze something in his fist for us to see. Although it was possible to take a guess, our Teacher would immediately understand that the student wasn't turning on his or her Third Eye.

In general, it's much more difficult to "look" at an inanimate object than at a human being. That's why I say that a diagnosis of a person in no way represents a high-level of Third Eye function.

During our training with a Teacher, the following system was adhered to: we were required to guess the object in his hand three time in a row before he would move ahead with his teaching. This demand was obligatory for his personal students. Once the Third Ear and Third Eye began functioning, we had to take an examination to pass to the next level of the program and develop further.

Second Story

In 1998, I attended a conference in China on Qigong. Because I had been living more in the former Soviet Union than in China, the conference leaders decided to check how my Third Eye was working. Since I hadn't shown anything for a long time, they had doubts. The test involved the following: a die was placed in an opaque vessel, and I had to see the top of the die and the number on it. I tried several times, because it's very difficult to direct energy to a numeral on a die. The challenge was complicated by the fact that I had to see the upper surface of the cube with the numeral, and not simply the cube or another side. This is why I at first did some practice attempts—a preliminary shot—and then three times in a row I called out the numeral correctly.

With the Third Eye, you can see through objects. Therefore, to learn how to see a specific place, serious training is needed. Without it, you'll be unable to focus energy in the necessary place. And then practice is required for each task, as with the die; otherwise your glance passes through the die and you see nothing. With a "preliminary shot," determine where its side is, and then what's on it. As probability theory teaches us, you can guess twice, but three times in a row—probably not.

Third Story

At one time during my Qigong studies, we played a game that involved seeing how much money a pocket contained. In 1989, I was already working in the programming center of the Chinese Academy of Science and lived with a friend in a hotel. He possessed certain abilities, and he later went to work in the main journalism department in Beijing. But then…then we played with each other. The game was very simple: whoever correctly saw how much money was in the pocket of the other would get a watermelon. I love watermelon, so for me this was a very good stimulus. Sometimes I was amazed how this was pulled off: you look in the pocket, and you see how many paper bills and coins there are; meanwhile my friend doesn't know exactly either. Then he takes out the money, begins counting, and is amazed that the amount is exactly as stated.

When we bought the watermelons, we also used the Third Eye: we looked at the thickness of the skin and determined how ripe it was.

We also trained our Third Eye playing a Chinese card game in which several participants played for money. In one stage of the game you take cards from the deck until you get a certain combination. After taking each card and see it you try to guess what the next one is. You think then "Should I take this card or not." I have a good acquaintance who has the same ability; she's a physician. When the three of us played this game, she played in an original manner—she looked with the Third Eye. And that wasn't easy at all.

It was necessary to learn to change the focus of the mind to be able to pass through objects with a glance. When you look at the page of a book, you see what's written on it, but then you must know how to pass through it with your energy so you can see the following page, and not one further on.

Diagnosing Your Own Body

For diagnosing yourself (or a patient), employ the Moon, which we work on with the seventh preliminary exercise, or a red ball from the lower Dan Tian. For this, we make the ball pulsate so it becomes bigger, then smaller; the red light also pulsates. Then we move the ball to the organ we want to diagnose. The ball gives off red light and illuminates the organ. We can then move it to the next organ, and so on. Once the diagnosing is complete, we return the ball to the lower Dan Tian.

1. Sit comfortably and relax. Place your hands on the lower Dan Tian, focus your attention there, and feel the energy ball in the lower Dan Tian. Feel the warmth of the ball. Visualize it. It's emitting red light.
2. With your hands, move it to the middle Dan Tian. Look how it emits red light. Everywhere inside is red light. Feel the ball in your middle Dan Tian.
3. Feel how the ball becomes bigger, then smaller. It pulsates: bigger, smaller, bigger, smaller... (Repeat a few minutes.) The red light also pulsates.
4. Move the ball to the upper Dan Tian and continue to shrink and enlarge the ball: bigger, smaller, bigger, smaller... (Repeat a few minutes.) The light also pulsates.
5. Return the ball to the middle Dan Tian. Look at the ball and red light in the middle Dan Tian, pulsating a few minutes.

6. Once again move the ball down to the lower Dan Tian, and everything inside is illuminated by red light. As usual the ball and the red light pulsate a few minutes.

7. Now begin looking at your bones, starting with your spine. Smoothly move the ball upward, illuminating the spine with its light. Examine all the details of the bone fiber: nuchal bones and their form, interdisk distances, and so on. In the same way, look at your joints and the bones of your hands and legs, your ribs, and so on.

8. After you've seen this, release the ball to the lower Dan Tian.

9. Now begin looking at the internal organs, illuminated by red light:

   • Move the ball to the intestines and observe the condition inside your intestines.
   • Move it a little higher, and look at your kidneys.
   • Look at your liver and gall bladder.
   • Look at your pancreas and stomach.
   • Look at your spleen.
   • Move the ball higher toward the middle Dan Tian, and look at your heart.
   • Look at your lungs.

10. Release the ball once again downward, to your lower Dan Tian. Open your eyes.

When doing this, if you saw something like a mirror or screen in front of your eyes with pictures of organs, this says that the Third Eye has been activated and can receive information from the surrounding world. If you continue working in this way, with time you'll see with more precision.

After this, try diagnosing another person.

You can also diagnose against the background of the Moon, illuminating organs and diagnosed parts with its light. To this end you have to slowly move the Moon from the upper Dan Tian downward, examining the spine and various bones, and then the internal organs. After the diagnosing is concluded, return the Moon to the upper Dan Tian.

Diagnosing a Patient

The principles of diagnosing a patient with the Third Eye are simple: energy moves to the place to be examined and returns with information—then you're able to see that place (Picture 35).

1. Look at the person you're preparing to diagnose. It makes no difference how many people surround him or her. Look at him or her first with your eyes opened. Look at the person's eyes.
2. Close your eyes and imagine this person; try to visualize him or her as being on an internal screen in front of you.
3. After this begin examining him with the Third Eye. Observe his organs as you did with your own body.
4. At the conclusion of the diagnosis, open your eyes.

In exactly the same way, we can mentally move the Moon from our upper Dan Tian to behind the organ that's in question. Then you can examine it on your own internal screen against the background of this Moon. Examine the patient starting with the head, and then move your attention downward—spine, lungs, and so on, step by step—in order to see where there's a problem and what the nature of the problem is.

While your energy is still limited, place yourself close to the object or person being diagnosed in order to see with the Third Eye. But when the amount of energy increases, when it becomes substantial, then your body itself will do the illuminating. From then on, special

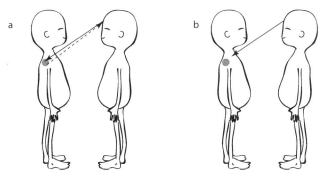

Picture 35: The Third Eye Functioning During Diagnosing
(a) Correct Focusing, (b) Wrong Focusing

illumination with the Third Eye isn't necessary. It's sufficient to focus attention on the part in question and then do the examining.

You know that around our body is a biofield covering, or aura. It surrounds the body like the atmosphere surrounds Earth. If you find yourself next to a patient at a time when you're already accumulating a lot of energy, your own energy will "cover" the patient, and you'll see only a white light and nothing more. From this it follows that *the more the energy you have—that is, the stronger it is—the further from you the object of the diagnosis can be.*

You may doubt the veracity of what you saw: Isn't this an image I created, a product of my imagination? Sometimes you may not know if you're really seeing something wrong with a patient. You may think you're just imagining it, especially if you possess information about the assumed or obvious illness.

How to Distinguish the Real Image from the Imagination

So, how can we separate the picture that we receive with the Third Eye from an image our own imagination creates? After all, we already have initial information about the patient, since he stands in front of us and we see him; we do react to his physical appearance.

No outsider will be able to determine this; you alone can make this distinction. *First,* if you create a picture, it's not stable, but moves. It isn't like a film of the workings of an organ; it begins to change randomly, in leaps. *Second,* in your heart you don't feel completely certain that what you see corresponds to reality.

If, in your thoughts, something changes, then the image also changes, because you created it. But if we really see with the Third Eye, the picture remains stable. Thus the *extent to which pictures are stable becomes the test to see if the Third Eye is working.* In addition, if you see the localization of an ailment with the Third Eye, every time when you diagnose this person you'll see the same picture—it will be stable and fixed. But if it's only your imagination at work, the picture may different.

Master's Story

I often discussed this question with my father many, many years ago. When I was still a youth and began to ponder over these questions seriously,

I told him about my doubts regarding seeing a patient's problems with the Third Eye. My father told me a very interesting thing: "This is all connected with energy and spirit. You can't think about illnesses, but you can think about normal organs."

If physicians are given the task of looking at a sick person, they can imagine and see all the organs because they know how the organs look and where they are situated. At the same time, however, they won't be able to determine the patient's problem and where it's located. But when you, in similar fashion, look at a person after appropriate practice, the opposite holds: you don't see healthy, normal organs clearly, but you do see unhealthy organs and problematic parts.

Thus, if you think something up about an illness, this almost never coincides with the real picture—unless you're a physician possessing vast knowledge and a great amount of practical experience. As a doctor you're able to establish a diagnosis and reveal the illness. There's no need to employ the Third Eye, because owing to your experience, you can propose with near certainty that a patient has, for example, a heart problem. But then, as a doctor, you must substantiate this with an examination and testing. If you simply employ your knowledge for the sake of coming up with conclusions on the basis of knowledge, you don't have enough detailed information. Questioning the patients serves this end, and then, on the basis of facts collected and examinations, you draw your conclusions.

If you work with the Third Eye, there's no need to get any information from the patient; in fact, it can interfere. If you listen to the patient's complaints about his or her condition, your knowledge begins to go to work. We can do without questioning the patient or measuring his or her pulse, and we don't need to employ diagnostic tools, but only our abilities.

But the patient almost always has the need to talk about his or her ailment, and you must allow this. This is why, for many years I questioned patients. They told me something in Russian very quickly and I understood nothing. By expressing themselves, however, they felt calmer. I recommend that my students question their patients but don't listen to their answers because of the temptation to establish a diagnosis with the help of knowledge and not the Third Eye. Sometimes establishing a diagnosis with the help of knowledge is significantly easier, but erring is also significantly easier. Diagnosing with the Third Eye is much more difficult, but making a mistake also becomes more difficult.

To employ your Third Eye intelligently, have a pure and clear mind. If you're positing a diagnosis on the basis of conjectures, you have preliminary information. If someone comes to you and says, "I don't know if I'm sick or not. Examine me," it's difficult to make a conjecture. This is good practice for the Third Eye because we don't know where to look. Disclosing the possible problem requires examining the whole person.

So, we can sum up in the following way: when diagnosing with the Third Eye, any pictures and images that you saw will be truthful if you didn't accept any additional information. But if you utilized your mind and made some conjectures in the process of such a "viewing" or "seeing," you can't come up with a correct diagnosis.

From my experience I know when I correctly determine a patient's problem and when I must still look. When diagnosing if I begin to think about the possible problem and I develop an opinion, the picture changes accordingly. For example, when I look at a head and run through possible options— the patient has high blood pressure, he has a headache, he has allowed unpleasant thoughts to take hold—the image changes. But if the Third Eye has already kicked in, the image doesn't change and no thoughts arise—I simply exam the picture and memorize it, so that I can later convey the diagnosis.

One of many such cases occurred in Moscow several years ago. A man came to me, and I saw immediately what was bothering him: a problem connected with his wife. I saw that she had appendicitis, and I said this. Time passed, and I forgot about our meeting. He came to me again with his wife and asked me to diagnose her. And I saw the same problem: appendicitis. While I remember illnesses, I usually don't remember faces; after all, I have a huge number of patients. This woman said that she had been to doctors but wasn't sure about their diagnoses because she had heard various conjectures: they said that most likely it was appendicitis, but such pains can also be caused by the pancreas or inflammation of the ovaries or the intestines. They advised her to come again for clarification of the diagnosis. But since I had seen and told her about the appendicitis, she already had faith in this diagnosis and was soon operated on successfully.

Thus I had twice established a diagnosis, and it didn't change. I talk about this case not only to emphasize the special characteristics of seeing with the Third Eye: the picture that is seen is always the same, as long as the condition of the person doing the diagnosing hasn't changed. That time this question arose: why did she want to be diagnosed twice? Sometimes a patient comes for a diagnosis, his problem is established, and he's treated. Time passes, and he again asks for an examination. With the second diagnosis, another ailment is found—so the problem changes. However, we encounter patients whose diagnosis remains the same.

This made me think about the difference between the work of the Third Eye and of our imagination. I also have moments when I'm tired and really am not up to working with the Third Eye. Lo and behold, I begin making conjectures. Then I begin to think about a likely problem: probably it's this, and then I reject it and think about some other that's also entirely probable. But since there's nothing approaching certainty here, I begin working with the Third Eye or propose to the person that he or she meet with me after I've rested. With conjecture, it's impossible to obtain certainty in a one-time diagnosis. But there can be no mistakes here. After all, we're talking about the health—and sometimes the life—of a person.

Distance Diagnostics

Sometimes diagnosing has to be carried out using photographs or other forms of information. For this you can use your body or hands. Energy travels any distance and through any barriers. For it, there are no distances. Therefore imagine the object to be diagnosed right in front of you. Then everything connected with him is also in front of you. With your hands, diagnose his organs in exactly the same way as if he were really in front of you. Employ your body when diagnosing this imagined patient.

These diagnostics are based on the programs in Stages I and II. It's done as if the person were standing in front of you. When diagnosing with your hands, you're able to sense the person's field, as if your hands are close to the person. With your eyes closed, you can imagine that the person is in front of you and employ seeing with the Third Eye in exactly the same way as if that person were in front of you in flesh and blood.

How to Develop the Third Eye

How can the Third Eye be developed? How can its possibilities be strengthened? Is there a memory of the Third Eye? These are questions that often arise in many practitioners.

It does happen that after a person dies, others thought about him and saw sickly organs. This, however, is actually a function or characteristic of our brain, and not of the Third Eye. Simply, in the training process there's a strengthening of the brain's ability to keep a picture our regular eyes see. For example, if there's a flash of light in front of your eyes, then with your eyes closed, you'll continue to see its trace. And the stronger the flash, the longer you can see it. Regular light isn't retained for a long time.

Over an extended period, a picture doesn't remain stable in our brain—it's always changing. But after training, our brain can be in a calm state for a time. Therefore if you calm your brain when accepting a picture, the picture can be retained for a lengthy period.

The workings of our brain and vision are characterized by definite traits: *with our eyes opened, the external signal (picture) is accepted, but when they're closed, it's erased.* A sequence involving acceptance of the signal and its elimination is repeated. After training in the state of calm, you can accept a picture, and it won't be erased for a long time.

You can check how well your brain enters the state of pause. Look at an object and close your eyes. If your brain can be in a state of Quietness and calm for a long time, the object will be in front of your internal gaze for a long time.

Practically all exercises of Stage III are intended to activate and open the Third Eye: Big Tree, in which we hold the ball on the level of the upper Dan Tian; acceptance of the Moon; moving the ball; and viewing the channel itself. All are methods for activating the Third Eye. In Stage I, we learned the Small Sky Circle. If you see poorly or don't see at all, you can practice all these exercises.

If you're studying Accepting the Moon from the Sea, you must practice it as much as possible, but then train the moving of this Moon in front of you: closer, further, closer, further. Then, with the goal of diagnosing, move the Moon behind the organ you want to see.

You can practice in the following way: relax, close your eyes, and lead your consciousness to the state of calm and Silence of Mind. Then, with your eyes closed, begin to look over the bone tissue of your body—all the bones, one after another. Of course, in the beginning you won't see this. Nevertheless, practice looking at bones. After some practice, you'll suddenly see white bones. A clear and precise viewing of white bone tissue indicates that the Third Eye is beginning to work. You can then begin diagnosing.

When you look at your own body with the Third Eye, you don't waste energy outside—it remains in your body. Then you have the opportunity to practice until you get a stable result. At first you'll see your own bones, until you develop a firm viewing. After a while, you'll be able to see the bone tissue of another person. With further practice, you'll be able to examine any organ, any tissue of the body, in the very same way. For example, if you need to diagnose the heart, you move the moon behind the heart of the patient, so that the heart is against the background of the Moon. Then you're able to examine the heart against the background of white light—the Moon illuminates it. In the next phase, you'll begin to see organs of other people.

If you wish to train your Third Eye to see material objects, at first simply develop its level. Here the technique is somewhat different from when a person is being diagnosed, since it's necessary to learn how to focus the Third Eye on the surface of what you wish to see. If you don't know how to do this, seeing anything is impossible.

However, don't forget that to see with the Third Eye, besides open points and channels, you have to have a sufficient amount of energy. Therefore it's necessary to practice exercises for accumulating Qi.

TREATMENT

In Stages I and II, we examined general approaches and learned some diagnostic and treatment methods. Before deciding on a course of diagnosis and treatment, there must be clarification as to the sickness at hand and at what stage it can be cured with Qigong methods, as well as in which instances it's necessary to resort to regular medicine or surgery. If, for example, disturbances occur in bone tissue or joints, Qigong alone won't help. Thus, if you have a fracture with a displaced or sprained joint, an alignment needs to be done to join bones as needed. You can employ Qigong methods for the final restoration, so that Qi is able to pass through this part. And this is very important.

Master's Story

I happened to be in Spain at a European conference on Qigong. From my perspective, this conference showed that each passing year has witnessed an ever-growing number of people from different countries taking interest in and studying Qigong methods. Since the day of the founding of the Chinese Republic in 1949, China has been a student of the West, absorbing its methods and knowledge. Those who are now around sixty remember that many Chinese young people were students in the Soviet Union. In the former Soviet Union, Europe, and America, there are now a very large number of Chinese students.

However, only a very small number of students from the West studied in China, mainly to learn Chinese. But now an ever increasing number of students from the West come to China to study Chinese medicine. And more and more students come to learn Qigong. I see that in Spain, Sweden, and Germany, Qigong is being studied very seriously, and they're publishing the results of research in this field. In Germany, Chinese medicine is very popular. In Spain, I worked in a Chinese center that was founded by Germans. There Chinese doctors do healing using massage techniques and Cheng Chui (acupuncture moxibustion) therapy. Five Chinese and two Spanish doctors worked in that center. In England and Germany, Chinese methods of treatment are very trusted.

In this conference in Spain, I met a very interesting woman from England. She had injured her leg in a car accident many years before. For over ten years, her leg was swollen and painful, and she had difficulty walking. Though she was treated by the finest specialists of England and Germany, their efforts didn't help. She also consulted a Chinese doctor specializing in bone tissue problems. And he told her that nowhere in the world would she find a doctor capable of relieving the swelling or medication to eliminate the pain caused by it.

An acquaintance of mine from the United States also participated in the conference in China. She was of Chinese descent, and had been practicing Qigong for a long time. Because she understood the capabilities of Qigong therapy, she advised the woman from England to seek treatment with me.

The results were magnificent. After seven sessions of treatment, the swelling completely disappeared. She brought her husband and their two children to me, as well as two friends. On her last day of treatment, I told her she could have her last treatment free of charge. I planned a certain procedure to fortify the effect. And, of course, I was going to discuss with her how she had to behave while her body was adjusting to a healthy state. My intention was to give her certain directives, to tell her that she had to take special care of herself at least for a month, if not two. And only when her health gained sufficient stability could she wear high heels. But that evening, after bringing her family to me, she put on high heels and went to a restaurant with friends. Finally she was able to dance like before. She was so happy!

But the next day she came to me unhappy again, because the swelling had reappeared. While it wasn't as bad as earlier, it was back. And I once again had to treat it. After five sessions, the swelling vanished. So here we have an example of improper care of one's own body.

In the course of providing treatment in the countries of Western Europe, I encountered a serious problem. Previously there had never been seminars of this type there, though they were rather popular in the lands of the former Soviet Union. However, people in Western Europe did have the financial means and were ready to spend big money, but only for treatment. With the overwhelming majority of patients who turned to me for treatment, the results were positive (only with two or three was the necessary effect not achieved, but there were particular reasons for this). However, since they didn't know what Qigong is and didn't practice, they behaved in the following way: as soon as they became better, they immediately and with a vengeance took up where they had left off, doing everything in life they wanted and were accustomed to, without allowing the healing to take root.

We in China usually adhere to the following course in treating people with this behavior. The patient is treated until he feels well (as a rule, this takes from four to ten sessions). But to make sure that this result remains firmly in place and that there's no relapse, the patient practices independently for a certain period; it's impossible to treat a person daily over a month or two. Even if this person is very seriously ill, breaks—time for changes in the body—are necessary. Therefore four to ten sessions are held and then, for the purpose of stabilizing and support-ing the result, the person is asked to work on himself or herself. Many people don't understand this, and many simply don't want to do it.

Now, it's possible to assess illnesses differently. For example, high blood pressure is a symptom—a phenomenon. But illnesses that cause this phenomenon vary from person to person. That's why, in the West, the same treatment seems to produce different results in different patients. That's because the cause and sources of an illness vary among patients; they only appear the same; they look like identical phenomena. However, if you consider them from the point of view of Qigong, it's immediately clear that the illnesses have different causes. You must keep in mind that sicknesses are connected with three systems: our physical body, our energy system, and our consciousness.

It seems to me that the time has come for the West to accept and study the systems of the East. And in thirty or forty years perhaps, these two systems, these two currents—East and West—should unite and create a single whole.

Musical Perception of the Organs During Treatment

Knowledge requires time and space. Abilities don't demand this: the capable person looks once and immediately knows what to do. That's why we must develop our abilities. Treatment is an art form, something akin to music or painting: you must possess deep sensitivity and precise vision. For example, if you pat certain parts to extract bad Qi from the body, you must perceive the pats as you would music—you need to hear the vibrations from the patting.

You already know from the Theory of the Five Processes (or Elements) that a specific element corresponds to each organ. Therefore each organ has its own emitting frequency, its own vibrations. If you possess the abilities and have a good ear, you can hear the workings of the organs very well. If you draw well, you can provide correct images of the ailments. You need only to transform your musical or painting abilities in accordance with the field of Image Medicine.

In ancient China, there were five different musical instruments that produced different sounds, and these were linked to various illnesses. The internal organs give out sounds with different frequencies, and the musical instruments were used to "tune up" the organs by synchronizing their frequencies with those emitted by the organs in their healthy state. Similarly, if our Third Eye sees five different colors that correspond to our internal organs, we can regulate these colors and carry out adjustments to treat illnesses.

Master's Story

Let's say that a person has a headache connected with high blood pressure. Well, I don't see the high blood pressure itself. But I see other symptoms that accompany it. So, for example, in the brain area there are many capillaries, and if the blood pressure is high, these capillaries try to widen because of the pressure. At that point they appear red to me, and I know that the person has high blood pressure or high intracranial pressure.

If you're inexperienced, you might think that what you're seeing is an inflammatory process, that the vessels simply became inflamed. However, if you already have experience, you know that this isn't an inflammatory process, but high blood pressure. And you convey this to the patient. The patient doesn't know what the vessels in his brain area look like. But he does know he's experiencing high blood pressure. If the vessels seem red but not widened, this means that the pressure was high, but it has fallen, probably as a result of taking medications.

The organs inside our body have different energies, which we spoke about in Stages I and II. If you try to approach this case from the point of view of what the Third Eye sees, the red vessels can be compared with infrared emanation. Though the sensation from this part is warmth, this isn't entirely correct. However, it's difficult to explain more exactly to a person who doesn't see with the Third Eye but knows how to feel energy. We say that the heart belongs to the element of fire because the sensation from it is warm.

You must know how to carry out a diagnosis before questioning a patient about his sensations, about his symptoms. This is what I normally do. First, I look at the patient and then I say what's not right with him and what he's feeling. I begin talking about his problems and the probable accompanying sensations. I then ask if he's in agreement with my diagnosis and if he wishes to add something. Usually the patient agrees with everything. After cases like this are treated, 50 percent of the ailment goes away because the patient trusts you—often after the first session. He trusts you because it wasn't he who told you about his problems, but you who told him.

We've already mentioned on several occasions that, in the majority of cases, it's necessary to employ treatment in the direction of all three aspects jointly: the physical body, the energy system, and the information system, or spirit. Such an approach is especially important during the awakening of restored capabilities of the body.

The treatment giver retained a picture in the consciousness, an image of the problem and how it must be corrected—that is, which energy and method must impact the zone of the illness. If the energy impacting is executed through the Contact method (as in Stage I) or if from this area the sickly Qi is expelled by patting, for example, (also by means of the Contact method), then all three directions - the body, the energy system, and the information system- turn out to be interconnected.

Sometimes nerve fiber is damaged in the spine. This can lead to disturbances in motor function; for example, it's difficult or even impossible for the person to walk. This problem provokes complications in the urino-genital sphere, with the bladder. A certain technology of combined treatment examined in the "Image Therapy" section permits restoration of the nerve fibers.

Master's Story

In 1991, I was conducting a seminar in the Ministry of Foreign Affairs of China. Many representatives of the embassies of various countries were there. One of the seminar participants had a problem with her leg due to an automobile accident; she dragged it, unable to lift her foot off the floor. According to the diagnosis, the nerve paths in her spine were damaged. To all intents and purposes, this was a sentence; not a single clinic was able to inspire hope in her. So, when I began to talk about a method of regenerating nerve tissue and how it was possible to restore the tissue, she stood up and said, "It's precisely with nerve tissue that I have a problem. Can you help me? Please restore for me. Regenerate it."

In those years, I would always treat several people at seminars to show the results that could be obtained by using this system. Her question, however, struck me as a challenge to my abilities. Later I learned that she had gone to the seminar after finding out about the program from some friends. She had decided to try yet another method of treatment.

I told her that I might be able to help her, but I couldn't give her a guarantee, since everything depended on the length of the damaged nerve. Regenerating a long nerve in the course of a few minutes isn't possible. And if a nerve is dying and then "dissolves," and this segment is filled by another connective tissue, then there's no room for the generation of a nerve. So I said, "Come for a diagnosis. I need to look. If I see a nerve there and its condition, I'll know if treatment is possible."

She had the results of the tests with her. Basically, the doctors' opinion was that nerve pathways in the lower part of the spine at the small of the back were damaged. So it was from there that I began to look. I shifted my glance upward and didn't see any problems until I got to the cervical section. I saw damage there, in a very small part.

Then I placed my fingers on that segment, sent energy of light there, and while continuing to observe with the Third Eye, gave an order mentally for the regeneration of the nerve. The energy of light exerts a certain influence on nerve fibers, and parts near the damaged area become very active. This leads to growth of the nerve tissue and eventually to the reconnection of the damaged area. In this woman's case, the process took about fifteen minutes. Then I removed my hand and said that the nerve tissue was totally united; there was no longer any damage, and the conductivity of the signals was restored. Then I asked her to walk around.

Very hesitatingly she made an attempt to walk normally. She was able to lift her foot off the floor; her leg could be raised. And then she began repeating, "My leg lifts up, my leg lifts up!" Then she began to run the perimeter of the hall, around the armchairs, exclaiming the whole time, "I can even run! I can even run!" And so it was, until everybody present began to laugh. For her, this was all very strange, something she couldn't believe: no pain, no suffering as a result of treatment—only my two fingers in the neck area, and after a few minutes she was already able to run.

I had a similar situation in Seattle when I treated a patient with nerve damage. Once he was cured, the man simply couldn't believe it. He exclaimed, "I can't believe this! It's impossible."

To me, this all seems very easy and normal, but for the patient, it's very difficult to believe in.

The most important thing is to determine the location of the problem and the magnitude of the disturbances in the beginning. Then it's important to use the appropriate method of treatment. Of course, there's no doing without the Third Eye, because present-day instruments still can't always find the actual location of an illness.

However, there were cases when I could do nothing, such as after a hand operation during which a large part had been removed, including channels and nerves. After some time, their place was filled with tissue of a different kind. In this instance, it was impossible to generate nerves, because a large segment was already occupied by something else.

About Spiritual Sicknesses

If the Third Eye and healing abilities are developed, it's possible to treat spiritual sicknesses. But for this, we have to know how to see them and treat them in a way that's unusual. In treating informational or spiritual illnesses, it's sometimes necessary to know how to solve a problem related to a different form of life. Spiritual treatment means that you must find a spiritual reason for the illness. If we look at a sickness of the physical body, sometimes it turns out that the reasons, the roots, of the illness are karmic. In this instance, the karma engendering the cause must be removed, and then the physical illness disappears. We can then say that the cause of the sickness was spiritual.

The technology of treatment in ZYQ is a combination of methods already known to you from Stages I and II and those you'll still have to master.

In Stage I, we learned four treatment methods, in Stage II, another two. In Stage III, we examine two methods.

Methods of Treatment

First Method: Group Treatment

This method can be used when you have not one patient but a group of people with the same illness. With it, you can treat not each person separately, but everyone together. *However, this holds true only under the condition that everyone has the same sickness.*

Seat them together as a group and mentally unite them in a single, collective image: form in your consciousness a single person, and imagine them as this person. Having done this, you'll be able to work with this image, with this collective phantom, as with one person. Of course, as with treatment in the preceding stages, it's desirable that patients in this group be in a relaxed state so that they can sit or lie comfortably and listen to the sensations in their body.

Apply any of the methods you learned in the preceding stages, doing everything that you would do with one patient, such as removing bad Qi along the channels with the hands or "plucking" bad Qi. You can also do Small Sky Circle or breathing with the body. And with any of your manipulations, such as removing bad Qi from the heart or liver of this collective image, each of the members of the group will feel that you're working specifically with him or her.

Second Method: Distance Treatment

If a person isn't with you, but in another city, use one of the eight principles of ZYQ in respect to energy: *distance doesn't exist;*

there is only the point your attention focuses on. This means that you'll use energy while excluding distance from your consideration.

For this, it's necessary to close your eyes and imagine that the person is in front of you. Then there's no difference where he actually is. For you, he's there. This method allows you to ignore the distance between you and the person.

Of relevance here is treatment by photograph, by telephone, or by using some other information about the patient independent of his location. After having looked at a photograph, it's possible to close your eyes and imagine that he or she is directly in front of you and to treat with the usual means. Here you can employ any of the six methods we examined in Stages I and II, in exactly the same way we extract bad Qi and in exactly the same way we send good.

Then distance has no significance since you're imagining that all the manipulations you're performing are with a patient in front of you. From the point of view of energy, whether the person is close to you or far away isn't essential. For spiritual treatment there are also no differences. Differences enter into the picture only in the physical part.

A you master diagnostic and treatment methods, and engage development the Third Eye and the practice of Pause, don't forget that in everything there must be balance. And *for the sake of practice and everyday affairs, don't forget about yourself.* If you feel that your health has worsened, practice familiar exercises that help you accumulate energy. Distribute it correctly and remove bad Qi from your body. Don't squander the time when you can still correct the situation. ***Don't wait until you become really bad off***, because the exercises you have to do then may be beyond your strength and abilities.

Master's Story

I once told a very good friend, "You need to take up practicing." He answered, "No, I'm not up to it now. Soon my circumstances will change. I'll have a little more time and a smaller load at work. I won't be as tired, and then I'll start practice."

Some time passed, and we met again. I repeated my earlier advice to him: "You seriously need to get involved with practice, even at the expense of other matters. You have an extreme need for this." He answered, "Only not now.

It's very cold. Soon the weather will warm up and then it'll be more enjoyable to develop myself. That's when I'll begin practicing."

In the spring, when I saw him again, he was clearly not doing well. He asked me what exercises he should be doing. I had to answer with the following: "Now you see and understand that you need to practice. But now, regretfully, you can't execute the required exercises." When an illness has become very serious and is causing great pain, it's often not possible to bring consciousness to the state of relaxation, calm, and quietness for proper practice.

If I see the future of a person and tell him what must be done, if I see what path he should take, but he doesn't listen or pay attention or do something else, I see and know how things will end for him. I know but can't change the situation because he himself does nothing. It's then that I become very bitter and deeply sad.

So, we must learn how to understand ourselves—understand what and when something needs to be done, and how to do it properly.

For this we practice Qigong.

Questions and Answers

1. In which current is it best to diagnose with the Third Eye?

You can see with the Third Eye from different viewing angles and from any current or direction, so it's of absolutely no importance in which current you look.

2. During the diagnosis, I felt very unpleasant, with palpitations and a sickly feeling. Also, there were some spots of light in front of my eyes, and they remained after the conclusion of the diagnosis. What does this mean?

Such a condition signifies that your channels aren't yet open. For this state to cease, so that all these sensations—the light spots included—end, you need to relax to the maximum, pat yourself in these zones, and then calm yourself and enter the state of Quietness. There you can execute Stage II breathing or breathing with the navel.

3. During any diagnosis, even with the hands, I expend a lot of energy and immediately feel tired and weak.

This is a psychological problem. It's not really a loss of energy—such a thing can't happen.

5. I experience painful pulsating in the Third Eye.

After a viewing, it's necessary to relax and enter the state of calm. Don't think, then everything will quiet.

6. Which exercises should be practiced for seeing, and how?

Use all the exercises we learned. At the same time, follow the basic principle of practice: "it seems it is, it seems it isn't."

7. Regarding the Third Eye, is it true that some people have an open Third Eye from birth and don't have to train it?

Yes, there are people who have always had an open Third Eye.

8. I had a viewing that seemed like streams of fog thickening, and from them emerged figures of some sort—like people and animals. They were similar to us, although stretched out. And they shined.

These are phenomena. You need only to study, and you'll see a lot more.

9. I had a sensation of movement occurring within me and, in some parts, of rotating in different directions. Can this be connected with a magnetic drill?

This doesn't depend on the condition of your environment. This is your energy beginning to move internally. When big channels begin to open internally, this movement is normal. Continue studying so that this can occur more quickly, and then the next phase will come.

10. Sometimes I experience the sensation of a strong weight during practice. When doing Yang-Qi, it becomes difficult even to stir, as with Chanzo practice.

These are normal phenomena. Great heaviness and great lightness normally accompany practice.

11. If a person is sick, don't we get his illness? After all, his sickly organ emits, and we take this in. If we must see it, doesn't that mean that we must receive it?

No. Don't think about this. You take back the light that you emit—light, and nothing more. If you don't think that you'll get something besides light, then nothing will come to you. You'll take back only your own light. I've often emphasized that the majority of you have very serious problems, about which I've spoken many times: when you begin to see some pictures or you experience phenomena of some sort, your consciousness begins to change. This is natural and normal, but many begin to think that someone is causing them, or may cause them, harm. Don't forget the goals of practice: you must be your own master—you and no one else: not the sky, land, paradise, God, or any other person. You alone must be master of your own life, actions, and behavior. Ignore everything else. Don't take it into account—as if it doesn't exist. Then, what will be, will be. It's namely your thoughts that create for you problems or good conditions.

12. I diagnosed acquaintances, and at first everything was fine. But then I suddenly stopped "seeing." Why did this happen and what can be done?

Actually, to diagnose well using the Third Eye you need to possess strong energy, since your own energy is being emitted in diagnoses. In the very beginning of such practice, you may feel very tired after a diagnosis, and sometimes a feeling of discomfort arises. But perhaps this is a situation where you see well the first time and the second time, but are unable to see anything at all the third time. This also happens, and rather often.

Seeing with the Third Eye isn't like seeing with regular eyes. If you simply look, you likely won't see anything at all with the Third Eye. To see with it, bring energy to that object or part that you wish to see. If there's little or no energy, you won't be able to see anything. Therefore, to really be able to see with the Third Eye, it's necessary to practice exercises for the accumulation of energy. And following the diagnosis, you should replace the expended energy.

13. When I relax and practice, I often see everything as if filled with fog. Why is this happening?

Fog is the first primary level of seeing Qi.

14. When diagnosing, I saw organs, not like in an atlas, but rather like on an X-ray—black and gray. What does this mean?

Usually, in the beginning, a black-and-white image appears, and then one in color.

15. I saw in a person I was diagnosing dark spots in several places. They were "filling up" the organs. This was in the area of the lungs and the liver. This person told me he had been afflicted with a serious case of pneumonia not long before, and as a result of many medications, he had begun feeling heaviness in the area of his liver. Can I conclude that these dark spots indicate unhealthy parts? Yet the pneumonia had already passed. What kind of treatment should be followed in such a case?

We stated that sickly, bad Qi in areas of stagnation has a dirt-like, gray color. So you were probably seeing correctly. If an acute inflammatory process in the lungs was suppressed with medications, the stagnant Qi in that place might still be present. In this case, Stage I methods can be employed—the extraction of bad Qi from this dark part and replacement with good Qi. As to how you saw this, it corresponds to the level at which you can see the quality of the Qi.

16. I tried diagnosing, but there were some strange sensations. At the lessons, something like lightning flashed several times in front of my eyes. And when I attempted to diagnose, I got something resembling tiny spots on the screen of an unfocused television set.

This is normal. It marks the beginning of the opening of the Third Eye. As a rule, initially flashes appear and then tiny spots—like snow. Next an image in black and white might show up, followed simply by various luminous spots and very often multicolored dots. Multicolored rays or luminous streams come next. Finally, everything halts and calms down, and you're able only sometimes at certain moments to see light of some sort. After this, usually a rather lengthy period is needed to increase your own energy, and only then will your Third Eye begin to function normally.

Since in the seminar, attendees receive a great amount of energy, the Third Eye becomes activated and begins to work. But after the seminar, when energy is no longer being given to you, you must employ your own energy for seeing. Therefore you need time to accumulate it.

17. I experience pain when I see with the Third Eye. It isn't at all like muscular pain, but dull and unpleasant.

That's to be expected when a person begins working with the Third Eye. Continue accumulating energy and to hone these abilities. Then the pain will go away.

18. In this area I feel strong pressure and vibrating, but other sensations and phenomena are absent.

This testifies to the fact that energy is already passing to the Third Eye. Then, when it becomes greater, "seeing" will reveal itself.

19. I was able to clearly see my acquaintance's spine and those places where he had disc problems, but I couldn't see his organs—only some washed-out, foggy spots. Why?

Bone tissue is usually easier to see than organs. Simply train your abilities further. This is also one of the phases of seeing. More energy, more training—and everything will manifest itself.

20. In the evening I treated my sister, who has hepatitis and lives in another city. In the morning I called her and asked how she was feeling. She said that in the evening she had the sensation of something beginning to be drawn out from her liver area, followed in ten minutes by the onset of lightness. Everything was normal in the morning, but toward evening she felt uncomfortable sensations again, albeit much weaker than earlier. I was using Stage I methods and worked with a photograph. Can the same thing be accomplished simply by imagining her image? Must the patient know about the treatment session?

If you know the person well, you can imagine him or her in front of you and work with this imaginary phantom exactly as you would with the actual person. But if it's someone you don't know, use a photograph to identify his or her image. Of course, it's best if the patient knows the time of the treatment. He or she should sit in a relaxed manner or lie down. And second, the patient should mentally "tune in" to the treatment process, which will strengthen your impact since you and the patient will be acting in a coordinated fashion. Your thoughts will flow in a synchronized way.

21. Why do pain and sickness often return with energy treatment?

You should know what happens in treating with this method. First, when you begin to administer treatment, the patient usually feels fine; the pain goes. But it returns after a while. Sometimes it can seem that patients became worse and their pain stronger. But they don't actually become worse; their nervous system becomes more sensitive and reacts with more immediacy to one and the same pain. Usually if a patient feels worse after treatment, this indicates that he or she will be able to recover more rapidly.

Second, after a one-time treatment, there might be no results whatsoever, but they appear after several days of treatment.

Or, third, with each day of treatment, the patient becomes better and better. Then there's a sudden, sharp deterioration. But after this the improvement process gains hold, resulting in total recovery.

This process plays itself out differently with different people. That's why treatment should be carried out for at least four days. If you administer treatment only once and do nothing further with the person, he or she can later become worse.

22. My blood pressure periodically rises. What should I do?

There are various reasons for a rise in blood pressure. It's best to employ the methods we learned in Stage I. But you can also pat the Yongquan point to have energy released downward.

23. When you work with patients, do you create the mental image or does the patient? Or is this done by some form of combination?

First you must get an image of the patient. From this image you'll learn what isn't working with the patient and what the problem is. Next you create an image that's able to correct the improper image. This way you correct the patient's problem with the image you form. In general, there's no reason for the patient to know what you're doing; he simply has to relax and rest.

24. Do bones and teeth change?

This practice changes bones and teeth. Those who reached one hundred still have all their teeth. With a regular person, teeth change twice: at first they simply develop, and at the age of seven or eight, they change. Then, if they fall out, it's for good and they never grow back. If, however, you practice, teeth can grow a third time. And third teeth will never fall out. This is established fact. However, why this is true, I don't know.

25. What causes premature grayness, assuming a person is without stress and healthy?

I don't know exactly. But I do know that in China, for example, a lot of salt is used in food, and therefore Chinese have black hair. If a person consumes almost no salt in youth, he or she will become gray early.

26. Is there a method to strengthen teeth for people who have either lost a part of their teeth or don't engage in Qigong?

I've met people well over one hundred who had all their teeth intact. When the teeth are already gone, it's said that one should eat ants every day. There was a monk who lived until eighty with very good, whole teeth. When writing an article about the monk, my journalist friend asked him what he ate. "Only ants—every day, very big, black ants" was the monk's answer.

27. In doing some of the exercises, we discard spent, bad Qi. Where does it go and who treats it? What happens with it?

These kinds of questions arise at all the seminars. In general, "bad Q" and "good Qi" don't exist. For example, is sunshine good or bad? Or water good or bad? Sunshine and water are natural. We say that water is bad when there's too much of it, when it causes us harm. We say that sunshine is bad if it causes us harm, if it's too strong. The same goes for energy: if it causes us harm, it's harmful. The energy that can be harmful to us at the very same time can be beneficial to another form of Life. For example, it can be beneficial to plants.

Hence, we can't speak in this way about Qi—that it's good or bad. If, for example, Qi of some sort should not be in this organ but should be somewhere else, we can say that the given Qi isn't needed, and is therefore bad for us. In other words, ***Qi in a place it's not supposed to be is bad for us.*** For example, if you're having problems with your liver, and it has Qi that you don't need, which we can label as bad for you, it's beneficial for trees. We extract this Qi from the liver area and direct it to a tree. And the tree loves the Qi of the liver; it's beneficial to the tree. As translated from the Chinese, Qi is not only energy, but also air. Therefore don't be concerned with what you discard. What you don't need is used by nature—the tree accepts Qi of the liver with pleasure, like we take in oxygen.

Chapter 4:
FUNDAMENTAL PRINCIPLES
OF ZYQ AND PRACTICE

EIGHT PRINCIPLES OF ZYQ
AND THEIR REFLECTION IN EXERCISES

In every significant system are certain internal rules and principles that must be followed if a deep understanding, successful mastery, and applicability of the system are to be attained. The principles discussed here are certain concepts employed in Qigong. Some of them are a completely integral theory, such as the first principle: the theory of Yin-Yang.

Naturally a question arises: Why do we need principles and what can we extract from them for ourselves? How can we understand them from the point of view of Qigong practice? How and to what purpose do we employ them?

The sensitive person may discover that his or her sensations correspond to theory, because the theory we're talking about was derived from the experience of practitioners over hundreds and thousands of years. *All these principles were deduced on the basis of experiments—* not of one person but of many people and many generations.

Knowledge of the theory allows for more effective practice. Many exercises can be explained from the point of view of these principles. We do them because they reflect the principles. The eight principles are a foundation for understanding the essence of the exercises, that is, why you must do a specific exercise and what its goals are.

In addition, we must realize that we're concerned here with models of reality and not with reality itself. It's to these models that all principles also pertain. And so it will be until we reach the state of Truth. Truth has no models, no principles, and no theories.

- **First Principle.** The principle of Yin-Yang as the unity, balancing, and development of opposites, as well the principle of the Five Primary Elements flowing from this.

- **Second Principle.** The uniting of the three external Yuan: of Sky, Earth, and Human.
- **Third Principle.** The joining of the three internal Yuan and the retention of "1" (the central channel).
- **Fourth Principle.** Zero begets one, or nothing produces something.
- **Fifth Principle.** There is no permanent, eternal method, and there is no permanent, eternal Teacher.
- **Sixth Principle.** Don't think about success, and don't expect a result.
- **Seventh Principle.** Time and space don't exist.
- **Eighth Principle.** You must practice the states of Relaxation, Quietness, Pause, and Stop in sequence.

Let's consider each of these principles in detail.

First Principle: Yin-Yang as the Unity, Balancing, and Development of Opposites

About the Concept of Yin-Yang

The First Principle concerns the concepts of Yin-Yang and the Five Primary Elements.

The theory of Yin-Yang is described in many books, and with particular detail in medical writings. This is the fundamental theory of Eastern philosophy. The Yin-Yang category is all-embracing. This means that you can see it in any representation of nature, in any sphere of human activity and being, as well as within the human body, itself. However, it's necessary to take into account the fact that the Yin-Yang concept is a relative category.

Remember that *the Yin-Yang concept assumes not only the material world, the world of things, but also the world of energy, the world of information.*

In general, *three aspects of this principle stand out.*

234

First Aspect

Yin and Yang are inextricably linked. For its development, each thing must possess both Yin and Yang. This means that in each Yin, Yang is very definitely present, and within Yang is Yin (Picture 36).

Or, said differently, without Yin there's no Yang, and without Yang there's no Yin. Yin and Yang don't struggle with one another, but rather rely on one another in the same way that men and women depend on each other. If Yin is absent, Yang suffers greatly. If Yin is removed, Yang ceases to exist, and vice versa.

Picture 36: Yin and Yang in a Balanced State

All of this exists in motion, in constant development. What do Yin and Yang signify if they unite? *If they come into contact with each other, movement arises.* This concept must be understood from the point of view of movement.

Second Aspect

Yin and Yang are balanced in the Universe. This rule is true not so much in each moment of time but over a certain period. For example, if we're talking about twenty-four hours, on the whole, Yin and Yang are balanced. But at a specific moment, true balance is six o'clock in the evening or morning. The same can be said about a period in the year also.

Master's Story

Of course you can read books, but it's my opinion that until you become familiarized with this theory, you can understand it through your own meditation.

In my youth, when I was still doing meditation, I was looking at where the Universe came from, and I "went" from the present to the past. At one point I saw two streams of energy rotating. It was then that I understood this as Yin and Yang energy, which holds together because of such movement. Yin and Yang must always be together; they are in a balanced state with each other. If Yin and Yang were able to separate, they would have no need to maintain mutual balancing.

But this theory says that if Yin exists, then for balancing purposes, Yang should also exist. If you have Yang, Yin is present in it. Without Yang,

Yin won't grow, won't increase; but without Yin, Yang also won't increase. In some treatment cases, it's necessary to engage in the regulating of Yin-Yang. For example, to increase Yin, you must first increase Yang. If you try increasing Yin alone, it won't happen; and Yang alone won't grow. When we talk about Qi energy, we must understand that the concept of Qi is based not on the world of substances, but on the energy world.

For a long time people have been speaking about the different approaches and philosophical bases in Western and Eastern medicine. In Western medicine, you won't find the theory of Qi, because Western medicine is based on laboratory investigation, which is the world of substances. Eastern medicine considers the energy part, not just the material. Even if we're talking about phytopreparations, the energy component is definitely taken into consideration in Eastern medicine. Everything that's connected with Yin-Yang theory, and with the theory of Sky and Earth and their fusing with the Human, is linked with the Eastern orientation—with Eastern philosophy and spiritual Masters.

Only when Yin and Yang are balanced in our body are we healthy. And if a society has the same number of men as women, usually no problems arise. Recent research shows that if a man or woman has no contact with the opposite sex, he or she will always have more illnesses than a normal person. And (I'm speaking here from personal experience), if a woman has several children, as a rule she won't get breast tumors or gynecological problems. Many single women with such problems have come to me as patients. Their troubles are caused by a Yin-Yang imbalance; internally a disorder arises in them.

Back in Stage I we mentioned that when diagnosing with the hands, an abundance of Yin is sensed as coolness and an abundance of Yang as warmth. This is the foundation for diagnosing problems in the body. If a patient has more Yang, you'll feel more warmth with your hands. If Yang is less and Yin more, you'll feel coolness. In Stage I, we trained our abilities in perception. The second preliminary exercise allows us to train our hands for determining Yin and Yang. It permits feeling the Yin of the Earth and Yang of the Cosmos.

If there's little Yin in a person, you can send him additional Yin (the sword method examined in Stage I). For this, inhale and imagine that you're receiving Yin energy from water, the Earth, or the Moon, then send it to the given patient. If Yin is in excess, add Yang by emitting Qi from the center of your palm, from the Laogun point. However, if in treating a patient and conveying energy to him or her, you don't get good results, this means that you don't know what kind of energy you need to strengthen in him or her.

The worst variation is when both Yin and Yang are in inadequate amounts. If they're also imbalanced, the patient may experience cold (he may begin shaking from chills), then heat. During diagnosis with your hands you may feel cold in some places and heat in others. The patient will also feel very, very weak.

When diagnosing, you may not fully trust your sensations because of insufficient experience or hand sensitivity. If that's the case, ask patients if they're afraid of heat or cold. If they say they're usually cold, it means that there's more Yin in their body. If they have a hard time dealing with heat, there's more Yang in their body. Patients who have problems tolerating both heat and cold lack both Yin and Yang. In this instance, you'll be able to check whether your diagnosis is correct or not.

Third Aspect

Yin and Yang change places, morphing into their opposite. We can often observe this at a specific moment during a state of imbalance, because as Yin and Yang strive to develop, they may exchange places. Each of these sides wants to develop itself. Where Yang dominates, Yin begins to "resist" this inequality and also wants to grow. Therefore everything flows and undergoes transformation.

For this reason, they are often imbalanced. The same pertains to our body with all it systems: very, very rarely is there a balanced state. During the day, when the sun is shining very brightly, there's almost no Yin. But then Yin begins to appear slowly. It emerges from "inside" Yang. As time passes, Yang begins to decrease, while Yin increases (Picture 37).

This also happens from midnight, with maximum Yin and minimum Yang, to the balanced state at 6:00 a.m., to maximum Yang

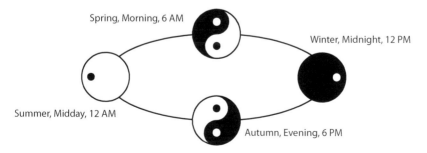

Picture 37: Transforming Yin and Yang into Each Other

and minimum Yin at12:00 p.m. This holds for the central regions, where the sun normally rises and sets. In the Cosmos, changes are constantly occurring, and they also pertains to the laws of Yin and Yang.

However, sometimes people artificially alter the relationship between Ying and Yang, as on poultry farms, for example. To maximize egg production, egg-bearing hens are raised but without roosters. As a result, chickens can't be hatched from these eggs: Yang is absent in them.

Now, how can we understand Yin-Yang in respect to ourselves?

Master's Story

Let's assume that you're a very good Qigong student, but after a year or two, you become a very poor one. Or perhaps you aren't a good student, but you become the best. Let's assume that right now your circumstances and health are either not very appropriate or simply bad. This can indicate that within you there's more bad than good. But improvement follows, and a balance is created. Now you think you're a good student, but time passes—some conditions undergo change or there's an overall change—and you quit practice.

What is the Path (Tao)? One Yin and one Yang comprise the Path. A man and a woman—this is the Path. Therefore, on meeting a bad human being, don't be overcome by fear. If you interact with that person and analyze what he or she is like, you'll see that even inside a bad person there's much that is good.

It may also happen that right now practice is very interesting for you; but later you only want to make money. But having a lot of money doesn't signify that you're a bad person. Do you think that people who ask for handouts on the street and in the subway system are able to develop our society? Of course not. Only a person with a rather high intellect, strength, and abilities can create conditions where he or she can make a sufficient amount of money. This means that you're in a state to give much more than you can utilize. In such a case, society can develop and become healthier.

Utilizing the Principles of Yin-Yang in Practicing

Let's consider how this theory helps practicing. You can choose a time for practice based on your goals at a certain time. Generally, it's best to study during the hours when Yin transforms into Yang and then reverts back, that is, between 11:00 p.m. and 1:00 a.m. You see, the Yin-Yang correlations inform us of the form and level of energy in the Cosmos at a specific time.

If everything is balanced and occupies the same level, then receiving distinct sensations is difficult. But when Yin approaches its minimum and Yang begins to grow, this is the best time for practitioners to accumulate more Yang. At this time everyone relaxes and calms down. Therefore you can consider this interval to be *the time of the state of Relaxation and Quietness.* For practicing higher levels—in contrast to the beginners—people practice at this same time also, but more often do nighttime practice.

However, if you're having health problems, it's better to practice in the morning, when Yin and Yang are relatively balanced. Then it's easier to balance Yin and Yang in your body.

In practicing nearly all of the ZYQ exercises, you can find manifestations of the principles of Yin-Yang balancing. If we do a given exercise eight times, in the beginning we do them eight times in one direction and eight times in another. This pertains to almost all of the exercises. A similar approach is found in Tai Chi: if you turn to one side, you must turn in exactly the same way to the other side as well.

Many exercises, such as the preliminary exercises, Big Tree, and Small Sky Circle, are directed at regulating the Yin-Yang balance; everything must be balanced qualitatively and quantitatively.

About the Principle of the Five Primary Elements

The principle of the Five Primary Elements is derived from the Yin-Yang principle. The Five Primary Elements are **Water, Wood, Fire, Earth,** and **Metal.** Here again, it's very difficult to understand things if we think of these elements as existing only in the material world. Simply we again employ phenomena or those signs, those symbols that originated in practice. If you enter the state of deep calm and Quietness, you'll see with the Third Eye that all the energy in the Universe can be divided into these five elements. And these five can control one another and support one another; they can produce one another. This principle tells us how balance is maintained throughout the entire Universe.

From my personal point of view, the principle of these five elements holds for our material world as well as for the world of energies and the spiritual world. But this isn't the only route that supports balance in the Universe.

In Stage II, we examined the principle of the five elements in detail when speaking about ***Wu-Xing theory***. We made clear that in this theory Metal doesn't signify the metal that we can touch, such as iron, copper, gold, and aluminum. We are therefore able to understand how metal can give birth to Water. If you look at the energy of Metal, you can see that it can change and be transformed into the energy of Water.

If we say that aluminum belongs to the element Metal, then this is correct. But metal isn't just aluminum; aluminum is only one of the metals. And Water is not the water we drink or that's found in the sea. But this water falls under the category of Water.

Everything we've just stated pertains to abstraction and not to the concrete "reality" we usually imply (Picture 38).

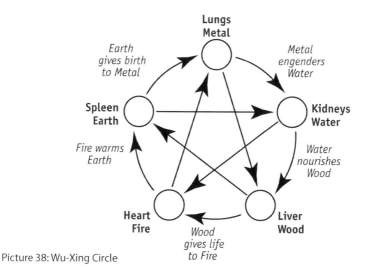

Picture 38: Wu-Xing Circle

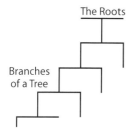

Picture 39: Inverted Tree

In this instance we go from the general to the constituent parts. Try to understand the conceptual level of what we're speaking about. The internal structure can be represented by an upside-down tree (Picture 39). And the opposite is possible: go from the component parts to that which unites these parts—to the "root." This resembles a tree that's turned inside out.

Master's Story

In ZYQ, the theory of the Five Primary Elements is used mainly to regulate the functions of the organs for the sake of good health. We also employ it to explain external manifestations.

So, for example, if there's too much water and flooding this year, there's an excess on Earth of the energy of Water. What will happen in the following stage? According to Wu-Xing theory, Water will impact and control another element—Fire. Then people have to think seriously about the rise of heart problems: if there's too much water, it lowers the Fire in people—the energy of the heart. People's minds won't function very well either. So there will be many patients with cardiovascular illnesses and problems with brain vessels.

What else can occur when there's a surplus of Water? Around ten years ago in China, there were very powerful floods. During the year after, many people came down with liver ailments. If abrupt changes in the environment take place in the correlation between the five elements, this exercises a strong influence on our internal five elements—the elements within our body that characterize our internal organs.

But if there's much less Water, what happens? About twenty years ago in northern China, powerful fires broke out. If there's an excess of Fire, nature automatically regulates this state of imbalance by seeking to return it to a balanced state. The country was simply unable to extinguish this fire, lacking the necessary technical means. After some time passed, stormy winds and very heavy downpours commenced. These put an end to the fires.

Second Principle:
Unity of the Three External Yuan: Sky, Earth, and Human

We employ this principle in all stages in all Qigong exercises. In any Taoist or medical book translated from Chinese, you'll see this reference. It speaks about the general philosophical approach and understanding of the ties of a human being with his or her environment. This means that this principle is applied everywhere.

In ZYQ, a human is looked upon as a small Universe, and the surrounding world as the great Universe. So these two Universes—small and great—should be joined together: humans and the their environment. If you're able to unite yourself with the environment

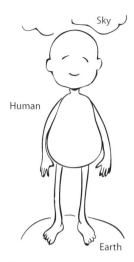

Picture 40: Unity of Human, Sky, and Earth

through certain methods—that is, unite your body with the Universe—you can understand through your body, through your sensations, everything that's happening in the Universe.

We must act in accordance with the position we occupy in the Universe. We've examined the model of the structure of the universe in ZYQ. We stated that there are twenty-seven levels of worlds, with the world in which we live occupying nineteenth place. This means that eight levels of worlds are higher than us and eighteen lower. If you wish to understand the essence of the Universe, then you must not separate yourself from the other worlds. We must know how to unite ourselves with both the upper and the lower worlds (Picture 40).

In Chinese, *tian* means Sky, but not that sky that we can see above us. Rather, this is the higher world; it's not the sky of the physical world but of the spiritual world—the world above us. *Diyu* means the worlds below us. A literal translation of this term is *Earth*, but this isn't the land on which we move; it isn't even our planet Earth. Rather, it's everything that's "under our feet"—the lower worlds.

If we understand the term *earth* as the land on which we move, or our planet Earth, and by the term *sky* we mean the sky that's above us, this is incorrect. In certain cases, this is true, but only because the land below our feet is a component of the general concept Earth. And the sky we see above us is a part of the general concept Sky.

We can use as an example related to how we use the pronouns *she* and *he*. If we're talking about a girl whose name is Mary, this is *she*. But if we say *she*, this doesn't necessarily mean "the girl Mary." Any girl with any name is *she*; and a woman is also *she*. If you say "Miss" or "Mrs.," we know that these belong to the category of *she*, and this is correct.

Tian and *diyu* are understandable to the Chinese, but can't be translated into other languages. They can be translated using a whole bunch of synonyms, and additional explanation can be offered, but there still won't be an exact equivalent to the meaning of these concepts in Chinese.

Sometimes Yin-Yang theory is used to explain *tian* and *diyu*. We can divide the entire Cosmos into two parts: Yin and Yang. *Tian* signifies Yang while *diyu* means Yin. So, it becomes clear that **tian** signifies sky—that which is higher than us, all worlds—whereas **diyu** means not only land but also everything existing below it, including all the lower worlds.

The human being is found between them, in the middle, and must join them together. Sometimes a question arises: "Why is this necessary? Why do we need to unite Human, Sky, and Earth in one system?" Because after we unite these concepts in us, we can perceive and realize what the Universe is.

While in deep meditation, Lao-tzo saw the Universe and understood that before its existence was something no word had yet described, so he named it Tao. But then it split up into two parts, Yin and Yang emerged, and they rotate like two streams of energy. The entire Universe consists of Yin and Yang. With their further development, they engendered three parts: Earth, Human, and Sky. That's why, to understand the Universe, it's necessary to practice all these aspects jointly.

For practice, we need Yin energy. We must understand ourselves; we must understand Earth (Yin), because all Yin energy comes from Earth. We also need Yang energy, and we're able to get all Yang energy from Sky.

Master's Story

Why do we say that we get Yin energy from Earth? Because nearly 70 percent of it is covered with water. In the Cosmos, we know that there's matter—stars, planets—and a material world. Therefore we need to understand the meaning of the concepts Earth and Sky from the point of view of energy. When we're able to feel the different types and structures of energy inside of our bodies, we're able to understand all of this.

When you come to the point that all of these three factors fuse in you, certain phenomena will begin to transpire. It's then that you'll learn why you're the way you are, why the Cosmos is as it is. We now have equipment that can investigate the brain: it provides "photographs" of your brain. Yet we have no equipment for testing the process by which Earth and Sky fuse in a human.

When uniting Sky, Earth, and Human, you'll be able to see and feel that, in comparison to Cosmos, Sky isn't as big as it seems to us and Earth isn't as small—they are approximately equal. A true picture when it reveals that Earth and Sky—Yin and Yang—are equal.

Why do we need to practice Big Tree? Because a tree joins with Sky and Earth. In the process of practicing Big Tree, we unite Sky, Earth, and Human. This takes place during Chanzo practice, when we develop the central channel and join them.

When practicing Big Tree, the moment will come when you suddenly see what Sky represents and what Earth represents. At that moment, a clear understanding will emerge in you; you will know why the Universe was divided into twenty seven worlds; what Sky is and why you unite Sky and Earth in yourself; and what you are and why you're in the middle. Before this image takes shape in you, you can imagine what Earth is, but this won't be sufficient, since you have no idea how to imagine Sky. But when this image appears to you, you'll see that Sky is a ball and Earth a ball, and you—Human—are in the middle. The ball over us was called Sky by the ancient Masters, and they called the ball under our feet Earth.

When carrying out practice, you'll get a certain result that can be understood at the moment you achieve it.

Third Principle:
Uniting of the Three Internal Yuan; Holding "1."

In the process of practicing, we must unite the three internal Yuan: Yuan-Jing, Yuan-Qi, and Yuan-Shen. This means uniting the three structures of energy, fusing the three Dan Tian into one. Doing this, in the process of meditation, we look at the central channel Zhong-Mai and retain a luminous, vertical tube resembling the figure 1 in front of our inner glance.

What does this unit signify? It means that we then acquire another quality and other functions. In this instance, the division into Yin and Yang disappears—they no longer exist; Sky, Earth, and Human are absent. This is why we join all three Dan Tian and do work, as if we're creating the central channel Zhong-Mai anew. Only after the realization of this principle can the soul go out beyond the limits of the body, and the practitioner begins his or her spiritual development.

The unifying of the three internal Yuan is described in more detail in Stage I and in the Chanzo exercise.

The principles described above are traditional. They're employed in Qigong and Chinese medicine and philosophy. But now let's examine principles that belong to the ZYQ system.

Fourth Principle:
Zero Begets One; Nothing Produces Something

Something is formed out of nothing: initial untruths and illusions lead to reality—with proper practicing.

How should we understand this principle? How are we to comprehend that we can get truth from untruth, reality from emptiness? In the very beginning of Big Tree practice, you don't represent a tree, but when you practice, you begin to feel like one. Here we're talking about your mind. If at the very outset of practice, you're asked to feel and see a ball in the lower Dan Tian, you won't see and not feel anything, because it's not there; in the beginning of practice, there's really no ball there. But then, gradually, you begin to feel warmth and heat; you begin to feel the ball and even see it.

This means that it's incorrect to speak about this ball from the very beginning; this isn't the truth. But after a while, it becomes the truth: the ball appears with the unfolding of practice. In Chinese, they say that from nothing something can emerge. Therefore, to get truth from untruth, we practice.

If you know about these principles, you won't analyze what the Teacher suggests that you practice or imagine and visualize. You'll understand that one day, as a result of practice; suddenly from nothing you'll feel or see that which had not existed.

You can see this principle in many exercises, beginning with Stage I. These include the energy ball in the three Dan Tian, luminous channel Zhong- Mai, the exercise with the Moon, and flight to higher worlds with the eighth preliminary exercise. Of course, there's no Moon in a lake; in reality, it's not the moon but its reflection; during the exercise we imagine this Moon. Of course we can't take it into our body—this is an untruth, a lie. Why do we do this exercise? After a while, as a result of studying, the Moon appears within: a lie gave birth to a truth.

The eighth preliminary exercise also looks absurd from the very beginning: after all, it's unreal to turn up in another world, in another space. Why do we practice this way? Because *one of the most important principles is manifested: zero can engender everything.*

This is the principle of the Cosmos: in the beginning, there was nothing; then it appeared. From a regular, normal point of view, this is illogical. This is very difficult to understand because everything is different with us in regular life. If there is 1 and we add another 1, we get 2. Or consider another variant: we have some kind of substance (first), we add to it another substance (second), and as a result of a chemical reaction a third kind of substance (third) is formed.

Master's Story

Let's try to examine this principle from within, to understand its deep, inner essence. What does this mean: "From nothing to get something"? At first glance, this principle is very simple, but it contains very deep meaning.

A being, the living, Life came from nothing, from emptiness. This is similar to the Tao Te Jing theory described by Lao-tzu. We mentioned this when considering the second principle. Lao-tzu would say, "How did the Universe happen? In the beginning, there was nothing, but before this, something existed. And since we don't know what to call it, let's name it Tao."

This is easier to understand if we refer to our very own practice. At first there's no ball in the lower Dan Tian, and then it makes its appearance; at first we don't have the energy needed for treatment, but as a result of practice, it arises in us; and seeing with the Third Eye is absent in us, but after practice it emerges. So, in the beginning, "there is not," but later "there is."

Where did the Universe come from? And what was there before it emerged? Logically a question arises: "And what was before this? Nothing?"

The opinion that the Universe is expanding is held in most scientific circles. It's possible that the average person looks on this idea as valid, but is it? From my point of view, this is an incorrect description. What is the Universe?

The Universe is that which has no age; it's boundless. But if it has no borders, how can you say that it's increasing in size? To understand or characterize the Universe, we can't rely on terms used in everyday life; we can't talk about bigger or smaller, higher or lower. For example, regarding defining small, *what is the very smallest particle?*

In X-ray radiation, for example, the particles are very small. But if we say that these are the smallest, this means that they do have size. Correct? If they have size, then what's inside them? If they're the smallest particles, can we break them down further into other particles?"

Many things are very difficult to understand, because we can't understand the Universe in categories on which we rely and to which we're accustomed. Thus Newtonian theory isn't applicable to big space—in it we must employ Einstein's theory of relativity. We can employ it where the speed of motion is close to the speed of light. And what if that speed is a lot greater than the speed of light? There are no tested theories for such cases.

Our thoughts travel much quicker than light. Recently scientists discovered beams and particles whose speeds surpass that of light. If you consider this question at night, when it's dark and very quiet, you may experience many interesting sensations.

There was a time when I very deeply and for a long time practiced the state of Quietness; at that time I still didn't know what the Universe was. After the state of Quietness, I entered the state of Pause. And then I saw the Universe as two opposing streams of energy that moved like the Yin-Yang ball. Then I saw that these two streams disappeared and **Emptiness**, **Nothing** *appeared. So, a theory revealed itself:* **Nothing gives birth to everything.** *And I understood that from everything there again takes shape Nothing, Emptiness. Everything comes to Emptiness.* **If you have everything, don't delight in it, and if you have nothing, don't be sad.** *Nobody knows when the situation will change, but it will.*

Fifth Principle:
There Is No Permanent Eternal Method;
There Is No Permanent, Eternal Teacher

E everything surrounding us can be our teacher. If someone is capable of teaching us at a given moment, it means that this person is our teacher. We can put it this way: *everything is changing; there is nothing unchanging.* teachers change, methods change, and it's unreasonable and wrong to cling to one thing all the time, since each human is constantly changing and his or her level of practice rises. Hence teachers and methods change. This becomes clearer after Stage IV.

There Is No Permanent Method

A method indicates what you must do, what practice you must engage in. We should emphasize that *what* you have to study is always changing. This means that there aren't permanent exercises; there is no permanent sequence of exercises or time allotted for their execution. There's no specific system you can select that will give you the opportunity to constantly develop and improve yourself.

How you practice depends on your level, at what step you find yourself, the conditions of practice, your state of health, and so on.

Master's Story

*Do you know how many currents and methods of Qigong practice there are in general in China? Many thousands. And do you know how many meditation methods are described in Buddhist books and how many methods Shakyamuni spoke about? There are as **many as the existing forms of life.** And we don't even know how many forms of life exist.*

Even for one person, at various times and with his or her varying states, various methods are employed. That's why we can't say that a given method is the very best and that there's no need to study others. If you meet a pharmaceutical salesman who says his medication is the best and suitable for all ailments, you won't take him seriously and likely won't trust him. If a Qigong Master claims that only his school is good and correct and that all others are bad then, from my point of view, he's crazy or dishonorable.

During practice, you're able to receive one and the same state under varying conditions. For example, the first time you get the state of Pause when practicing breathing with your body; the second time, you don't. Perhaps you achieve the state of Pause the second time, when you practice Yang-Qi. The third time you climb up mountains, and there you feel deep fatigue, sit down to rest, and at that moment enter the state of Pause. It depends on when and how you're able to relax completely.

Those things that are eternal in this world and really unchanging are changes themselves. They're unchanging because everything changes. And since you also are constantly changing, you can't employ unchanging methods for yourself.

*To determine the methods that are suitable for our practice— that is, which are more effective—you must **rid yourself of your mind and consciousness.** Forget all your methods and enter the state of no-consciousness to be able to practice automatically and naturally. Such opportunities are made available to us in the fourth stage, which provides not one method, but a guide or conductor. For example, you practiced a certain exercise, but the next day decided to repeat it. But when you begin to practice, you practice something completely different.*

There Is No Permanent Teacher

Let's assume that today you have a certain teacher. But as time passes, your level changes, and your teacher changes. Or your teacher's mission reaches completion or is altered, and then he or she is a different teacher to you.

Moreover, the concept of the Teacher in ZYQ doesn't signify a single person. There are many teachers: Teacher is everything that surrounds us. Any form of life, any form of spiritual being, and everything in Nature can be our Teacher—if this can help us, if we can learn something from it. We can be instructed by trees, chickens, dogs—any beasts or birds—mountains, a stone, situations, and so on.

Master's Story

If you're able to receive knowledge or experience from anything, all of this can be your teachers. And you can be a teacher for someone. You can teach a tree, a dog, a mountain. Try it. When your communication system develops to a sufficient degree, you'll discover that you're able to interact with a mountain or even other planets.

There are many kinds of students, and different students need different teachers. I'm convinced that if a person is accustomed to working well with children, for example, he or she will be able to teach kids better than I.

Any form of Life can be a teacher for us, so there's something like a "duty attendant" for us. For example, today a particular Teacher is "on duty," and tomorrow another. The one who's on duty may not know some of the exercises. This is understandable, because exercises are geared for the training needs of a specific person. And as we've already stated, methods number in the thousands. While there are general approaches, the variety is great.

When I was in India, I heard an interesting tale. Three gods are worshipped there—Brahma, Vishnu, and Shiva—and each and every person pray-

ing directs his or her prayers to all three of them. So it happened that a certain individual who was experiencing a problem began seeking help from these three gods. The first god said, "I am very busy and don't have time to help you, so ask the next one." The second answered, "Right now I'm with my wife, so ask the third god." The third one said, "I'm very busy. Ask one of the others." What does this mean? When you're seeking help, turn to one, and only one, source of support rather than too many. If you turn to several, they will say, "Well, this can be done by one of the others - he'll help you. Why should I also help?"

In ZYQ, Teachers aren't required to represent ZYQ alone. Any spiritual being who is able to render you help and support at a certain stage can become your Teacher.   Why is this? Because ZYQ is an open system or direction that aims at helping people. If you need help, you can turn to the person who is "on duty" right then and able to take care of you.

Sixth Principle: Don't Think About Success; Don't Expect a Result

This principle is very, very important. At first, its phrasing confuses and disappoints us, since it contradicts our usual thinking and experience. After all, when we don't know if we'll achieve success in an undertaking, we don't even begin it. We begin doing things only when we hope to succeed, or at least if we think we're likely to be successful.

But in Qigong practice, things are different because the principle beseeches us *to only practice and never think about the result.* You must, of course, practice and use your head. You must think about what you have to do and how to do it. But you have absolutely no idea when you'll achieve a given result, when it's you who will taste success.

If, during practice, you think that you should receive abilities of some kind—for example, the ability to open the Third Eye or knowledge of how to receive something through teleportation—it won't happen. If you simply practice without displaying any desire to achieve something, you'll progress along the normal road of the development of your abilities and be able to achieve a goal. But if you do this in accordance with your own personal notions of things, you'll go off course and open the way to problems. Why?

Qigong is a very special field. Everything in it is at variance with Western thinking. For example, if you're engaged in your usual work and always thinking about the result you expect; if you're constantly striving for it, focusing your attention on it, you can succeed in your work. But with Qigong, it's necessary that the internal energy of the practitioner moves in harmony with the energy of the Cosmos, in the same direction. If you're thinking about results, you introduce disorder into the movement of the energy—its direction changes and you won't be able to attain a high level.

By thinking about results and counting on them, you put a brake on your own development.

Master's Story

Sometimes people think they're ready to advance their abilities and want to stimulate them sooner. They think they occupy a high level, but this is only in their imagination. Sometimes **what you think about yourself isn't the truth***. This becomes clear if you continue studying.*

During Qigong studies, apply yourself and don't think about results, because whether or not your lessons are successful is something that you yourself often cannot determine.

Several years ago, when I was in Tyumen, Russia, one of the seminar attendees questioned me regarding whether I could tell him whether or not he would be successful. He said that if he didn't receive a positive answer, he wouldn't practice, because the lessons took up a lot of time, and he didn't want to waste time. After all, if you study in a university, do you know for sure ahead of time that you'd achieve success after obtaining knowledge in your major? Usually people have intuition about their own future. Perhaps you don't trust your intuition one hundred percent, but you experience a sensation, a feeling that you will achieve success. You often encounter situations in which you never imagined that suddenly and unexpectedly success would come your way. That's why I can't predict your possibilities in Qigong field.

According to the book **I Ching***, the future can be predicted. But who really knows their future? And who can guarantee that your future will not change or that your fate will not change? I can say only this: I guarantee that you'll live less than 150 years.*

Fate directs your life journey in a certain direction and maintains it at a certain level. But if certain events occur, this could impact your fate. Then your life changes and may diverge from its earlier course. As a consequence, much can happen in a way that would have been different had there not been the interference of these events.

251

This is why you need to practice without giving thought to success and without caring about the result. If you think about the result all the time, about what you should receive, you'll never be able to enter the state of deep Quietness and Pause, because your brain will be working all the time. Your brain will be occupied with finding the way to realize your desire, with an idee fixe.

Based on my personal experience, I can say that if you really wish to achieve success, don't think about—don't plan—your future. Again this contradicts our habit of thinking. We're used to planning our life and calculating what we'll be doing in five years. In your Qigong practice, no plans whatsoever should be constructed. If you're thinking that this year you're going to Shaolin to open a "seeing" with the Third Eye, I'm absolutely certain that you won't receive this. In spiritual development, and particularly in Qigong, a result comes out of nonconsciousness—without preparations, without plans and in a nonconscious form. This isn't a state of unconsciousness, but a state of nonconsciousness. This means that to receive an unexpected result, you need to employ nonconsciousness; you need to be in a state of nonconsciousness.

My Teachers used to instruct me by taking this into account. When I was a child, my Teacher usually told me to do something, but would often not specify what I should do. So when I began to practice, I experienced interesting phenomena. I told him about them, and he uttered only one word: "Correct." Sometimes he would add "Continue," and I would go deeper into the practice. When I did this, I had no idea what I would be studying later and how I would employ it. The thought never even entered my mind that later I would be involved in instructing others, that I would use this knowledge to make a living and get set up in life. My motivation was only a sincere and deep interest. I had no interest in a future application of my practice; it was the process itself that interested me. While still a school kid, I felt a pull toward research, and I had a strong desire to become a scientist, with Qigong serving me as a hobby. But Qigong attracted me powerfully.

When I was eleven or twelve and still in middle school, I would jump on my bicycle after school and race to another village that was about six miles from my home to visit my Teacher, an old nun.

This is often the way it is when you're strongly interested in something. For example, you study something only because it's interesting to you, you don't even think about how it might benefit you in the future. Then suddenly it turns out to be useful to you in places and at times that you would never have expected. Only after I completed college and graduate school with a major in computer technology did I realize that my knowledge in spiritual development, medicine, and Qigong was much more useful than all my knowledge in computer technology. Interestingly, at that time, which was many years ago, I thought every physician knew how to diagnose with the Third Eye.

Seventh Principle:
There's No Time; There's No Space

We utilize this approach at all stages, but at first it leads us to a dead end. You see, we live in a three-dimensional space, in a space of three measurements, where speed is limited by the speed of light. This means that the speed of light is the highest of existing and possible speeds in our world. We're used to this because we live in this world. We don't understand what lies beyond the boundaries of our three-dimensional space. To understand the world beyond these limits, we must jump over these borders, these limitations of speed and time. But this is achievable only by our soul, our consciousness. That's why we must train our soul: so it can surmount this world's limitations, exit it, and comprehend another world and its laws. If we were limited by time or space, we wouldn't be able then to depart for other dimensions and travel wherever we desire.

But to receive such abilities, you must adhere to certain rules. When you're getting ready to practice, don't think, for example, that the room is too small and uncomfortable for practice, so find a more comfortable and convenient place. Don't think of your practice as not going well, telling yourself that later it'll get better. ***Don't use the temporal categories "right now and later"; don't use the spatial categories "small and big, external and internal." During each lesson, get into "here" and "right now."***

Very often we employ this principle in relation to our mind and consciousness. So during meditation, don't think about how long you want to practice it.

When doing Big Tree, you sometimes become as large as the Universe; you unite with Nature—and for you both space and time are absent. Don't limit yourself in your thoughts with space and time; don't take time into consideration, don't take space into consideration.

If you accept the energy of Sun or Moon and practice the fifth preliminary exercise, with your mind, you'll be extending your hands into infinity and taking in the needed Qi. But don't think, for example, "The Sun is far away, so how will I be able to get energy from it?" If you imagine there's no space and the Sun is right next to you—or that your arms extend the needed distance—this isn't difficult for you.

Using Stage I treatment methods, we draw out sickly Qi from the patient and direct it to the soil. We imagine that from the sickly part this Qi immediately turns up deep in the earth. With this we can examine the thesis that the movement of Qi depends only on the point where our attention is focused and that it doesn't traverse the usual path between two points but goes with a leap and turns up in the earth.

When diagnosing with a photograph, think that there's no distance, no space. If you glance at the photograph and think that the person is very far away, how will you be able to diagnose him or her? But if you simply imagine that it's not a photograph in front of you but a real person, you can diagnose him as if he's real and standing in front of you.

What's more, in the Qigong system there's no time because *we can know the past and the future.*

For example, several years ago, somebody died. According to some theories, this person's energy went far away, as if the space began to expand. But when you're in a state of Qigong, your speed of motion is much greater than the speed of this soul. And you can receive information very quickly—"catching" it. At the same time, you'll experience certain sensations: you'll understand where the information is coming from—from the present, past, or future.

Therefore no matter where you practice, if you employ categories of time, place, and duration of practice, you'll never be able to transcend the boundaries of this world, because in other worlds time is completely different, as are categories of distance.

If you think in our categories, you'll never go beyond the boundaries of our world.

Master's Story

We can also talk about the theory of multidimensional space. In general, we speak about three-dimensional space in our reality. If we add time, we get four-dimensional space. But space can be five-dimensional, six-dimensional, and so on.

Time can flow not only in the direction of increase, but also in the opposite—that is, the axis of time can have both positive and negative values (Picture 41). When you're able to reject the limits of time, your level will rise significantly.

Picture 41: The Axis of Time

*We need not move **in** time; we need to move **outside of** time.*

In Stage IV, we study the use of methods that allow us to receive information from another time and space. But for this, certain laws must be mastered.

Once, in Yekaterinburg, Russia, the soul of one of my students exited and went for a stroll. It flew to the monastery in Shaolin, where it turned up when Damo was still living there. It was halted by the gatekeeper, who asked, "Who gave you permission to get near this place? Where's your entry pass?" I have students or apprentices so that they can receive this entry pass to certain places of other worlds. There's a special method by which a Teacher can introduce his students there. The spirit can do whatever it thinks about doing and immediately go wherever it wishes, but the body can't achieve such desires. That's why that world is better than ours: there all your desires are realizable.

Eighth Principle:
Practicing the States in Sequence:
Relaxation, Quietness, Pause, Stop

In ZYQ we practice and master states sequentially. As a consequence, we acquire *wisdom.*

Such sequential practice contributes to the development of our soul and spirit. Systems and methods that lack sequential development of these states are directed at solving only partial, concrete tasks and not general ones. For this reason, their employment doesn't assume the development of the spirit and may give only a partial effect in a certain current, for example, in health restoration or psychology.

In Stage I, it's sufficient to realize only the state of Relaxation, and in Stage II, to enter the state of deep calm and Silence of Mind. This state allows you to heighten your sensitivity. In it you can also enter into contact with the environment. Learn how to relax very quickly and enter the state of Quietness.

In Stage III, you can practice the state of Pause, and then of Stop. During your stay in the state of Pause, you'll be able to interact easily with the entire surrounding environment—to receive information from the external world and know who has what desire. During Pause, your soul may depart, and during Stop it may study in the highest worlds.

Later you'll be able to return to a natural state, to nature, if you will, and your behavior and movements—everything that you'll do—will be natural.

Master's Story

It's very easy to pronounce the word relaxation, *but achieving the state of relaxation is very difficult, especially if we encounter situations we don't like. If we consider a situation to be unfair, it's difficult for us to contain our emotions and maintain a state of relaxation. But if we analyze the surrounding world, it becomes evident that total fairness is impossible. For example, during a powerful storm, the branches of an enormous tree break off. Or you're walking along, and you trip, fall, and bruise your knees. You won't fault other people for this; you can complain about the weather and that the ground is slippery and the road uneven, but you won't complain about another person. What can a tree do? Can it be upset with the fact that it was so windy that its branches didn't hold out?*

It's difficult to see justice over a short period. But if we examine justice over a century, the situation begins to look different. For example, today you lost one hundred dollars, but in a year you acquired one hundred dollars; the balance is restored.

On this Earth, every form of life has to get along well with the environment; every form has a self-preservation instinct; every form suffers; and every form experiences happiness. When we look at other people, we usually notice only what they have and the reasons for their happiness. But regarding ourselves, we turn our attention to what we don't like and what causes our suffering. We're bewildered, and we complain about problems.

What do we understand by the term wisdom*? It's manifested when we look at others and see their problems and their suffering, but when glancing at ourselves, we realize what we have and we are happy. With wisdom, you feel dissatisfaction and disappointment less often and experience happiness more often. This world is created in such a way that no one can be permanently happy. Not* *a single family can be rich permanently. No big trees can always be the biggest.* **Changes are eternal.** *Therefore if you're dissatisfied with your conditions, with your home, or with your financial worth, don't worry; continue living, and when conditions are different, everything will change with you also.*

THE CONNECTION BETWEEN ZYQ PRINCIPLES AND OUR PHILOSOPHY

So, we've reviewed the system's eight principles, which help us to understand the approaches and principles of practice. However, when we consider the big picture, they go far beyond the limits of ZYQ practice, since they're universal. These principles give shape to our thoughts. They point the way to the correct method of "thinking." If you base your life on these eight principles, you can get many different ideas and use many methods.

All our exercises are movements based on these eight principles. We apply the principles when we execute exercises. Or better yet, the exercises are an outgrowth of these principles. Later you'll be able to see these eight principles in all exercises. (Other systems have some different principles.)

It may seem that these eight principles are easy to understand, but after five years, you'll have a new understanding of these principles. And with the passage of ten more years, you'll see that once again a new meaning, a new understanding, has crystallized. That's because these principles are common to and suitable for the Cosmos in its entirety. Right now you may understand them in a small part, in a limited number, but as your understanding of yourself, Universe, and Life as a whole expands, you'll perceive them in their totality.

If you understand the eight principles, this is equal to understanding the brain or the very foundation, essence, or base of the ZYQ system. And you can try to use these eight principles in your work and life in general.

Accompanying Phenomena

A number of phenomena accompany practice and relate to these eight principles. The most significant of these is the effect of the activation of energy. The Chinese term connected with this phenomenon is difficult to translate. In general, it signifies "the action of energy" or "the active nature of energy."

You know that external and internal Qi exists. After the beginning of practice, internal Qi begins to move, to work, and we feel something. This "feeling" is a result of the activation of energy.

Usually after the first and second day in seminars in Stage I, various sensations arise in the attendees: some feel pain; others have a desire to move; some want to cry. Other sensations make themselves known, including warmth, cold, heat, and a feeling of tiny insects creeping through the body. This is because the energy is becoming active inside our body. This is the effect of activated energy, activated Qi.

If you suffer from illnesses, certain segments of the energy channels are spasma-clogged or blocked. When Qi tries to go through these segments, sensations of pain arise. In Chinese medicine, it's well known that Qi passes freely through normally opened channel segments, and its movement doesn't cause any sensations. But if the channels are blocked, the passing of Qi through them triggers pain. Qigong practice heightens sensitivity, and this is why you begin to feel sickly zones more strongly. In a number of cases, the pain is strong. But this doesn't mean that the illness has become more acute. Sometimes before Qigong lessons, before a seminar, the attendee experiences no painful sensations, but after two or three days of practice, he or she does.

Master's Story

A classmate of mine who had worked in the United States began taking the Qigong courses. She considered herself healthy because she'd never felt illness or pain. After two days of study, she felt pain in her stomach area. On the second day, the pain was so great that she went to the hospital. An examination disclosed the presence of a cancerous tumor—unfortunately too late.

Sometimes a person is sick and totally unaware it. Only when an illness reaches an advanced and dangerous stage, when it has become terrifying, does the person begin to feel that things aren't right. The Qigong system can disclose an illness at an early stage. By analyzing pain symptoms, we can determine how dangerous it is. Is it really serious, or can it be cured independently through Qigong? If the pain is strong and doesn't ease up on the second or third day of practice, the person must have a doctor check that part of the body. But if the pain lessens with each day of practice, it makes sense to continue practicing actively.

Sometimes doctors can't determine what to do with a patient, because there are no medications or cures. Problems then arise, but not because there are no treatment methods or the doctor is bad. Perhaps the illness isn't fatal, but the patient is dying nevertheless. This can happen when the patient thinks that he has a dangerous illness and might die. Even if this isn't the case—he dies because he thinks about it all the time. This prompts the question: if a doctor knows that his patient has cancer, for example, should he tell the patient? This depends on the patient.

There are different types of people. On finding out that they have cancer, some people work quickly and intensely to attain healing. Others do the opposite: they put up their hands and await their end.

This is why students in Qigong training aren't told precisely what sensations they should experience during a given exercise: some begin thinking about sensations the whole time. This prevents them from feeling what may be inherent only to them. In addition, their targeted thoughts interfere with the natural flow of practice.

*Therefore **teaching the Qigong system is very difficult. You must instruct in a way that the attendee receives truthful information**—information that isn't thought up, that isn't the product of his or her own imagination, but is the natural result of practice.*

Conclusion
HOW TO PRACTICE FURTHER

Master's Recommendations

After each stage, seminar attendees put forth this question: How should I work with the various exercises spelled out for each stage? There are many different exercises in Stages I, II, and III. How should they be practiced?

As you know, there are two kinds of practice: one uses the front part of our brain; the other uses the back part. For practice involving application of the back part of the brain, it's necessary to keep the mind in a state of calm. To do this, you load this part with work. If you often have to switch on your mind, you should not do exercises requiring active work of the back part of your brain.

During movement, you can practice that which makes demands on your mind, for example, moving or mixing energy between your hands, breathing with your skin, or doing Qigong while walking.

For exercises, one thing can be said: if you practice them more deeply and for longer periods, you'll discover that each can give you much more than you first thought.

We examined the eight principles of ZYQ in great detail. They should help you understand the general approaches to independent practice. We know the goal of each stage. But it's also necessary to know and understand the goals of each exercise. Then it becomes clear what you must practice and when. For example, if you want to enter the state of Pause, you have to develop skin breathing and the Bigu Shiqi exercise.

If you want to accumulate a great amount of energy, practice Big Tree, taking in Qi from the environment as indicated in Stages I, II, and III.

If you wish to strengthen your mental abilities and activate your brain, practice Small Sky Circle.

If you wish to realize within yourself the qualities of a healer, spend more time practicing everything connected with the development of sensitivity in the hands.

You must use your knowledge to analyze what you need to practice in each case. However, after the fourth stage, you no longer need to think about what you should practice, because your body executes what it needs to on its own.

Before you begin practicing Stage IV, orient yourself on how your sensations relate to your conditions. If you feel that you're short on energy, practice what's connected with the lower Dan Tian. If you're sufficiently strong, if you have a lot of energy and your health is in order, you must practice the upper Dan Tian—everything that's connected with the acquisition of wisdom.

Everyone lives in different circumstances, which are constantly changing. There's no single method for making decisions about daily practice. There's no method that's suitable for everyone. That's why everyone must find his or her own path, his or her own methods of study. Without a doubt, your practice will vary, as do the time and conditions.

No method is constant and eternal, but changes are endless. Therefore study in accordance with your own conditions. And since your conditions change, so must your practice.

In ZYQ, you must choose a method for your practice that matches the possibilities of your physical body, your spirit, and your desire. Practice will be different for people of different ages and varying states of health. For children, dynamic exercises requiring exertion are generally in order, while adults—and especially the elderly and sick—are better off with the exercises of Quiet Qigong for relaxation.

While children are still small, all they do is eat, sleep, and play, and most aren't overwhelmed by stress as adults are. They have no worries, no serious mental preoccupations, so relaxation is natural for them. That's why it's necessary to do gymnastic exercises with them so that their muscles and consciousness are challenged. Adults are normally pressured, so they need to learn how to relax.

It's well known that the life cycle of males is about eight years and of females, seven. Therefore, when boys reach sixteen and girls, fourteen—when the second cycle is reaching completion—they're capable of assimilating and practicing everything.

In China, it's believed that the foundation of a person's development in paranormal abilities and practice of the Yin-Shen soul's exiting must be in place before the beginning of the fourth cycle, that is, by the age of twenty-five for males (3x8 = 24) and twenty-two for females (3x7 = 21).

In the first life cycle, the basic life functions are established, and the need arises for a great amount of physical movement. Consequently, as early as preschool age—five or six years old—children are taught Qigong. The second life cycle is a period of active physical development and the formation of secondary sexual indicators.

The eight-year cycle after sixteen—roughly from seventeen to twenty-four—is the best period of practice for men, because it's when the brain develops very actively and can grasp everything. In addition, this is the time of very rapid changes in the hormonal system, so it's when wisdom and paranormal abilities can develop very quickly.

If these changes are already ensuing, adding something when natural changes are taking place is usually very easy. But if the situation is stable, introducing changes is difficult. For this reason, developing paranormal abilities in men over the age of twenty-four becomes more difficult. Problems don't arise when developing normal abilities, but it's not so easy to develop paranormal ones.

For girls, the third cycle—from fifteen to twenty-one—is the best for developing paranormal abilities. It is the period of maximum effectiveness. Various methods can be employed to lift energy to the brain, especially the Small Sky Circle.

For young people, there's no need for supplemental practice, let alone for an extended period of practice; their energy is already great, and elevating it to the brain is very easy. Everything is more complicated with the elderly, because when they practice the lower Dan Tian, it's difficult for them to feel heat and even warmth. No sooner do children begin to open this zone than they immediately feel fire; energy can be lifted to their brain very easily.

However, at this most advantageous period for practice, it's very difficult for young people to practice since they are attracted by many external things that they find interesting. But later, when people begin to understand that they need to practice, they realize they let valuable time pass by.

But perhaps the circumstances in which you find yourself are different. For example, you're burdened by family obligations. Or you want to attain a certain position in society, such as becoming the president of a company. Maybe you're occupied with scientific work or ideas that are far from Qigong practice. Should anything like this be yours, you must practice in a different way. You must practice two hours a day in Stage III and Stage IV, as well as seek help that allows you to do your practice better and more intensely. In other words, during these two hours you must employ all your energy to practice in this time intensely. You must concentrate totally on this intensive practice and succeed in constructing the route between Dan Tian.

If you need to do many things in your everyday life, don't use all your energy for Qigong practice; leave a portion of it for the carrying out of your usual work. And you can still achieve success in the practice of Qigong. What do we mean by *success*? Normally, success means getting what we want. You may have your own idea of success, while another person has a different idea. When you consider yourself to be a successful or happy person, you experience a certain sensation. In what cases do others characterize you as a person who has attained success?

In the Qigong system, there's a standard of success; you've achieved success only when you're able to unite with the surrounding world and interact with it, only when you acquire happiness inside of your heart, and only when you understand the laws of the Cosmos. Only then would we say that you've achieved success, because you became master of yourself. But you should forget to have a rest, and not only practice (Picture 42).

If you ask me which exercises are best—those from ZYQ, other Qigong systems, or some form of meditation, I answer that *all systems are the same. This depends only on you.* You should select a system best suited for the realization of your goals. If your goals are high, choose a system that enables you to attain them. Usually there's not a big difference between various systems. The difference lies in how suitable it is for you and how you select it and a teacher. A good teacher saves you time by helping you to achieve stated goals very quickly. A bad teacher wastes a lot of your time. Whether a teacher is good or bad depends on whether he or she simply provides you with information, or leads you to your goals via the shortest and safest route.

I'm convinced that by following Qigong practice, we become more intelligent and are able to make our lives simpler. We gain the ability to simplify many complex things. Don't think that a certain individual is bad and another good, or that everyone is bad. This will give you a headache. If you accept every person as good, if you experience love toward him or her, if you consider all people to be great, life will be happy—your life and the life those surrounding you.

Live in such a way that you like your life. ***Don't postpone anything that concerns your life. Zhong Yuan Qigong practice isn't your life, but it can raise the quality of your life and make you happy.***

Picture 42: During and After ZYQ Workshops

Picture 42: During and After ZYQ Workshops

Picture 42: During and After ZYQ Workshops

Picture 42: During and After ZYQ Workshops

Picture 42: During and After ZYQ Workshops

APPENDIXES

Appendix 1:
THE CAUSES OF ILLNESSES

In this appendix we bring to your attention the ideas of ancient Chinese philosophers and medical workers regarding the interaction among a person's way of life, emotions, and desires on the one hand, and his state of health and longevity on the other.

1. For the "Emotions and Desires" Section of The Yellow Emperor's

Classic of Internal Medicine by Emperor Huangdi[9]

All illnesses arise because of a disturbance in the dynamics of the movement of biological material. While there are very many causes of illnesses, Chinese medicine divides them into three basic classes:

Class I. (a) disease-producing factors resulting from impact of environmental and climatic conditions—cold and frost, heat, dryness, humidity, dampness, etc. State of atmospheric (weather) conditions. (b) disease-inducing principles of an infectious character (various microorganisms);

Class II—abnormal (extreme) changes of a mental and emotional character: outbursts of anger, grief, sorrow, joy, various stresses and emotional shocks. Seven different emotions induce seven kinds of qualitative changes: joy, anger, rage, sadness-longing, thought and concern, grief and sorrow, fear, horror and panic;

Class III—errors in nutrition; overwork; injuries and bites from animals; sexual excesses.

Circulatory system, heart responsible for joy, merriment, euphoria.

Choline system, liver—for malice, anger, hot temper.

Digestive system, spleen, pancreas—for grief, sadness.

---

9   These are abstracts from the Russian translation with explanations by A. Yazon, "Matter of Qi: A Bible of Yatros," Kyiv, Ukraine, IT Centre, 1999.

Respiratory system, lungs—for sadness, longing, melancholy.

Urogenital system, adrenals-kidneys—for fear.

If a person becomes angry with another, then during the argument his face becomes crimson and ears red, while after the flare-up pains in the right and left sides might be felt.

Chinese medicine believes that rage, anger, and irritation trigger a rousing reflex of the functional system of the liver, which leads to hypertension. An outburst of anger leads to a blockage.

Anxiety is harmful to the spleen and pancreas. As a result of a bad mood and feeling in the dumps, a person loses his appetite.

The liver preserves the spirit and provides for a clear consciousness, and normal and calm sleep. When problems emerge with the liver, nightmares and unease are experienced. Anger and rage harm the liver.

2. "Physician Khe"[10]

by Chuang Tzu, Historical Classic of Ancient China (722-468 B.C.)

The sky has six states of Qi, which produce and give rise to five taste sensations, transform into five colors, and are confirmed in five sounds; while an excess of them engenders six illnesses. The six states of Qi are Yin, Yang, winter, rain, darkness, and light. Separating, they form the four seasons of the year; available in sequence, they form the sequence of five principles. When one of the six Qi is excessive, sickness arises. Thus, if there's too much Yin, there arises illness-causing cold; too much Yang, illness-causing heat; too much wind, illnesses of the extremities; too much rain, internal illnesses; too much darkness, insanity; and if too much light, emotional disturbances. For intimacy with a woman you need an object possessing Yang and a dark time of the day. An excess of Yang and darkness lead to internal heat and an insane curse....Curse—this is insanity triggered by sexual excesses.

---

10 From here to the end of appendix 1, we used abstracts from Ancient Chinese Philosophy/ Collection of Texts, 2 vols., USSR Academy of Sciences, Institute of Philosophy (Moscow: Mysl Publishing House, 1972).

3. From the Treatise "Han Feizi"

by Han Fei, an outstanding theoretician of antiquity
(288-233 B.C.)

If a person has a lot of desires, his calculations lose balance. When calculations lose balance, desires increase. When desires increase, cunning predominates. When cunning predominates, the (normal) course of affairs ceases. When the (normal) course of affairs ceases, unhappiness and difficulties manifest themselves. From this it's obvious: unhappiness and difficulties appear because of cunning, while cunning is engendered by that which can stir up desires....Thus that which can arouse desires causes, at the highest echelons, harm to the ruler, and at the lower levels, suffering among the people—a great crime. Hence the saying: "there's no greater misfortune that that which triggers desires." With this as a foundation, the sage is not tempted by an array of colors, nor is he seduced by sonorous music, while the clearly understanding ruler scorns diversions and distances himself from corrupting beauty.

A person has neither a hide nor feathers. If he doesn't dress, he'll be unable to battle cold successfully. Above he doesn't belong to sky phenomena, and below not to earth. His intestines and stomach are his foundation. If he doesn't eat he won't be able to live. With this foundation of his, it would be impossible for thoughts not to manifest themselves regarding self-gain. Thoughts reflecting the desire to obtain that which furthers his self-interest are inescapable and represent the source of his concerns in life. Therefore, if clothing is sufficient to battle the cold, and food to quench hunger, the sage would no longer be concerned with anything. Regular people are not this way....Thus the saying: "There's no greater misfortune than ignorance of the limits of one's desires."

Therefore excessive desire for self-gain leads to concerns. If there are concerns, illness arises. Illness sets in and the efficacy of wisdom is weakened. If the efficacy of wisdom is weakened, then a sense of measure is lost. If a sense of measure is lost, actions are undertaken is disorderly fashion. If actions are undertaken in disorderly fashion, unhappiness and suffering ensue. Unhappiness and suffering ensue, and illness takes hold of the very core of a person. If, then, illness takes hold of the very core of a person, this leads to sufferings. A person outwardly unhappy arouses woe. If suffering and pain penetrate the intestines and stomach, they injure a person harshly, triggering torturous pain. If injured cruelly, a person backs off from the pain and reproaches himself. Thus backing off and reproaching oneself are caused by the desire for personal gain. So it is said that "there is no greater danger than the desire for advantage."

4. From Encyclopedic Classic on the History of China

Philosophy, Everyday Life and Morals, from Li Sixun Tzu (third century B.C.),

By nature water is pure. Since, however, it mixes with soil, it becomes turbid. By nature, a human being can live for a very long time. But when he is seduced by things he does not reach his life expectancy. Things are intended to satisfy the needs of people, not to subordinate to them people's lives.

In our day errant people, for the most part, subordinate their lives to things. This means that they don't know what the main thing is, and what it is not. Not knowing what the main thing is and what it is not leads to viewing the main thing as not the main thing and that which is not the main thing as the main thing. As a result, every action suffers failure. Following this path, a ruler becomes a blind man, a state official a troublemaker, and a scholar a windbag. When any of these factors is present a state becomes unhappy and fatally doomed....

Therefore the sage possesses things for the purpose of using them to preserve his natural, holistic essence. When a person's nature is whole, then his soul becomes calm, eyes sharp-sighted, ears keen, nose sharp, tongue sensitive, and the 360 joints will function properly....

Premature death and unhappiness, ruin and demise do not come by themselves but are the product of people's errors. The exact same thing holds for a person's life expectancy and a country's calm. Therefore he who has achieved Tao studies not that which can be prompted, but that by which something is prompted. Only in this way can a desired result be attained. You cannot be ignorant of this principle. Let's assume that strongman You Ho, with all his strength, pulls his bull by the tail such that the tail rips off, while the strongman's strength is exhausted. Meanwhile, the bull hasn't moved an inch. This happens because a man is going against nature. Now, let's imagine a boy who is five qi tall. He leads the bull by the bridle and the animal submits to him totally. This occurs because the person we're discussing is following nature....

A long life is obtained by adhering to the natural life. People act contrary to nature when they are motivated by their passions. For this reason, the sage limits his desires. In large premises there is a lot of Yin, while in a high tower Yang is plentiful. When there is too much Yin a person can take sick with rheumatism. If there's an excess of Yang the tremors can afflict a person. This is also harm resulting from an imbalance in Yin and Yang. Hence, wise rulers of ancient times did not desire to live in big houses. They did not build high towers, consume dishes that were too tasty, or wear excessively warm clothing. If you dress too warmly you can cause a blockage in the blood vessels, and such an obstruction can result in qi circulating not normally in the blood. When an excess of tasty food is eaten, the stomach gets blocked up. And constipation can cause apathy. Apathy, then, can result in qi in the blood not circulating normally. Do you really think that pursuing this route will bring you a long life?

Both useful and harmful for man are what the sky engenders: Yin and Yang, cold and heat, dryness and dampness, alternating seasons, and a change of things. The sage, observing what is in accordance with the strength of Yin and Yang and clarifying what the useful characteristics of various things are, directs them to the service of human life. When the soul in the body is calm, then a person's life will be long-lasting. A long life occurs not because a short life is joined to its continuation, but because a person to the end utilizes the quantity of years allotted to him. For a person to make use of the number of years allotted him he must get rid of everything harmful to him.

What does getting rid of that which is harmful for a person mean? Excessive consumption of things sweet, acidic, bitter, spicy and salty—overfilling the body with all of these five kinds of food is harmful to human beings. To display excessively feelings of joy, anger, sadness, fear and sorrow—overfilling the soul with all of these five sensations is harmful to human life. Excessive cold, heat, dryness, dampness, wind, rain, and fog—all of these seven elements when they impact a person's thinnest qi are harmful to his life. Therefore, in order to support life you need to know its source. If you know the source of life, there'll be no illnesses appearing from anywhere.

Flowing water does not spoil; a door rod does not get worn down by a wood borer. This is so because they are constantly in motion. The same holds for the human body and Qi. When the body does not move, then even the thinnest of qi in the blood does not circulate. When the thinnest qi in the blood does not circulate, then lumps form from them. The appearance of these lumps in the head triggers the illness and headaches; in the ears the illness of deafness; in the eyes the illness of blindness; in the nose—blockage; in the stomach—pain; in the legs—cramps.

Where the water is light you'll find many people with herpes/shingles and malignant tumors; where it's heavy, many people with swollen legs who are incapable of moving; where it is sweet, many well-built and beautiful people; where it has a bitter taste, many people with incurable ulcers; where it is bitter, many ugly and hunchbacked people.

You should not excessively eat refined dishes and that which stirs up a sharp sensation, as for example, a strong wine. All of this is labeled the source of illnesses. When a person eats properly, he is free of ailments.

Going hungry and overeating should both be avoided. This is the best way to calm the five internal organs. The mouth should always sense a pleasant taste. Then the state of a person's spirit will be harmonious, his outer appearance firm; and he'll be the recipient of wonderful qi. All his joints will experience a pleasant lightness and freely be nourished by qi from the blood....

By freeing oneself of sadness and merriment, joy and anger, passion and greed, the heart can restore its former state. A person's emotional state requires calm and quiet. When there's no excitement and hustle and bustle, harmony takes over on its own.

Sky brings justice, Earth evenness, and the Human Being strives for calm. Spring and fall, winter and summer—these are the four seasons of Sky. Mountains and hills, rivers and plains—here is the richness of Earth. Joy and anger, belonging and estrangement—these are the manifestations of the feelings and strivings of man. Therefore the sage, changing with the times, does not himself change; keeping up with changing things, he remains in one place. He who is able to be just and calm can be firm. With a stable heart, the ears and eyes become sharp, and the hands and legs strong. Then it can become the receptacle of the thinnest of qi.

A human being's life is normal if he is in a state of calm and balance. He will always lose it if he displays in excess joy and anger, sadness and sorrow. Hence the best means for restraining anger is poetry, for getting rid of sorrow music, for restraining merriment ritual, for observing ritual deference, and for observing deference calm. When a person's internal state is calm and outer appearance deferential, primordial nature will return to him and firmly establish itself in him. As regards food, the following holds: excessive consumption harms a person's physical state; insufficient consumption triggers a condition by which one's bones jut out and the amount of blood diminishes. The establishing of a happy medium between excessive and inadequate consumption of food is referred to as the achievement of harmony. Then the finest qi find their receptacle, from which reason arises. When the mode of nutrition is upset it is necessary to undertake required measures. When a person is full he should move around quickly. When a person is hungry he should avoid mental stress. When old he should be free of concerns. When he's full and does not move around quickly, his qi will not go to the four extremities. When he's hungry and not free of mental pressure, he cannot deal with the hunger; when he's old and not free of concerns, his physical state deteriorates and his death is hastened. A person should have a big and open soul, an expansive character and social instinct—then he will always be in a calm state. He who: is able to maintain a holistic outlook, while ignoring countless petty matters; in the face of personal gain does not succumb to temptation; confronted by danger displays fearlessness; is freedom-loving and humane; is satisfied with his own life—this person possesses the ability to direct qi! Then the thoughts and actions of such a person will function like a clear sky.

The normal life of a human being should be founded on that which is pleasant to a person. Sadness undermines his routine, while anger throws him off balance. Where there are sadness and sorrow, joy and anger, there is no place for the presence of Tao. Calm your passions, eliminate your mistakes and errors, don't hold back what's leaving and don't pushback what's coming—then happiness will return on its own. Tao itself comes to us, and you can seek advice from it. Tao can be gotten by means of calm, while hastiness brings about its loss. Tao, as the most miraculous qi, is to be found in the heart of a person. It comes and goes. It can become so small in size that nothing can pass through it; and so big that it will not have external borders. It gets lost because the hastiness of a person causes him harm. If a heart is in a state of calm, then Tao on its own is maintained in it. With a person who possesses Tao, his qi goes out in all four directions, through pores and external organs, and his internal state is not subject to disturbances. Thus the limiting of a person's passions leads to a situation in which things are unable to cause him harm.

Appendix 2:
ABOUT RESEARCH ON PARANORMAL PHENOMENA

In all eras, people have been drawn to the unknown, be it natural oc-currences, profound aspects of the human psyche, or simply "white spots" on a map. Such is the structure of humans. And, of course, whatever doesn't fit into the customary framework of perception in the usual range of our sense organs has always remained under intense scrutiny.

If people can't explain a phenomenon, they called it a miracle, while amazing abilities of separate individuals are treated as hocus-pocus. When it became clear that these were very special phenomena, people began to give them names. Animal magnetism; prophetic visions; duality; telepathy; mediumship, or sensitivity to the extrasensory; levitation; telekinesis; psychometric abilities; and seers—these are just a few of the terms used since the nineteenth century. All of the terms have been placed in the categories of "paranormal occurrences" and "extrasensory perception." Everything beyond the limits of the existing scientific paradigm was classified this way.

Systematic research into these phenomena began in the second half of the nineteenth century. Thousands of experiments, tens and hundreds of par-ticipants, and endless analyses and quests for explanations have provided no conclusive results. Below we provide a brief introduction to this area.

In 1919 in the former Soviet Union, the first secret laboratory of was created. By the middle of the twentieth century, a great amount of experimental material had been collected, and in 1956 the first seri-ous conference on extrasensory perception took place.

In 1975, an article was written to survey the history of the study of paranormal perception; it included a detailed account of sci-entific experiments in various countries of the world.[11] The nature of the perceptual channel discussed here was studied in experiments in the electronics and bioengineering laboratory of the Stanford Research

---

11 Harold E. Puthoff and Russell Targ, "A Perceptual Channel for Information Transfer over Kilometer Distances: Historical Perspective and Recent Research." Proceedings, Institute of Electrical and Electronics Engineers 64 (1975).

Institute. Experiments of this type were called "remote viewing," that is, the observation of objects at a distance from the test subjects. The latter were volunteers who tried to create visual images of objects of a topographical and engineered nature—buildings, roads, laboratory equipment—that were far from them. The accumulated data indicated that this phenomenon isn't strongly dependent on distance and that shielding with the help of a Faraday camera didn't noticeably improve the quality and precision of the perception. Based on the results of their research, the authors point to areas of physics that could serve as the foundation for a description or explanation of the phenomenon. H. Puthoff is well known as the author of the book *The Foundations of Quantum Electronics* (it is also translated into Russian).

A few years later, the same journal[12] published an article by Robert G. Jahn, "The Ageless Paradox of Psychophysical Occurrences: Engineer's Approach." Written in the form of a survey in a very literary, imaginative, and not at all technical style, the article gives the reader a systematized presentation of the state of the question of psychophysical phenomena in commentaries and scientific research. Included is a discussion of religious and philosophical treatises, of spiritism and the unconscious, of clinical research, and of the creation of a technical base for systematic scientific experiments—beginning in the middle of the twentieth century. Detailed discussions are offered of such notions as psycho kinesis and poltergeists, as are descriptions of experiments with interference (with operators impacting various objects) and perception (with the perception of distant objects, the depiction of which was conveyed by the operator-transmitter).

In no area of research and concomitant commentary were difficulties so often encountered as in the study of extrasensory perception—the ability to reveal distant objects or occurrences that aren't based on the usual sensory processes. It's been over a century that occurrences of this type have served as the subject of scientific examination, yet many in the scientific community react to them as something mystical and unreliable. Indeed, they have been viewed as out-and-out falsification or, at best, as experiments set up in a shady fashion.

---

12 See footnote 11

For this reason, the above-mentioned works of H. Puthoff, R. Targ, and R. G. Jahn became classics in research on psychophysical phenomena and various kinds of informational interaction, in particular, between the consciousness and psyche of a human being and different types of random number generators. They are remarkable examples of work done setting up and executing experiments in the field of revealing extrasensory perception or remote viewing (or, in the language of Qigong, the work of the Third Eye, Third Ear, and Second Heart).

Many principles of the above mentioned articles—far from losing their relevance over the last quarter century—still describe the state of things in this area.

It's been established that the consciousness and will of a human being-operator can affect certain correctives in the workings of a mechanism. As a result, R. Jahn developed the concept of a quantum mechanical interaction between a person's consciousness and physical systems.

Further developments in science and technology have disclosed certain formations accompanying the various forms of energy-informational interaction between a human being and the environment. These luminous formations of irregular shape are called **signatures**. They can be photographed with a photo camera or a video camera. They are most often encountered where a person is involved in a tense mental process or during a lecture on themes that are of interest. Such structures have been studied for over thirty years. You can see them only with the Third Eye, or rarely with usual vision with an out-of-focus glance.

Within the confines of the contemporary scientific paradigm of the West, these formations are explained as plasma structures or clusters, or blocks of solitons, which arise as a result of the interaction between the biofield of a person and his or her consciousness on the one side and environmental space—certain surrounding fields—on the other (Picture 43).

According to quantum mechanics, any material object is, in the final analysis, a large wave packet of solitons.

We can also explain such phenomena from the standpoint of Qigong. In Stage III, we practice the upper Dan Tian and the region of the Third Eye. Then—and with good practice sometimes even after Stage I—you'll be able to see these structures. Then you'll be able to understand: why they vary, as in the case if someone is relaxing or concentrating (for example, on tying a tie, if the procedure has not yet become automatic); why in most cases we observe spherical forms of complex structure, differing in size and density; and what, in general, they represent.

In recent years, information theory, quantum theory, and neurophysiology have appeared and continue to develop, and the current notions of human possibilities have begun to change. Research into brain activity through noninvasive methods using technology reveal such possibilities for humans that were difficult even to imagine before the appearance of squids, quantum tomographs, thermovisors, and other equipment. Of relevance here is the work of the Saint Petersburg scientist S. Karpov.

As before, for the majority of scientists, the most mysterious area of perception is the ability to get information about the past and the near and distant future. For many millennia, this has been explained in Qigong as a certain level of development of the Third Eye. Today, from the point of view of fundamental physics, there's no barrier to conveying information from the future to the present. And it's possible that the moment isn't so distant when trustworthy scientific research will explain the nature of phenomena long known and obvious to Qigong but still amazing and enigmatic to our regular world.

Picture 43: Certain Energy-Informational Structures (Irregular, Arising Near People with Various States, and Spheres of Various Sizes and Colors)

Picture 43: Certain Energy-Informational Structures (Irregular, Arising Near People with Various States, and Spheres of Various Sizes and Colors)

 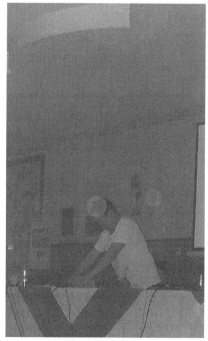

Picture 43: Certain Energy-Informational Structures (Irregular, Arising Near People with Various States, and Spheres of Various Sizes and Colors)

286

Picture 43: Certain Energy-Informational Structures (Irregular, Arising Near People with Various States, and Spheres of Various Sizes and Colors)

Made in the USA
San Bernardino, CA
09 June 2014